CUENTOS:
Stories by Latinas

CUENTOS:
Stories by Latinas

Edited by Alma Gómez
Cherríe Moraga
Mariana Romo-Carmona

KITCHEN TABLE: Women of Color Press

Text Design by Olga Urra.
Cover design by Susan Yung.
Cover Photo by Ann Chapman.
Printed on acid-free paper in the United States by Patterson Printing.

First Edition. Fourth Printing.

Cuentos: stories by Latinas / edited by Alma Gómez, Cherríe Moraga, Mariana Romo-Carmona. — 1st ed. — New York: Kitchen Table, Women of Color Press, c1983.

xx, 241 p. ; 22 cm.

English and Spanish.
ISBN 0-913175-01-3 (pbk.)

1. Short stories—Hispanic authors. 2. Short stories—Women authors. 3. America—Literatures. I. Gómez, Alma, 1953-   II. Moraga, Cherríe. III. Romo-Carmona, Mariana, 1952-

PN6120.92.H56C8   1983   83-202778
                      813'.01'089287—dc19
                                        AACR 2   MARC
Library of Congress

ISBN 0-913175-01-3 paper
ISBN 0-913175-20-X cloth

GLORIA EVANGELINA ANZALDÚA: "El Paisano Is a Bird of Good Omen," copyright ©1981 by Gloria Evangelina Anzaldúa, first appeared in *Conditions*, reprinted by permission. **CENEN:** "Hunger's Scent," copyright ©1983 by Cenen, printed by permission. **ROBERTA FERNÁNDEZ:** "Amanda," copyright ©1979 by Roberta Fernández, first appeared in *Prisma*, reprinted by permission; "Zulema," copyright ©1983, first appeared in *Massachusetts Review*, reprinted by permission. **CAROLINA MARÍA DE JESÚS:** "Childhood," an excerpt from *Bitía's Journal*, a novel unpublished in the original Portuguese, copyright ©1982 by the estate of Carolina María de Jesús translation reprinted by permission of Marilyn Hacker, first appeared in *13th Moon*. **ROCKY (RÁQUEL) GÁMEZ:** Gloria Stories," copyright ©1981 by Rocky Gámez, first appeared in *Conditions*, reprinted by permission. **ROSARIO MORALES:** "I Never Told My Children Stories," copyright ©1983 by Rosario Morales, first appeared in *Sojourner* under the title, "What Me Write Fiction?", reprinted by permission. **CÍCERA FERNÁNDES DE OLIVEIRA:** "We Women Suffer More Than Men" from *Cícera Um Destino de Mulher* (Sao Paúlo: Editora Brasiliense, copyright ©1981) by Cícera Fernándes de Oliveria and Danda Prado. English translation reprinted by permission of Linda Shockey. First appeared in *13th Moon*. **ELVA PÉREZ-TREVIÑO:** "Character Sketch of a Woman Looking," copyright ©1982 by Elva Pérez-Treviño, first appeared in *Sinister Wisdom*, reprinted by permission. **HELENA MARÍA VIRAMONTES:** "Snapshots," copyright ©1983 by Helena María Viramontes, first appeared in *Maize: Notebooks of Xicano Art & Literature*, reprinted by permission. **IRIS M. ZAVALA:** "Kiliagonía," from *Kiliagonía* (Mexico; Premia, copyright ©1980) reprinted by permission from the author.

Contents

UNO

DOS

TRES

By Word of Mouth

TESTIMONIO

Mi abuelita constantemente en la cocina, con la cuchara
en la olla. Mi mami planning what we're going to do. This
one needs money...who can lend it to them. Tú sabes....
There were those centers in our lives. But when you read
stories, none of that was there. (Mariana)

Most Latinas, in looking to find some kind of literary
tradition among our women, will usually speak of the
"cuentos" our mothers and grandmothers told us. This knowledge is what we hold close to our hearts when leafing
through volume after volume of anthologies of literature
—"American" and Latin American—and seldom seeing a
name or a line by a Latina writer that speaks accurately
of our experience. For the most part, our lives and the lives
of the women before us have never been fully told, except
by word of mouth.

But we can no longer afford to keep our tradition oral—
a tradition which relies so heavily on close family networks
and dependent upon generations of people living in the same
town or barrio. This way of life that kept our tales re-told
is falling apart; for they have taken the story-tellers and
scattered us all over the world. The written word, then, becomes essential for communication when face-to-face contact
is not possible. Particularly for so many Latinas who can no
longer claim our own country, or even the domain of our own
homes—barely holding la tierra below our feet—we need una
literatura that testifies to our lives, provides acknowledge-
ment of who we are: an exiled people, a migrant people,
mujeres en lucha.

vii

LAS RAICES DE "LA CULTURA DE SILENCIO"

As Latin American women, we are heirs of a culture of silence. Even so, women have managed to write—from Sor Juana Inés de la Cruz in the seventeeth century on through to Rosario Castellanos, Clarice Lispector, María Luisa Bombal, and Julia de Burgos in the twentieth century. These writers, however, are virtually unknown in the United States. "El" so-called "Boom" del escritor latinoamericano has only meant that norteamericanos have discovered that Latin American *men* can write. Because of this, the Latina in the U.S. not educated in Spanish, is deprived of any knowledge of her own female literary legacy.

The question remains, however, to what extent can most Latin American women writers be considered our literary legacy when so many, like their male counterparts, are at least functionally middle-class, ostensibly white, and write from a male-identified perspective. True, the woman writer in Latin America, as in the U.S., *is* constrained by her sex in terms of subject matter and recognition. Class, race, and education, however, as it combines with sex, are much more critical in silencing the would-be Latina writer than discrimination on sex alone. As long as the Latin American woman writer tows the line of her brothers, there will be a place for her in their literary milieu.

Unlike the Latin American writer in Latin America, the U.S. Latino writer is considered a "non-white" person and as such, a "minority writer." Writing is so dependent upon education that most people of color, because they are poor, are deprived of access to recorded history or written artistic expression. This is further complicated for Latinos by the fact that we are largely born not speaking English.

With the Third World liberation movements in the Sixties, a generation of people of color gained entrance (although limited) to the University. There, our "cuentos" grew into literature. But even our "official" story-tellers—mostly male— did not tell our stories as women. The Latina fiction writer was the last to be fostered and recognized. And, the Latina as subject seldom extended beyond the role of virgin or puta. Latinas in the U.S. have been, as Mariana states, "fucking

viii

silent and fucking silently." We oftentimes put our countries first, our identities as Latin people first, and subvert what are considered "personal" needs for "political imperatives." The total silence about the lives of la lesbiana is the most glaring example of how deeply Latinas have been censored. We cannot mention so many facts of our experience because they are considered taboo by our culture.

EL PODER DE LA PALABRA

In *Cuentos* our intent is to mention the unmentionables, to capture some essential expression—without censors—that could be called "Latina" and "Latina-identified." In short, we sought writings which put the concerns and struggles of the Latin woman first. And that in the naming, our cuentos could empower Latinas to believe we have the right to feel what we feel, in all its complexity.

There *is* power in the word. Each of us knows what it means to find something out through a book. As Cherríe says, "When you don't grow up with books around your house, your first introduction to them is so valuable. It's like you realize you can be a *thinker*. Then you begin to see books as potential movers and shakers, capable of changing people because they have worked to change you." It is with this conviction that we took upon ourselves the task of making *Cuentos*. And, it is with this same conviction that literacy campaigns are conducted in countries undergoing socialist revolution.

Most of the writers in *Cuentos* are first-generation writers.* This means that your mother couldn't have written this story—or even helped you write it. On these writers, then, rests the responsibility to be the first de nuestra gente to describe what it means to be sixteen, female, Puerto Rican, and New York. "Jane Eyre never gave me this!" Alma says. "This is my life on paper. No getting out of it."

QUIENES SOMOS

We are New York and Island Puerto Rican, Los Angeles

* This concept was introduced by Tillie Olsen in her book, *Silences* (New York: Delta, 1979).

Chicana, and Chilena. We are Latina writers and activists who identify as U.S. Third World women.

In compiling this book, there was a certain zeal in our working together. "Hunger" is the word Alma used. In other working relations so often we have felt that part of us had to stay outside a room when we entered it. A part of us had no place to go, no place to find expression. During our discussions with each other, we spoke of the common tired phenomenon of educating people about Latino values.

"I am who I am. I'm sick of being a damn anthropologist for people about myself." (Alma)

In working together, certain things didn't need explaining, including the fact that we all look different from each other and are still Latina.

There *are* issues that divide Latinos — color, class, language: "Los cubanos son así. Los puertorriqueños no saben hablar," etc. But in working together, we tried to be respectful of and sensitive to the cultural differences between us in the hopes that it would make us more sensitive editors in terms of working with the wide variety of expression in the material we selected.

LA POLITICA DE HACER CUENTOS

At bottom, we wanted to create a book that made feminist the connection between Latin American women here and in Latin America. We wanted to "defunct" the myth that only white people live en los estados unidos. We wanted latinoamericanas to recognize that there are Latinas here, too. But as Latinas in the U.S., our experience is different. Because living here means throwing in our lot with other people of color.

Cuentos goes against a grain of privilege we have been told is necessary for the development of "good"—meaning white—writing. Our aspirations are not to be more European. Instead, we claim "la mezcla," la mestiza, regardless of each author's degree of indio, africano, or european blood.

As Latinas living in the U.S., the issues of bilingualism and bi-culturalism are crucial. In este libro, we wish to stretch la imaginación—help the reader become accustomed to seeing two languages in a book, learning to make sense of a thing by picking up snatches here, phrases there, listening and reading differently. *Cuentos* validates the use of "spanglish" and "tex-mex." Mixing English and Spanish in our writing and talking is a legitimate and creative response to acculturation. It doesn't mean that we are illiterate or assimilated as we are sometimes labeled by the anglo and Latin American elite. Our audience is first and primarily the bi-cultural reader: the Latina in the U.S.** *Cuentos* is written for her sensibility. Hopefully, one day the book can be translated entirely into Spanish to reach a wider Spanish-speaking audience.

Who appears in this collection reflects the ethnicity of the editors and the Latin population in the U.S. As editors, our intent was not to develop a comprehensive volume, representative of all Latin American women. But, we hoped the sentimiento of these writings would mean something to many Latinas of different national origins. The range (in geography, language, theme, story, character) that does appear elaborates on and recreates the richness and complexity of being Latina in the U.S., the Caribbean,, or Latin America. *Cuentos* is only one version of the many stories of our lives to be told.

We see this version, however, as a powerful one where the Latina as a breed of writer—political, tercermundista, feminista, and familial—is clearing new ground. These stories are the first upswing of the tool, the first hoe in the soil, digging up what for too long has not been spoken between us.

What hurts is the discovery of the measure of our silence. How deep it runs. How many of us are indeed caught, unreconciled between two languages, two political poles, and suffer the insecurities of that straddling.

All of us are very protective of our words—their arrangement, their meaning—but it is essential that the realities of our lives be named in our own tongue, however mixed. To wait until later, when they have europeanized our style and

** For this reason we have only translated Spanish references in works written predominantly in English and where the references are critical to understanding the work. We have not italicized the Spanish or footnoted the translations in order to have the text visually reflect the bi-cultural experience.

the material of our lives, would be too late.

This book is bound together con la esperanza that we can stop apologizing for nuestros deseos, nuestras voces—how our words run together, how our voices rise and fall with the quick change of heart.

Alma Gómez
Cherríe Moraga
Mariana Romo-Carmona
with Myrtha Chabrán

April 1983

De Boca En Boca

TESTIMONIO

Mi abuelita constantemente en la cocina, con la cuchara
en la olla. Mi mami planeando lo que íbamos a hacer.
Este necesita dinero...quién le puede prestar. Tú sabes...
Allí estaba nuestro centro, pero cuando leíamos historias,
no había nada de eso. (Mariana)

Al buscar una tradición literaria entre nuestras mujeres
la mayoría de nosotras probablemente recordará los "cuentos"
que nuestras madres, abuelas y hermanas nos contaban. Esta
memoria es la que llevamos junto al corazón cuando hojeamos
tomo tras tomo de antologías de literatura, "Américana" y
"Latinoamericana," y no encontramos ni el nombre, ni
siquiera una línea por una autora latina que refleje con
exactitud nuestra experiencia. Ni nuestras vidas ni las de
nuestros antepasados han sido relatadas adecuadamente,
excepto de boca en boca.

Pero ya no podemos mantener una tradición exclusivamente
oral, una tradición que depende del contacto familiar, de la
residencia de generaciones en un mismo lugar. Las condiciones
que aseguraban la continuación de nuestras historias y el
mismo esquema de nuestras vidas ha cambiado; las cuentistas
han sido dispersadas por todo el mundo. Por eso necesitamos
la palabra escrita para comunicar la historia que todavía nos
une como latinas.

Para tantas latinas que ya no podemos reclamar nuestra
patria, ni siquiera la tierra bajo nuestros pies, necesitamos
una literatura que sea testigo de nuestras vidas. Que reconozca
quiénes somos: gente en exilio, gente emigrante, mujeres en
la lucha.

LAS RAICES DE LA CULTURA DE SILENCIO

Somos herederas de una cultura de silencio. Aún así, hay mujeres en Latinoamérica que se han atrevido a escribir— desde Sor Juana Inés de la Cruz en el siglo diecisiete hasta Rosario Castellanos, Clarice Lispector, Julia de Burgos y María Luisa Bombal en el siglo veinte. Estas escritoras, sin embargo, son prácticamente desconocidas en los Estados Unidos. La latina criada en los EEUU, por lo tanto, no tiene acceso a su propia herencia literaria. El llamado "boom" de la ˙novela hispanoamericana sólo indica que los norteamericanos han descubierto que los hombres latinos saben escribir.

Aún así, es necesario determinar hasta qué punto la mayoría de las escritoras latinoamericanas puede considerarse nuestra herencia. Al igual que los escritores, muchas de ellas funcionan en una clase media ostensiblemente blanca, y escriben con una perspectiva e identificación masculinas. Es cierto que la escritora en Latinoamérica, como en los EEUU, es limitada por su género; clase, raza y educación en combinación con el género de la persona, son determinantes mucho más críticos al silenciar la posible escritora latina. La escritora latinoamericana tiene su lugar asegurado en el mundo literario siempre y cuando baile al compás de sus hermanos.

A los latinos en los EEUU se nos considera personas de color, por lo tanto el "U.S. Latino writer" es además un "minority writer." La capacidad para escribir depende tanto de la educación, que la mayoría de la gente de color en los EEUU, porque son pobres, carece de acceso a la historia y al la expressión literaria. Para la gente latina este hecho se complica ya que el inglés no es nuestra primera lengua.

Con el comienzo de los movimientos tercermundistas de liberación en los años sesenta toda una generación de gente de color logró algún acceso a las universidades. Allí, nuestros "cuentos" pudieron transformarse en literatura. Pero aún nuestros cuentistas "oficiales"—casi siempre hombres—no contaban las historias de nosotras las latinas. La escritora latina fue la última en ser reconocida y apoyada. Y la latina como personaje pocas veces pasó más allá del rol de bruja o virgen.

"Nos hemos quedado jodidas en silencio, y en silencio nos han jodido," dijo Mariana una vez. Simpre colocando a nuestros países en primer lugar, nuestra identidad como gente latina primero, negando lo "meramente personal" por la "imperativa política." El silencio total sobre la vida de la lesbiana latina, por ejemplo, da una idea de lo efectiva que ha sido la mordaza. ¡Hay tantos hechos de nuestra existencia como mujeres que se consideran tabú por nuestra cultura!

EL PODER DE LA PALABRA

En *Cuentos* nuestra intención es decir lo "indecible," capturar una expresión esencial—sin censura—que se pueda llamar "latina." Escritos que coloquen la experiencia y la lucha de la latina en primer lugar. Y que al nombrarlas, nuestros cuentos convenzan a nuestras lectoras de que todas tenemos derecho a sentir lo que sentimos, en toda su complejidad.

La palabra encierra poder. Cada una de nosotras sabe lo que significa comprender algo a través de un libro. "Cuando uno crece sin libros en la casa, esa primera introducción es tan valiosa," cuenta Cherríe. "Es como si te dieras cuenta de repente que tú puedes ser una pensadora. Entonces los libros parecen capaces de mover, de sacudir, capaces de cambiar a la gente porque a ti misma te cambiaron." Con esto por entendido es que se llevan a cabo las campañas de alfabetización en las naciones en el proceso de revolución socialista. Y es con esta convicción que nos entregamos a la tarea de formar *Cuentos*.

La mayoría de las escritoras en *Cuentos* son las primeras de su familia y de su generación.* Esto quiere decir que la madre de una no podría haber escrito este cuento, ni haber ayudado a escribirlo. Sobre estas autoras cae la responsibilidad de ser la primera de su gente en describir, por ejemplo, lo que significa ser una puertorriqueña de dieciseis años en Nueva York. "¡*Jane Eyre* nunca me habló de esto!" observó

---

* Tillie Olsen en su libro *Silences* (New York: Delta, 1979) introduce este concepto.

Alma, "pero en estas páginas se encuentra mi vida. No lo puedo negar."

QUIENES SOMOS

Somos puertorriqueñas de Aquí y de Allá, chicana de Los Angeles y chilena inmigrante. Somos escritoras latinas y activistas que nos definimos como mujeres tercermundistas en los EEUU. Recopilando el material para estre libro sentimos un nuevo entusiasmo, una ansia de comunicarnos. "Hambre" es la palabra que usó Alma. En otras relaciones de trabajo a menudo teníamos la sensación de que una parte de nosotras debía esperar fuera del cuarto cuando entrábamos. Una parte de nosotras no tenía dónde ir, no podía expresarse. En nuestras conversaciones discutíamos la faena de tener que educar a la gente sobre los valores latinos. "Yo soy lo que soy," dice Alma, "y ya estoy harta de ser una jodía antropóloga para los blancos." Cuando trabajamos juntas no teníamos que explicar, incluso el que todas lucimos diferentes, pero igual somos latinas.

Entre los latinos existen divisiones históricas de color, clase e idioma: "Los cubanos son así. Los puertorriqueños no saben hablar," etc. En nuestro trabajo hemos tratado de reconocer las diferencias culturales entre nosotras con la esperanza de poder ejercer ese mismo criterio al evaluar y desarrollar el material que hemos elegido.

LA POLITICA DE HACER CUENTOS

Para empezar, queríamos crear un libro que hiciese feminista la conección entre mujeres latinas aquí y en la América Latina. Queremos acabar con el mito que en los EEUU sólo hay gente blanca. Queremos que las latinoamericanas sepan que aquí también hay latinas pero que nuestra experiencia aquí es diferente, porque vivir aquí significa compartir la suerte de todas las gentes de color.

Las historias en *Cuentos* van contra la corriente de lo que se supone es necesario para el desarrollo de "la buena literatura." No se trata aquí de ser más europeo. Al contrario, nos identificamos como "la mezcla," la mestiza, sea cual sea la proporción en cada autora de sangre India, Africana o Europea.

Para nosotras las latinas que vivimos en los EEUU el issue del bilingüismo y biculturalismo es decisivo. En este libro queremos extender la imaginación de nuestras lectoras a su límite, para que nos acostumbremos a ver dos idiomas simultáneamente, a comprender algo gradualmente—una frase aquí, un retazo allá. Aquí validamos el uso del "spanglish" y el "tex-mex". La mezcla del inglés y el español en el habla y la escritura es una expresión legítima y creadora ante el fenómeno de la aculturación. No somos ni analfabetas ni asimiladas como a veces nos califican las elites norte-y latinoamericanas. Nos dirigimos primeramente a la lectora bicultural: la latina en los EEUU.** Es un libro escrito para su sensibilidad. Esperamos que pronto se pueda traducir para un público más numeroso en español.

Quien aparece en esta colección refleja la etnicidad de las editoras y de la población latina en los EEUU. No intentamos desarrollar un tomo completo, representativo de la mujer latinoamericana, pero esperamos que la sensibilidad de estos escritos alcance a muchas latinas de diverso origen nacional. La latitud que aparece aquí, en cuanto a geografía, tema, carácter y personajes elabora la riqueza y complejidad de ser latina en los EEUU, el Caribe y la América Latina. *Cuentos* es sólo una versión de los muchos cuentos que están por escribirse.

Nuestra versión, sin embargo, es poderosa porque presenta una raza de escritoras latinas—política, tercermundista, feminista, familiar—que labra un nuevo terreno. Estas historias son el primer azadón en la tierra, desenterrando la palabra sepultada por demasiado tiempo.

Lo que duele es descubrir la medida de nuestro silencio. Lo profundo que corre. ¡Cuántas de nosotras nos hallamos atrapadas sin reconciliación entre dos idiomas, dos polos políticos sufriendo las inseguridades de estar a horcajadas!

Todas protegemos nuestras palabras—el arreglo, el querer decir—pero es esencial que la realidad de nuestras vidas se

** Por este motivo sólo hemos traducido las referencias en español en los trabajos escritos mayormente en inglés, donde es crítico comprender dichas referencias para apreciar el trabajo completo. Tampoco hemos italizado el español ni anotado las traducciones para que el texto sea fiel visualmente a la experiencia bicultural.

nombre en nuestra lengua, mezclada y con cualquier acento. Si se espera hasta más tarde, cuando ya hallan inglesado nuestras voces y nuestras vidas será demasiado tarde. Este libro nace con la esperanza de que ya podemos dejar de pedir disculpas por nuestros deseos y nuestras voces —cómo nuestras palabras se confunden, cómo nuestras voces se levantan y caen al son del latir del corazón.

Alma Gómez
Cherríe Moraga
Mariana Romo-Carmona
con Myrtha Chabrán

abril de 1983

AGRADECIMIENTOS

Gracias a nuestras madres who gave us/taught us language.

Gracias to the women of Kitchen Table: Women of Color Press:
Myrtha Chabrán who took the job of copyediting *Cuentos* to heart. Gracias for keeping us honest and away from rhetoric. We don't know what we would have done without you.
Barbara Smith who early-on had a vision of and commitment to this collection.
Susan Yung for her generous help in the graphic design of *Cuentos*.
And to all the other collective members—*Leota Lone Dog, Audre Lorde,* and *Sonia Álvarez.*

Special thanks to *Adriana Romo* for her support. *Regina* who accepted Alma's one o'clock in the morning phone calls. *Marilyn Hacker* for connecting us with Brazilian writers. *Olga Urra* for her patience, perseverance, and affection as production consultant. Also thanks to las mujeres who typeset *Cuentos,* and to *Cora, Sonia,* and *Nancy* for those last-minute jobs.

And, of course, thanks to all the funders of this project— private donors and *The Astraea Foundation.*

Finally, gracias to all the contributors who endured a sometimes difficult editorial process who kept faith in us and in the meaning of *Cuentos.*

Las Editoras

AGRADECIMIENTOS

Gracias a nuestras madres que nos dieron/nos enseñaron el lenguaje.

Gracias a las mujeres de Kitchen Table: Women of Color Press:
A *Myrtha Chabrán* que se dió el gran trabajo de editar *Cuentos* y por ayudarnos a mantener la integridad literaria de las autoras.
A *Barbara Smith* por su visión y lealtad a esta antología.
A *Susan Yung* por su generosa ayuda en el diseño gráfico de *Cuentos*.
Y a todos los otros miembros de la colectividad—*Leota Lone Dog, Audre Lorde,* y *Sonia Álvarez*.

Agradecimientos especiales para *Adriana Romo* por su apoyo. A *Regina* que aceptaba las llamadas telefónicas de Alma a la una de la mañana. A *Marilyn Hacker* por conectarnos con las escritoras Brazileñas. A *Olga Urra* por su paciencia, perseverancia, y afecto como consultante de producción. También gracias a las mujeres que hicieron el trabajo litográfico de *Cuentos* y a *Cora, Sonia,* y *Nancy* por trabajos de último minuto.

Y por supuesto, gracias a las fundadoras de este projecto y *The Astraea Foundation*.

Finalmente, gracias a todas las escritoras que soportaron el proceso editorial, a veces dificil y quienes mantuvieron la fe en nosotras y en el significado de *Cuentos*.

Las Editoras

Cuentos
Stories by Latinas

uno

There is a level of passion we possess for which there is no legitimate outlet. Feeling like we were born with too much inside of us and that should we decide to express ourselves in any deeply felt way, they will think us crazy, sick, or senile. The characters in these stories are "possessed"—possessed in opposition to the forces that deny their humanity.

Puerto Rico is la mujer latina. La mujer latina is post-Allende Chile.

Hay un nivel de pasión que poseemos para el que no existe salida. Nos sentimos como si hubiéramos nacido con algo muy grande dentro de nosotras mismas, y si alguna vez decidimos expresarnos con profunda y verdadera emoción, nos van a decir que estamos o locas o enfermas o seniles. Los personajes en estas historias son mujeres que se hallan "poseídas," poseídas en oposición a las fuerzas que niegan su humanidad.

Puerto Rico cautivo es la mujer latina. La mujer latina es post-Allende Chile.

La confesión

Gloria Liberman

Hoy me regalaron unas hermosas margaritas. Son las flores que más me gustan, tienen un aroma especial que me evoca las tardes de paseo en el jardín del sanatorio. Trae agua, que se me van a secar las margaritas. Ya te voy conociendo déjame darte un besito. Quiero aire, una sorpresa cobijada bajo mis ojos. Ya me acostumbré y no siento nada. Un rayo de luz se cuela por la ventana. ¿Dónde está la gente? Seres blancos marchan por el pasillo, se esconden, cavilan, tienen miedo. Yo tengo miedo, siempre tengo miedo. Veo ese charco de sangre. Vete, escóndete. Abrázame, hermano. Quizás sea la última vez que nos veamos. ¡Putas! se cagan en un inocente. Queríamos un mundo mejor. Liberen a los esclavos. Este país es una mierda. Háganse humo que ahí vienen los comecacas. Me gusta sentarme en el banquillo del patio y ver pasar al hombre diáfano, al hombre mudo. Insólito paraje donde la mente ha quedado apuntando hacia otro espacio, más libre, más humano. ¡Ven, acércate! ¿Cómo te llamas? A mí no me vienen con cuentos. Tú lo viste todo. Adoro las margaritas. Cuando me porto bien yo también me llamo Margarita. El doctor me habla. Otro nudo aprieta mi cuello. Esta vez será una soga larga; la del recuerdo de mi casa, escondido en el velador.

¡Arturo, pobre hermano! El Arturo sí que era bueno, todos lo decían. Tenía muchos amigos. Le gustaba pasear y reír.

Tienes que pensar en el futuro, darle una tierra más fértil a tus hijos, una tierra donde exista un rincón libre y puro.

No me gusta el invierno, ni el corredor oscuro.

Otra vez me llaman.

Olvídese de todo. ¡Pobre de usted si abre la boca!

Aquí venden un hermoso vestido; mamá. ¿me lo compras?

No tenemos plata. Olvida tus estúpidos sueños.

Déjenme tranquila. Les juro que no diré nada.

Estoy amarrada, adónde me llevan, me torturarán. A lo mejor me matan como a mi hermano.

Yo no sé nada. Tengo la garganta seca. Por el amor de dios...tráiganme agua.

¿Dios? ¿acaso yo lo he nombrado?

¿Hiciste la primera comunión? ¿Te bautizaron? El te debe protección. Donde está.

Me duele todo, vomito sangre.

Me encantan las flores.

Tú los viste cuando entraron. Yo no vi nada. ¿Viste cuando mataron a tu hermano?

Sangre, mucha sangre. Todo el grito de la noche clavado en mi lengua. Un filo helado urgueteando en su vientre. Todo se desparrama, invade. Un océano espeso de aguijones irrumpe violentamente en mi alma, sus aguas violáceas me empujan, me viajan. No puedo dejar a Arturo. ¡Alejandra! ¡Alejandra!

El doctor dice que yo me llamo Margarita y eso me complace, porque entonces es cierto que soy bella como una flor.

¡No lo maten! No tengo a nadie.

¡Escúchenme! Yo no diré nada. ¡suéltenme por favor!

Es mejor así. Confesará de todos modos. Trae un cigarro.

Fuego, dolor. Se aplasta en mi piel. Grito. Desgarro ancestral, viene de muy adentro.

Es lejos. No escucho.

Así nos aseguraremos de que no hables.

¿Si le cortamos la lengua?

A veces me quedo largamente en el patio. Todos caminan silenciosos. Serán mudos como yo. Pero yo hablo. Sí, yo hablo

con las flores, ellas son mis hermanas.
Tuve un hermano. A él lo asesinaron. ¡hijos de puta!
¿Dónde estoy?
¿Conoces a Gerardo Rodríguez? Era un amigo de tu hermano.
Quiero margaritas en mi pieza. Pásenme un florero. Los
floreros son tristes. Siempre callados. Viven del silencio.
Viven y dependen de las flores. A lo mejor soy un florero.
¡No! ¡No me den nada!
Ya oscurece. Escóndete, te vendrán a buscar y te matarán. No
quieren testigos. Y desde ahora vas a sentir siempre que sobras.
Está de Dios, hijita! No se amargue más. Bastante ha sufrido
con lo del Arturito, váyase lejos...
Yo soy margarita. Déjenme en paz.
Será mejor internada en un sanatorio. Diremos que se volvió
loca.
Ellos lo mataron. Yo lo vi todo. Lo acuchillaron, pero no
quieren que nadie se entere, por eso yo estoy aquí.
No, yo estoy aquí porque soy margarita y pertenezco a este
jardín.
Me llaman. El doctor me dijo que si sigo portándome bien seré
como una de ellas. ¡Qué suerte! Estoy segura que con el tiempo
tendrán que enterrarme. Porque soy una margarita ¿o no?

Doña Marciana García

Rocky Gámez

August in the lower Rio Grande Valley of Texas is a true hell-hole. The sweltering subtropical heat presses down like a lid on a pressure cooker, making both day and night unbearable. The searing rays of the sun along with the suffocating humidity scorch every form of vegetation and give the landscape a depressing gray-green color. The Mexican people of the delta call this period la canícula—dog days— when every ounce of energy in a living body evaporates leaving only an inert blob. During these dreadful sluggish days of summer even the horned toads and the lizards shy away from the blistering sun and surface only to search for food. Everything is in a state of inanimate suspension. The heat has no beginning nor end—it is always hovering like a steaming blanket over every inch and every cell of the valley floor.

It was during one of those searing days, that doña Marciana was hurrying along the road which headed straight back into the barrio. She had to explain things to the neighbors before Esperanza arrived there. But because of her age and the arthritis that had deformed her toes and ankle bones, the hunch-backed woman found it excruciating to walk as fast as she wanted. Her worn-out huaraches buried themselves in ankle-deep sand with every step she took.

The sum total of her existence, that epithet for which all of us work during our lives, depended on that race she was now running. If she hurried, despite her painful joints, she would arrive in town before the younger woman, and her reputation as a good and wise curandera would be saved. If she didn't, then all those years she had served the community as a source of comfort and security would have been in vain. The villagers would never remember her as she deserved to be remembered. They would only think of her as the crazy old healer who had been responsible for Susana Mendoza's death. Life, she thought, was filled with very cruel irony. When the time came to expel the final breath nobody gives a damn for all that one does in a lifetime. The summation of one's entire existence was generally condensed into one very small and simple sentence and nothing more. In her case, seventy-five years of selfless devotion to the healing of the sick would be reduced to that unfortunate second when Susana emitted her last sigh, and she would always be known as la curandera que falló, the healer who failed. That was life! And if she could manage it, Esperanza would be the one to chisel that epithet when Marciana's final hour came. Marciana could see it glaring at her from the marble slab:

Aquí la vieja hierbera
que por su culpa murió Susana

But she was not going to let that happen; Carajo!; No faltaba mas!

Esperanza was a young woman who came from the same barrio of Guadalupe where Marciana had lived all her life. She had recently graduated from nursing school and for the past year or so had been talking bad about Marciana's healing practices to the village women, trying to discredit her vast knowledge of herbal medicine, midwifery and occasional witchcraft. Most of the older women in the barrio didn't believe the young nurse because Marciana had always cured them of their ailments or delivered their babies without complications. But Marciana worried about this younger breed of women. They, with Esperanza's help, were beginning to have serious doubts about her abilities. The barrio was now teeming with younger people—hundreds—whom Esperanza had been encouraging to go to doctors across the railroad tracks instead of to Marciana's humble consultorio. She had been telling them not to have their babies at home like their mothers and grandmothers, but to go to the hospital because it was equipped with the latest of modern facilities and their post-natal care would be better. She even had the audacity to dispute the existence of evil spirits invading the human body, calling them archaic superstitions, and suggesting that anyone who believed in such things should have their heads examined.

Old Marciana knew that Esperanza had the words to convince many people. But up to now her ammunition had been very limited. Marciana had not ever made an error in judgment, something that Esperanza had anxiously awaited. Up to that tragic day there had not been a single doubt as to her ability. She could cure anything from anemia to zoster, mend broken bones as well as shattered hearts, extract evil spirits and impacted teeth better than the best physician in the world. And she would not even demand payment for her services because that was the trademark of a good healer. But now she had failed with Susana, and now Esperanza had the evidence she needed to convince the people that it was the time to change, that Marciana was indeed more dangerous than she was beneficial.

The name of the young nurse was beautiful, it meant "hope," but in Marciana's mouth it left a bad taste. She was a new phenomenon in the barrio, the product of the new crop of fools that had emerged from the local university. She, like dozens of others from the barrio, had gone to school to free themselves from the bonds of ignorance and had come out worse fools than they were when they went in. Marciana could not think of a crueler trick that fate could play on a human being. Esperanza entered the university an innocent and honest Mexican and emerged totally Americanized, casting away her old customs, traditions and beliefs, betraying not only herself but also everything that la Raza held sacred.

And here she was, doña Marciana García, a white haired old woman who had spent a lifetime practising healing and fearing God, now running away in fear of that five pound wailing baby she had delivered only 23 short years before— a wispy skinny thing that called herself a nurse and couldn't yet tell the difference between a wart and a fart. Carajo! No faltaba más. She even had the nerve to laugh at her nostrums as she took them out of her medicinal bag. That had hurt her the most.

"No pienses, Marciana," the panting and perspiring old woman told herself over and over again, "thinking wastes energy. Just hurry! Hurry!"

Her brown face gleamed with beads of perspiration. She grunted and groaned making the necessary strength that would enable her to trot faster. Neither the sizzling heat nor painful feet were going to keep her from reaching the barrio first. She had to let the people know that Susana's death had not been her fault.

But, how was she going to explain the young woman's death when she, herself had not understood what had gone wrong? Pregnancy was not an illness; it was the most natural thing for a woman of Susana's age. She couldn't understand what had actually happened during labor.

She had not done anything different than she had in thousands of other deliveries. There was no reason for that death, unless it was Susana's time to leave this world, unless God had a special need for her in heaven. If only her legs could carry her fast enough to explain this to the people... if only she could get there before Esperanza! The older people were bound to believe her side of the story.¡Seguro que sí! But, what about the young ones? The ones that Esperanza was beginning to infect with her concept of logic? Would they believe her? They would when she told them that Esperanza had arrived first at Susana's house, that she must have done something to her own cousin before she arrived. Esperanza had been with Susana since early morning while Marciana was delivering another baby in the adjacent barrio. She could not have just been sitting there holding the woman's hand waiting for the curandera to appear.

The first stage of Susana's labor was exactly like all the others she had attended, from the onset of the contractions to the complete dilation of the cervix. The pains came every three minutes, then they came more rapidly. Everything happened as it should but the fetus' head never appeared.

"Ándale, Marcianita, apúrate!; Apúrate!" She kept urging herself to speed up her steps. "Don't think! Thinking is not food for you right now."

10

But she couldn't stop herself from thinking. The reel of memory kept spinning inside her burning skull. The fetus could not be expelled, she thought, because it was dead. Esperanza had, no doubt, done something to cause its death. Marciana was sure of this. She probably had administered an injection of some sort that neither mother nor child could tolerate. Modern medicine people were very quick with the needle. Why else would Susana close her eyes and not open them no matter how loudly she had screamed at her to wake up? Women just didn't fall into a deep sleep during labor. She had died.

Marciana wiped the streams of perspiration with her wrinkled underskirts. She felt a strong urge to relieve herself but fought it. There was not enough time to find a private spot for that. Every minute of that race was precious. If it came to where she could no longer hold the waters it would have to be done on the run and she would have to disregard her sense of dignity. Besides, it was not the first time she sprayed her legs. Lately her bladder had begun to give her a lot of trouble.

The sandy road seemed twice as long and her legs twice as shaky. The burlap bag she carried with an assortment of medicinal herbs, votive candles and the clay statuette of the virgin de Guadalupe weighed more than it had earlier this morning. She thought of tossing it behind a nearby clump of brush and returning later to recover it, but guilt held her arm. She could not dispose of those things she believed in and held sacred. These were the tools of her trade. So she decided to carry the bag to the end of the road, although now it was only a cumbersome weight instead of the reliable nostrums she prized for her work.

She paused in the middle of the road for a moment to catch her breath. Her heart was pounding so loud against her ribs she could hear it thumping. She looked over her shoulder to see if Esperanza were catching up to her, but she couldn't see anything in the shimmering haze. ¡Gracias a Dios! Thank God, she still had a chance to get to the barrio before the young nurse. There was nothing in the merging distance but a white blur. It was possible that Esperanza was delayed because she had to walk across the fields to deliver the tragic news to Susana's husband. And for a brief moment, Marciana felt sorry for the nurse. It was not easy for anyone to give the saddest of all news. She resumed her rickety running certain that in all of Esperanza's glib attitude she would still be very kind to the young man.

The blazing sun rose higher, intensifying the sweltering heat., Marciana's toothless mouth felt parched, her throat burned and tightened. The flat heel on one of her old huaraches came loose. But she continued her feeble trot across the burning sands. Her thighs and her lower back felt like they didn't belong to her anymore; they were artificial appendages threatening to come unhinged at any moment. In the distance ahead, she saw something on the road that appeared to be a white gelatinous blob. The faster she walked, the farther away the mass slithered. She knew now that her eyes were playing tricks on her, perhaps irritated by the burning, cutting sand, or from the torrents of perspiration falling from her forehead. Something in her head moved as if it were shifting positions inside her skull, sending a tremor through her entire exhausted body. She lost her balance and almost fell sideways into the culvert filled with the stagnant water of the previous rain.

She forced her wrinkled eyelids to open wide in an attempt to wave away the cumulus haze covering her pupils, but the stubborn old hoods were no longer obeying her command. Her groin ached from the labored walking and the weight of her full bladder. Once or twice she sank to her knees from exhaustion, relieving herself of the full sack that was pushing on everything inside her abdomen.

As far as she could estimate, she was only halfway home. She wrapped her twiggy arms around the burlap bag and pressed it to her sunken chest, protectively leaning forward, hoping that walking in such a position would induce her tired old legs to move faster.

Somewhere along that straight and narrow road she felt that she had done something wrong, although her waning memory could not discern what it was. She felt she had made a turn but she told herself that that was utterly ridiculous. That same desolate road was as familiar to her as the palms of her gnarled hands. There was no need to turn anywhere.

It was a straight road that led directly to the barrio. Under normal conditions, taking her natural easy strides, she made the trip home in the amount of time it took her to recite a full rosary—something she always did when she walked those lonely roads to tend to her patients. This time, however, since she had left her rosary beads by Susana's bed, she couldn't really tell how far away from home she was. Suddenly, Marciana felt a cool breeze surrounding her. The thorny brush lining the road moved closer, and the buzzing cicadas almost brushed the top of her black shawl. She heard the ripping of cloth on her shoulder, on the side of her long brown skirt, and the backs of her cotton stockings. Startled, she stopped and searched about. For as many times as she had walked that road she could not remember a creek nor an old bent mesquite tree with the name "Lupe" carved in a heart on its trunk. She had never come so close to the clumps of cacti with their menacing spines. The road had shrunk into a thin slice leading her into what appeared to be a refuge for wild animals. A brood of black birds squawked at her from the treetops and lizards and horned toads scurried brazenly in every direction. She stretched her shiny wrinkled neck in alarm, surveying the unfamiliar surroundings through a dizziness that was clouding her vision.

There were all sorts of strange sounds and furtive movements behind the thickets. She stood rigid for a long time, afraid to step any further lest she disturb a wild animal that would not welcome an uninvited visitor. By now the right side of her body had become heavy with a frightening numbness and her pulse had become accelerated to the point where she could almost hear it pounding against her eardrums.

She soon realized that she had, indeed, made a turn off the long straight road. There was no doubt about that. But, in what direction? Right or left? She felt very confused. The sun had already begun to disappear behind the treetops, making everything, even the dwarf shrubs, cast big shadows. She knew what she had done wrong and why. She had not been a curandera too long for nothing. La canícula spared no one. She knew right away that she was her latest victim.

In a helpless rage, the old hunch-backed woman hurled herself on the cracked baked earth and began to weep long painful sobs, hammering her fists into the ground until the dried skin cracked and blood oozed between her tightly clenched fingers. The long sorrowful wails penetrated the thickness of the chaparral, frightening a covey of morning doves into a flurry of movement that left the bushes showered with tiny gray feathers.

By now Esperanza would be in the barrio spreading the news of the tragic happening. By now everyone had already judged her and no doubt passed sentence on her. It was a strange fact of human nature that people would always believe the first account of a story.

She tried to pick herself up but she was a bundle of dead weight. She could no longer feel her legs under her. Instead, she crawled toward the sound of the small creek, and when she finally reached it, she dipped a bloodied hand, hardened now like a claw, into the cool water. She had to cool her body in whatever manner she could. Heatstrokes were very dangerous especially to the elderly like herself.

"Ah, the miracles of God! How great they are!" She said to her reflection. One drink had made her heart's pounding subside. A second had cooled her dehydrated mouth and the third had relieved the numbness in her body. All of a sudden nothing mattered to Marciana anymore, except this feeling of well-being. As far as she was concerned, Esperanza could do with her reputation whatever she wanted—let the neighbors think what they would. She knew now she would not have to face them again. Marciana took a long deep breath and felt a soothing coolness all over her body.

"Que sea lo que Dios quiera."

After the blazing sun had dropped completely into the horizon, a young woman with long brown hair, dressed in faded jeans and a white shirt several sizes too large for her, walked into the dense thicket where two neighbor-men had found the old woman by the creek, a clump of earth in her still-clenched fist. The young woman was followed by a thin man in bib overalls and a denim jacket. He was holding his straw hat in his hand and was shaking his head slowly back and forth. With his free arm, he held the woman protectively.

"I had to find this," Esperanza said, picking up the burlap

bag the men had forgotten in the thicket. "Her bag must be buried with her."

"Pobre Marcianita." the young man replied. "She had to have felt terribly sick to leave Susana in the middle of her labor. She must've known her end was near."

"It's hard to say, Fernando." Esperanza took Marciana's rosary out of her pants pocket, and put it into the sack.

"During the middle of Susana's labor, the baby was just about to crown when all of a sudden Marciana grabbed her head as if someone had dealt her a hard blow and began screaming all sorts of strange things, yelling at Susana to wake up. She took out her rosary from her skirt pocket and flung it at me crying that Susana was dying and that there was nothing she could do about it. Then she picked up her medicine bag and ran out the door. That was the last I saw of her."

"I should've taken her into town to have a doctor look at her," Fernando said. "The minute I met her at the gate this morning I knew she wasn't feeling well. She looked redder than the sun and she could hardly talk to me. But I was so worried about Susana, I couldn't think of anything but her and the baby."

"We were all thinking of that, especially doña Marciana," Esperanza said softly. "But what I don't understand is why didn't she tell us she was so sick?"

"Some people are just like that, Esperanza," Fernando replied, "unselfish to the end."

Snapshots

Helena María Viramontes

It was the small things in life, I admit, that made me happy; ironing straight arrow creases on Dave's work khakis, cashing in enough coupons to actually save some money, or having my bus halt just right, so that I don't have to jump off the curb and crack my knee cap like that poor shoe salesman I read about in Utah. Now, it's no wonder that I wake mornings and try my damnedest not to mimic the movements of ironing or cutting those stupid, dotted lines or slipping into my house shoes, groping for my robe, going to Marge's room to check if she's sufficiently covered, scuffling to the kitchen, dumping out the soggy coffee grounds, refilling the pot and only later realizing that the breakfast nook has been set for three, the iron is plugged, the bargain page is open in front of me and I don't remember, I mean I really don't remember doing any of it because I've done it for thirty years now and Marge is already married. It kills me, the small things.

Like those balls of wool on the couch. They're small and harmless and yet, every time I see them, I want to scream. Since the divorce, Marge brings me balls and balls and balls of wool thread because she insists that I "take up a hobby," "keep as busy as a bee," or "make the best of things" and all that other good natured advice she probably hears from old folks who answer like that when asked how they've managed to live so long. Honestly, I wouldn't be surprised if she walked in one day with bushels of straw for me to weave baskets. My only response to her endeavors is to give her the hardest stares I know how to give when she enters the living room, opens up

16

her plastic shopping bag and brings out another ball of bright colored wool thread. I never move. Just sit and stare.

Mother.

She pronounces the word not as a truth but as an accusation.

Please, Mother. Knit. Do something. And then she places the new ball on top of the others on the couch, turns towards the kitchen and leaves. I give her a minute before I look out the window to see her standing on the sidewalk. I stick out my tongue for effect, but all she does is stand there with that horrible yellow and black plastic bag against her fat leg, and wave good-bye.

Do something, she says. If I had a penny for all the things I have done, all the little details I was responsible for but which amounted to nonsense, I would be rich. But I don't have a thing to show for it. How can people believe that for years I've fought against motes of dust or dirt-attracting floors or bleached white sheets to perfection when a few hours later the motes, the dirt, the stains return to remind me of the uselessness of it all? I was always too busy to listen to swans slicing the lake water or watch the fluttering wings of wild geese flying south for a warm winter. I missed the heart beat I could have heard if I just held Marge a little closer.

I realize all that time is lost now, and I find myself searching for it frantically under the bed where the balls of dust collect undisturbed and untouched, as it should be.

To be quite frank, the fact of the matter is I wish to do nothing, but allow indolence to rush through my veins with frightening speed. I do so because I have never been able to tolerate it in anyone, including myself.

I watch television to my heart's content now, a thing I rarely did in my younger days. There were several reasons for this. While I was growing up, television had not been invented. Once it was and became a must for every home, Dave saved and saved until we were able to get one. But who had the time? Most of my time was spent working part time as a clerk for Grants, then returning to create a happy home for Dave to remember. This is the way I pictured it:

His wife in the kitchen wearing a freshly ironed apron, stirring a pot of soup, whistling a whistle-while-you-work tune, and preparing frosting for some cup-cakes so that when he drove home from work, tired and sweaty, he would enter his castle to find his cherub baby in a pink day suit with newly starched ribbons crawling to him and his wife looking at him with pleasing eyes and offering him a cup-cake. It was a good image I wanted him to have and everyday I almost expected him to stop, put down his lunch pail and cry at the whole scene. If it wasn't for the burnt cup-cakes, my damn varicose veins, and Marge blubbering all over her day suit, it would have made a perfect snapshot for him to keep.

Snapshots are ghosts. I am told that shortly after women are married, they become addicted to one thing or another. In Reader's Digest, I read stories of closet alcoholic wives who gambled away grocery money or broke into their children's piggy banks in order to quench their thirst and fill their souls. Unfortunately I did not become addicted to alcohol because my only encounter with it had left me senseless and with my face in the toilet bowl. After that, I had never had the desire to repeat the performance of a junior in high school whose Prom date never showed. I did consider my addiction a lot more incurable. I had acquired a habit much more deadly: nostalgia.

The habit began after Marge was born and I had to stay in bed for months because of my varicose veins. I began flipping through my family's photo albums, to pass the time and pain away. However I soon became haunted by the frozen moments and the meaning of memories. Looking at the old photos, I'd get real depressed over my second grade teacher's smile or my father's can of beer or the butt-naked smile of me as a young teen, because every detail, as minute as it may seem, made me feel that so much had passed unnoticed. As a result, I began to convince myself that my best years were up and that I had nothing to look forward to in the future. I was too young and too ignorant to realize that that section of my life relied wholly on those crumbling photographs and my memory and I probably wasted more time longing for a past that never really existed. Dave eventually packed them up in a wooden crate to keep me from hurting myself. He was good in that way. Like when he clipped roses for me, he made sure the thorns were cut off so I didn't have to prick myself while putting them in a vase. And it was the same thing with the albums. They stood in the attic for years until I brought them down the day after he remarried.

The photo albums are unraveling and stained with spills and finger prints and filled with crinkled faded gray snapshots of people I can't remember anymore, and I turn the pages over and over again as I once did shortly after Marge was born, to see if somehow, some old dream will come into my blank mind, like the black and white television box when I turn it on. It warms up then flashes instant picture, instant lives, instant people.

Parents. That I know for sure. The woman is tall and long, her plain, black dress is over her knees, and she wears thick spongelike shoes. She's over to the right of the photo, looks straight ahead at the camera. The man wears white, baggy pants held high up above his waist with thick suspenders. He smiles while holding a dull-faced baby. He points to the camera. His sleeves are rolled up, his tie undone, his hair messy, as if some wild woman has driven his head between her breasts and run her fingers into his perfect grease ducktail.

My mother always smelled of smoke and vanilla and that is why I stayed away from her. I suppose that is why my father stayed away from her as well. I don't ever remember a time when I saw them show any sign of affection. Not like today. No sooner do I turn off the soaps when I turn around and catch two youngsters on a porch swing, their mouths open, their lips chewing and chewing as if they were sharing a piece of three-day-old liver. My mom was always one to believe that such passion should be kept to the privacy of the home, and then, there, too, be expressed efficiently and without the urgency I witness almost everyday. Dave and I were good at that.

Whenever I saw the vaseline jar on top of Dave's bedstand, I made sure the door was locked and the blinds down. The anticipation was more exciting than the actual event. Him lifting up my flannel gown over my head, slipping off my underwear. The vaseline came next, he slipping into me, coming right afterwards. In the morning Dave looked into my eyes and I could never figure out what he expected to find there. Eventually, there came a point in our relationship when passion passed to Marge's generation, and I was somewhat relieved. And yet, I could never imagine Marge doing those types of things that these youngsters do today, though I'm sure she did them on those Sunday afternoons when she carried a blanket and a book, and told me she was going to the park to do some reading and returned hours later with the bookmark in the same place. She must have done them, or how else could she have gotten engaged, married, had children all under my nose, and me still going to check if she is sufficiently covered? Mother? Marge's voice from the kitchen. It must be evening. Every morning it's the ball of wool, every evening it's dinner. Honestly, she treats me as if I had an incurable heart ailment. She stands in the doorway.

Mother? Picture it. She stands in the doorway looking befuddled, as if a movie director had instructed her to stand there and look confused and upset; stand there as if you have seen your mother sitting in the same positon for the last nine hours.

What are you doing to yourself? Marge is definitely not one for originality and she repeats the same lines every day. I'm beginning to think our conversation is coming from discarded scripts. I know the lines by heart, too. She'll say: Why do you continue to do this to us? and I'll answer: Do what? and she'll say: This—waving her plump coarse hands over the albums scattered at my feet—and I'll say: Why don't you go home and leave me alone? This is the extent of our conversation and usually there is an optional line like: I brought you something to eat, or, let's have dinner, or, come look what I have for you or even, I brought you your favorite dish.

I think of the times, so many times, so many Mother's days that passed without so much as a thank you or how sweet you are but I guess I am to blame. When Marge first started school, she had made a ceramic handprint for me to hang in the kitchen. My hands were so greasy from cutting the fat off some porkchops that I dropped it before I could even unwrap my first Mother's day gift. I tried gluing it back together again with flour and water paste, but she never forgave me and I never received another gift until after the divorce. I wonder what happened to the ceramic handprint I gave to my mother.

In the kitchen I see that today my favorite dish is Chinese food getting cold in those little urn like containers. Yesterday, my favorite dish was a salami sandwich, and before that a half-eaten rib, no doubt left over from Marge's half hour lunch. Last week she brought me some Sunday soup that had fish heads floating around in some greenish broth. When I threw it down the sink, all she could think of to say was: Oh, Mother.

We eat in silence or rather, she eats. I don't understand how she can take my indifference. I wish that she would break out of her frozen look, jump out of any snapshot and slap me in the face. Do something, I beg. Do something. I begin to cry.

Oh, Mother she says, picking up the plates and putting them in the sink. Mother, please.

There's fingerprints all over this one, my favorite. Both woman and child are clones, same bathing suit, same ponytails, same ribbons. The woman is looking directly at the camera, but the man is busy making a sand castle for his daughter. He doesn't see the camera or the woman. On the back of this one, and in vague pencil scratching, it says: San Juan Capistrano.

This is a bad night. On good nights, I avoid familiar spots. On bad nights I am pulled towards them so much so that if I sit on the chair next to Dave's I begin to cry. On bad nights I can't sleep and on bad nights I don't know who the couples in the snapshots are. My mother and me? Me and Marge? I don't remember San Juan Capistrano and I don't remember the woman. She faded into thirty years of trivia. I don't even remember what I had for dinner, or rather, what Marge had for dinner, just a few hours before. I wrap a blanket around myself and go into the kitchen to search for some evidence, but except for a few crumbs on the table, there is no indication that Marge was here. Suddenly, I am relieved when I see the box containers in the trash under the sink. I can't sleep the rest of the night wondering what happened to my ceramic handprint, or what was in the boxes. Why can't I remember? My mind thinks of nothing but those boxes in all shapes and sizes. I wash my face with warm water, put cold cream on, go back to bed, get up and wash my face again. Finally, I decided to call Marge at 3:30 in the morning. The voice is faint and there is static in the distance.

Yes? Marge asks automatically. Hello.

21

I almost expected her to answer her usual "Dave's Hardware." Who is this? Marge is fully awake now.

What did we, I ask, wondering why it was suddenly so important for me to know what we had for dinner. What did you have for dinner? I am confident that she'll remember every movement I made or how much salt I put on whatever we were, or rather, she was eating. Marge is good about details.

Mother?

Are you angry that I woke you up?

Mother. No. Of course not.

I could hear some muffled sounds, vague voices, static. I can tell she is covering the mouthpiece with her hand. Finally George's voice.

Mrs. Ruiz, he says, restraining his words so that they almost come out slurred, Mrs. Ruiz, why don't you leave us alone? And then there is a long buzzing sound. Right next to the vaseline jar are Dave's cigarettes. I light one though I don't smoke. I unscrew the jar and use the lid for an ashtray. I wait, staring at the phone until it rings.

Dave's Hardware, I answer, Don't you know what time it is?

Yes. It isn't Marge's voice. Why don't you leave the kids alone? Dave's voice is not angry. Groggy, but not angry. After a pause I say:

I don't know if I should be hungry or not.

You're a sad case. Dave says it as coolly as a doctor would say, You have terminal cancer. He says it to convince me that it is totally out of his hands. I panic. I picture him sitting on his side of the bed in his shorts, smoking under a dull circle of light. I know his bifocals are down to the tip of his nose.

Oh, Dave, I say. Oh, Dave. The static gets worse.

Let me call you tomorrow.

No. It's a bad night.

Olga. Dave says my name so softly that I could almost feel his warm breath on my face. Olga, Why don't you get some sleep?

The first camera I ever saw belonged to my grandfather. He won it in a cock fight. Unfortunately he didn't know two bits about it. but he somehow managed to load the film. Then he brought it over to our house. He sat me on the lawn. I was only five or six years old, but I remember the excitement of everybody coming around to get into the picture. I can see my grandfather clearly now. I can picture him handling the camera slowly, touching the knobs and buttons to find out how the camera worked while the men began gathering around him expressing their limited knowledge of the invention. I remember it all so clearly. Finally, he was able to manage the camera, and he took pictures of me standing near my mother.

My grandmother was very upset. She kept pulling me out of the picture, yelling to my grandfather that he should know better, that snapshots steal the souls of the people and that she would not allow my soul to be taken. He pushed her aside and clicked the picture.

The picture, of course, never came out. My grandfather, not knowing better, thought that all he had to do to develop the film was unroll it and expose it to the sun. After we all waited for an hour, we realized it didn't work. My grandmother was very upset and cut a piece of my hair probably to save me from a bad omen.

It scares me to think that my grandmother may have been right. It scares me even more to think I don't have a snapshot of her. So, I'll go through my album, and if I find one, I'll tear it up for sure.

Como el cristal al romperse

Luz Selenia Vásquez

I

A veces se despertaba con coraje, porque se levantaba con la bata mojada. Las sábanas siempre estaban pegajosas y se pegaban a sus piernas. El olor a orines siempre la sacaba de sus sueños de playas y palmas. Por esa razón, se despertaba con coraje. Las enfermeras la forzaban fuera de su cama, pero nunca la dejaban quitarse la bata hasta que acababa con el desayuno. Eso le daba más coraje. Tenía que andar así, mojada y apestosa; tenía que comer con el olor de la bata que le daba náuseas. Por eso a veces vomitaba el desayuno. Pero después de mirar el vómito manchar la bata y sentir su calor por el cuello y la cara, después de tocarlo y sentirlo con sus dedos, venían siempre las enfermeras para desamarrarla de la silla y llevarla a la ducha. Siempre era lo mismo, las mismas palabras, la misma pelea.

La Rubia siempre la miraba con asco y decía:

"OK, Carrera, strip."

Nunca le gustaba quitarse la ropa allí delante de la gente.

"Carrera, I said strip, come on take off the nightgown. We haven't got all day."

Lo peor era que nunca la dejaban dormir con ropa interior. "Look Carrera, either you undress or we undress you. Shit,

24

this is an everyday thing with you, you know damn well that we'll take it off for you."

No le gustaba que nadie la viera desnuda.
"McConnell, help me get this off of her, if not we'll be here all day."

Siempre le quitaban la bata y exponían su cuerpo de sesenta y cinco años. Siempre las mismas palabras:
"Oh God, she smells. Carrera, get under that shower."

Y después venía el frío del agua que penetraba sus huesos, que siempre mataba aquel olor.
"OK, Carrera, you can get out now."

La secaban con las mismas toallas blancas y peinaban su pelo gris.
"Get her clothes on and put her out in the day room. I got to check on Briggs, she's screaming again."

Siempre la misma pelea. Nunca hablaba con las otras. No valía la pena tratar de comunicarse con ellas, nunca la comprendían. Siempre, siempre las mismas palabras.
"Carrera, don't touch that radio. Can't you see we're watchin' TV?"

Esas voces extranjeras siempre se mezclaban con las voces que venían de adentro.
"Nurse McConnell... Nurse McConnell, get Carrera away from the radio."

A veces no podía oír esas voces porque escuchaba a las otras, las que hablaban español.
"Let Carrera turn on the radio. If not, she'll start screaming."

Y como siempre prendía el radio y buscaba la emisora hispana. La voz del cantante se mezclaba con la de la televisión y llenaba ese cuarto.
        "Si quieres separar nuestro destino... Ya nunca
        me verás en tu camino..."

"Carrera, turn down that radio...Nurse McConnell..."
Tú vivirás sin mí...Yo moriré sin ti...¡Ay!,
   es el destino"
Pero nunca las oía, las voces de ellas siempre se mezclaban con
las otras, con las que hablaban en español. Las que la llamaban
por su nombre, Lupe...Lupita...Doña Lupe...
   "Más nunca, me verás...Jamás, jamás, jamás...
   en tu camino"

Siempre la misma pelea.
"Carrera, I'm going to turn off that damn radio if you don't
turn it down."
   "Yo no regresaré...Jamás, jamás...
   A ver qué cosa fue...de ti, de ti"

Y despúes, despúes empezaba a bailar y no le importaba la
gente ni sus palabras. La gente y su voz desaparecían. Sólo
quedaba siempre el radio, y las voces, las que venían de adentro,
las que en español hablaban de sus recuerdos...
   "Si quieres separar nuestro destino...
   Ya nunca me verás...en tu camino...
   Tú vivirás sin mí...Yo moriré sin ti...
   ¡Ay! es el destino...más nunca me verás...
   Jamás, jamás, jamás...en tu camino."

II

Los miércoles siempre servían "spaghetti". Sabía que era
miércoles por el olor de siempre en el corredor cuando venían
con la comida. Por esa razón, a la hora de almuerzo, siempre se
quedaba cerca del radio. Siempre era la misma escena. Los
muchachos venían con los carros de la comida y los dejaban
en el comedor. Siempre las mismas palabras.
"Alright girls, chow time, come and get it! Damn, you've only
been screaming all morning that you're hungry."

Todo eso le daba más razón para quedarse cerca del radio.
Siempre trataba de esconderse, de hacerse bien chiquita y
esconderse debajo de una silla. Pero la música del radio siempre
la delataba. Siempre estaba tocando fuerte.

26

"Si quieres separar...
Nuestro destino...
Ya nunca me verás en
tu camino..."

Siempre había la misma pelea. La Rubia la buscaba debajo de la silla y la halaba hasta hacerla salir. "Come on, Carrera, it's lunchtime. Why do you always have to give me such a damn hard time? You know you have to eat!" Y después, después la llevaban a la mesa y ponían el plato frente a ella.

"OK, Carrera, no funny stuff this time, just eat and clean that plate. McConnell, keep an eye on her, will ya?"

Nunca le gustaba esa comida. El olor impregnaba su nariz y le daba asco. Siempre trataba de ignorar el olor pero no podía respirar más sin oler esa mezcla de salsa de tomate y plato sucio. Siempre llegaban las mismas palabras. "Carrera, pick up that fork and start eating. I'm not in the mood to force-feed you today."

Y la Rubia siempre se acercaba para mirarla, para amenezarla que si no comía ella iba a hacerla comer. Por esa misma razón siempre intentaba recordar la música, oír el radio que estaba en el otro cuarto.

"Tu vivirás sin mí...
Yo moriré sin ti...
¡Ay! es el destino"

Y a veces, a veces las voces la acompañaban. Las que hablaban en español, las que la llamaban por su nombre, Lupe...Lupita... Doña Lupe. Las voces siempre se mezclaban y el resto del mundo desaparecía. Sólo escuchaba las voces del radio que hablaban en español, las que la llamaban por su nombre. Pero eso nunca duraba mucho. Siempre eran interrumpidas.

"Alright Carrera, you've had long enough. Now, open your mouth, you're gonna eat whether you like it or not."

Siempre la misma escena, siempre la misma pelea. Trataba de permanecer con la boca cerrada. No le gustaba que la forzaran a abrir la boca y por esa razón la Rubia tenía que forzarle la quijada manteniéndola abierta con sus manos. "McConnell, you shove the food in while I hold her mouth open." Ella, mientras tanto, trataba de escuchar el radio que se oía desde el otro cuarto. Sin embargo, cada vez que la comida se le acercaba a la boca la olía y le daban náuseas. Después la sentía en la boca. Siempre estaba tibia y nunca tenía sabor. Las náuseas le invadían el cuerpo entero hasta que sentía que si tragaba la comida, tendría que vomitar el alma. Por esa razón empezaba a hacer arcadas. Brotaban las mismas palabras. "Carrera, don't you dare throw up."

En ese momento siempre trataba de escuchar el radio que se oía desde el otro cuarto para poder olvidar el olor.
"Yo no regresaré
Jamás, jamás...
A ver qué cosa fue...
De ti, de ti."

Y por eso mismo siempre tragaba la comida sin vomitar. Despues de tragarla toda, volvía siempre al otro cuarto. Podía volver y escuchar las voces en paz, las que le hablaban en español, las que la llamaban por su nombre.

III

De noche las otras miraban la televisión. A las ocho siempre venía la Rubia a prender la televisión.
"OK, Girls, it's prime time, what'cha want to watch, Channel 7 or Channel 4? The best shows are on Channel 4 tonite."

Después venían todas para sentarse en fila en frente de la televisión. Las enfermeras regresaban a la oficina a preparar las recetas. Durante esas horas ella se quedaba cerca del radio. No le gustaba la televisión, no la entendía. Permanecía en su rincón tocando el radio y bailando. Venía la misma pelea. Las otras se enfurecían porque el radio las molestaba. Decían

28

siempre lo mismo.
"Carrera, turn off that radio, we're trying to watch TV. Nurse McConnell, Nurse McConnell, tell Carrera to turn off that radio. We can't hear the TV."
Siempre lo mismo. Ella nunca las oía. Estaba preocupada con la música y las voces que venían de adentro. Y siempre desaparecía el resto del mundo. Solo oía ese radio.
"Si quieres separar-
Nuestro destino-
Ya nunca me verás-
En tu camino."

Después llegaba la Rubia.
"Carrera, we go through this every night. You have to keep the radio low, because the rest of the girls are watching TV. When are you going to learn Carrera, when?"

La Rubia bajaba el radio hasta que apenas lo podías oír. Esa noche la Rubia regresaba a la oficina cuando oyó el radio tocando duro otra vez.
"Yo no regresaré-
Jamás, jamás,
A ver qué cosa fue...
De ti, de ti...

En eso la Rubia volvió al rincón y empezó:
"Look, Carrera, I'm not going to play this little game with you tonite. Now I'm going to turn this radio down, one more time, and if you turn it up, I'm going to turn it off, and I mean it Carrera, I'm not kidding."

La Rubia volvió a bajar el volumen del radio y empezó a caminar hacia su oficina. Pero llegó al mismo sitio, cuando oyó otra vez:
"Si quieres separar nuestro destino
Ya nunca me verás en tu camino
Tú vivirás sin mí, yo moriré sin ti"

La Rubia se enfureció y se acercó.
"OK, Carrera, you asked for it. I'm taking this damn radio back

into the office with me. You can just live without it for tonite.
That's just what you get for trying to be funny."
La Rubia desenchufó el radio y se lo llevó en sus brazos a la
oficina. Sólo se podía escuchar la televisión.
"Join the Pepsi people...
feeling free, feeling free.
join the Pepsi people...
you be you, I'll be me..."

Las voces habían desaparecido. Se quedó parada en el rincón
tratando de oír las voces, pero no podía. Sólo quedaba el ruido
de la televisión.
"All across the nation
Join the Pepsi generation,
Here today, here to stay..."

Trató de recordar la canción pero la televisión interfería con
sus pensamientos.
Entonces se dio cuenta de que las voces nunca más volverían.
No era como antes, ahora no podía hacer que todo desapareciera.
Levantando las manos, quiso volar. Levantando las manos trató
de imitar a los pájaros y volar a otro sitio. Tenía que ir en
busca de las voces. Echó a correr, echó a volar en círculos,
volaba en círculos en frente de la televisión. Alquien dijo:
"Carrera, stop that! We can't see! Nurse McConnell, come get
Carrera. She's blocking the view!"
Siguió volando más y más ligero en círculos. Las otras seguían
gritando. Estaba tratando de encontrar las voces, de oír la
música otra vez. Vino la Rubia.
"Carrera, I'm going to put you in restraint. Stop it right now!
You hear me, Carrera?"

Ella se dio cuenta que venían con la camisa de fuerza. Tenía
que volar, tenía que escapar. Vio la televisión y supo que la
única manera de salvarse era usando la televisión. La Rubia
estaba bien cerca. Siguió volando en círculos pero después,
después se estrelló de cabeza contra la televisión.
Vidrio. Podía oír el vidrio romperse cayendo sobre el piso.
Cristal. Podía oír el cristal cayendo al piso. Se podía oír como
si fuera el ruido de botellas al romperse, como los vasos al
quebrarse, como el cristal del espejo al romperse.

Selecciones de su novela
Kiliagonía

Iris M. Zavala

Yo que veía el llanto y sabía la causa, consolaba a las hermanas con las mejores razones. Ellas para divertirme y engañarme decían que no había otro mejor remedio que apartar la memoria de la hermosura. Los enemigos encantadores transformaban el día en noche y no se podía ver y diferenciar las cosas. Aparecieron de pronto muchas lunas pequeñas de resplandecientes espejos y todo lo miré y todo lo noté bajo el asombro. Entonces vi que la luz estaba encubierta porque nunca se había alzado del suelo. En mi alma anochecía la noche al volver a la casa.

Volvamos a la casa. Era grande, labrada de muchos pilares y losas. Cada hermana atravesaba la sala y se sentía en tierra extraña. Presa magnífica de tardes sin prisa, con libertades de lenguaje. Al vuelo las flechas lanzadas al aire. Profesionales de la santidad aquellas tardes ensanchaban sus límites al apretar los cercos de la noche. Infierno abreviado cada noche, cada tarde vencida por el sueño. Las miradas se volvían a cada viento que alargaba su cola de cometa. Vivir receloso aquél, que fabricaba la red para la trampa. Cada día era un cuchillo, cada mirada un farol que perseguía engaños. Cuentan que se eschuchaban de noche hasta los sueños. Sospechaba el pueblo las peores calamidades, derribadas tan bajo cuan alto querían subir. Optima razón para cerrar las puertas y hacer huir la luz. Incursión por regiones mal exploradas. ¡Qué derroche de ingenio! Se daban alas por cada ilusión; genios errantes abrían la razón y los ojos como puente de cristales para engañar la luz. El campo de sus delaciones era cada habitación en sombra. Método excelente. El cúmulo de mentiras imaginadas se explayaba a su antojo cada noche, heraldo casi oficial de remolinos internos que mataban la luz baja los resquicios. Sonaban los golpes, contaban tentaciones con ojos entornados. Era propiamente encomendarse al diablo en el vacío, trazos de hurtarle tiempo al tiempo, haciendo creer que la espera era ayuno voluntario. Estos peligros les dejó la vida en perpetuo silencio. Por eso soy del parecer que el dolor se acaba con la vida.

Pasando revista a todo lo que vi y la ciudad y lugares en los que había estado, observé que los habitantes de Ponce no tenían ningún interés en conocer palacios, casas y calles, sino únicamente las cosas que se supieran habían sido hechas por ellos. Me sorprendió mucho, así que les pregunté por qué menospreciaban los magníficos objetos y sólo se ocupaban de los hechos y asuntos relacionados con ellos. Me fue dicho que la vida de los habitantes es tal que sólo se preocupan de las normas, leyes y honras. Nunca sobre las cuestiones del alma, que son innumerables. Pronto pude comprobar cúan ansiosamente buscan este tipo de conocimiento y cómo penetran en la memoria de todos para apropiarse de cualquier cosa. Tienen tal habilidad en esta tarea, que realizan la operación de saqueo con gran pericia. Tal es su vivo deseo de penetrar en la memoria de los demás, que son cristales. Se deduce de esto que viven en un mundo de sombra. Retirándome un poco, sentí que la luz de mis ojos empezó a volverse oscura y velada. La forma interna del rostro se me transformó, pensando en las hermanas. A través del mal conocí el bien y conocí el bien a través de su contrario. Entonces me fui contenta, llena de dispuesto ánimo.

Estos casos y cosas que suceden en el mundo sobrepasan la imaginación y así no son tenidos por verdaderos. Mi buen crédito no permite que pasen por apócrifos. He buscado algún remedio para aquel pueblo donde moraban dragones, con los cuellos alzados y los ojos abiertos para velar. Que jamás los cerraban, ni pestañaban, de tal manera que perpetuamente estaban en vela. El tiempo giraba allí hacia la noche y llenaba de espesas tinieblas los ojos. Fascinada por el espejismo, si metí en el agua un rostro no lo reconocí.

La verdad es una esfera bellamente circular con el centro en alto equilibrio.

Dígase la verdad. Nadie preguntaba en la casa. Todas las hermanas engañaban y guardaban secreto. De noche oían sus conciencias. De golpe entraba, hablando, aporreando el alma. Duplicada, cada hermana escuchaba con licencia frescamente a su sombra. Gastaban el aire con las quejas cuando éste no estaba en su lugar. Cortesías infinitas cada día. Viéndose tan solas y desfavorecidas intentaban conciliar las voluntades. Plaza de armas la sala. El natural recato impedía mezclar favores con quejas. A tientas y ciegas caminaban por las calles. Entonces ardían las miradas, adulterios de la verdad, siniestros de la información. Pólvora sorda que avisaba a los contrarios. El pueblo era casa con dos puertas encontradas. En la mañana saludaba el amanecer con cantos y los despedía con nocturnos pájaros. Todas las fachadas eran ostentosas, hacían gala de igualarse. Prodigios eran los ojos de la envidia. Salían de sus lóbregos desvanes con solapada alabanza. Estimaban las cosas por de fuera sin atender a la substancia.

XVI

Las puras y limpias aguas de la fuente, a pesar de la pesadumbre, mostraban su claridad. Eran corrientes de líquidos diamantes formados, que cruzando por todo el pueblo, sierpes de cristal parecían. Allí tenían todos cautiva su libertad y no querían ni acertaban a cobrarla. A sus felices nuevas atenta, qudé admirada de la desenvoltura de las aguas y los rostros.
Madrugaba el amanecer para forjar azogues. Narciso reflejado en mil ojos donde peligraba más que en la fuente. Tanto espejo derramado en olas mientras el filo del viento creaba nuevas constelaciones. Se consumían todas las hermanas prisioneras, se consumía el pueblo, que excomulgaba a los intrusos. Todo quedaba a solas para el homicida de narcisos, despectivo y burlón Minotauro de la Casa del Linaje.

El marino vuelve a encontrar, contento,
su apacible río, tras haber viajado
por lejanos bordes, donde veía deslizarse
los barcos.

XIX

De nuevo queda Paloma obligada a poner el bajel en vela
con el próspero viento. Apartándome a un lado del camino,
sentada a orillas de un río, yo torno a mirar atentamente.
Lo que menos me conviene es equivocar el cielo. Remedo de
immensidad en aquellas latitudes. Un viento de vanidad
trastornó el juicio. Allí yo no pude dejar de condenar la
descuidada naturaleza que expone al engaño. No convienen
las tardes, los objetos no permanecen. El alma se retira a su
quietud. No bastan los párpados, con la vista duplicada los
vecinos cuelan las palabras, previniendo de antemano las
vueltas y reveses. Sin discernir la verdad de la mentira escuché
las voces que resonaban en las calles. Recatados disgustos se
detuvieron en los balcones. Descubrí a la gente murmurando
entre sí con una voz baja y compasiva. Esta extraña visión
a tales horas y en tal despoblado bien bastaba para poner miedo
en el corazón.

Famosos hechos de hazañas immortales enorgullecían al
pueblo, puerta principal de la isla, coronado de varonil decoro.
Allí asistía lo mejor. Todo concurría en especial calidad. No
era de maravillar la cortesía de las palmas. La fuente, equívoca
de aguas y fuegos, se deslizaba siempre huyendo de los
peregrinos que seguían sus cristales. Picados en lo vivo, en
la tarde los labios salían del leberinto de sus enredos sin osar
palabra. Los ojos andaban sin libertad; poca o ninguna vez
salían de la casa. Mentira continuada cada casa donde el sol
se vengaba eclipsándose por puntos. Con furor corrían a
oscuras los ojos, tropezando unos con otros. Portentos seme-
jantes eran natural efecto en aquel pueblo poblado de balcones
y persianas. En él se andaba apenas tropezando con las puertas,
pocas y cerradas. Mirar equívoco que de la ajena gloria hacía
infiernos. Cada labio mordíase por entrar, dando vuelta a las
casas.

Es cosa de ver las vueltas y revueltas de las calles. Casas
de llanto, donde las fiestas del contento son vigilias del pesar.

Trampa encubierta cada entrada, cada pórtico que saludaba con todo cumplimiento. Allí se revolvía todo sin dejar cosa en su lugar ni tiempo. Por desmentir al tiempo, a veces se permitían victorias. Pero en la noche, burlado el engaño, se trocan los gestos y todo el mundo engañando o engañándose, halla contento alegrándose de tener tanto bien en sus conciencias. La noche sólo deja lastimado el corazón y misterios en los ojos. Yo, muy a salvo, dejé el sitio; esta gente, aunque vencida, medrosa y sin armas, podría rehacerse y buscarme.

Les pregunté a las hermanas sobre Ponce y a qué semeja desde su casa. Respondieron que desde allí se ve muy grande, mucho más grande que desde las demás. Dijeron que llegaron a saber esto a través de las ideas que los ángeles tenían. Añadieron que había un calor excesivo, dada la circunstancia de la proximidad con el infierno. Pero debo decir que el calor no procede de la proximidad del pueblo al infierno, sino de la altura y densidad de la atmósfera del aire. También hay que observar que el calor varía según la incidencia de los rayos, que puede ser oblicua o perpendicular. Los que habitan en lo recóndito del pueblo están desnudos, pues están en estado de inocencia. Otros están desnudos, pues están en estado de inocencia. Otros están vestidos de ángeles, cosa que no es una mera apariencia, sino realidad. Los ángeles tienen muchos vesitdos y se los ponen y quitan continuamente. Estos son todos los particulares que me dieron a conocer las hermanas respecto a Ponce y sus habitantes.

Se vierten lágrimas por las desgracias,
y el hado mortal conmueve la mente humana.

Se contaban cosas y casos portentosos. En aquel pueblo se decían cosas grandes. Oíase en los estanques cantar a los cisnes todo el tiempo y cuentan que una de las hermanas hizo subir el agua de los ríos. Tenía extremadas manos, que daban vida a todo aquello en que las ponía. Era la remediadora de dichas y sus manos un ardid contra el engaño. Mejoraba los rostros mismos, de modo que de la noche a la mañana se desconocían mudados los pareceres. Esta hermana vivía favorecida de las fantasías. Hacíase ojos y saludaba a todos con la reverencia debida. Miraba los rostros por ver si podía brujulear alguna realidad. A veces era en vano. Sólo sus tres hermanas sabían cerrar las ventanas curvas con celosías muy espesas, otras con vidrieras. Todas de burla y engaño, le hablaban no con su voz sino con la ajena. Se dice que ella llevaba más atravesado el corazón cuanto más del él se apartaba. Maga, hechicera, encantaba a las personas. Me hablaron de Lupe con gran variedad. Se contaban raras maravillas. A ella una misma cosa le era dos veces tormento, primero deseada y después aborrecida. Vivía entre los pueblerinos perseguida y admirada. Relumbraba en sus célebres prodigios. Alternaba, curiosa, certeza y perfecciones. Un día, en los reflejos de la fuente, advirtió que era ella misma a quien creyó otra. Remirábase contemplativa, recta de cuerpo, sin dobleces en el ánimo. Sutilizaban, discurría, suave e inflexible. Admiración y gusto que allí tuvo. Toda ocupada en verse, atendía sus acciones duplicadas. Nunca pudo, corte de confusiones, solicitar favor o poder para rescatar su otro yo cautivo en el estanque. Torcía el espejo a un lado y a otro. Allí, rara maravilla, no pudo salvar el perfil de su sombra. Escondida, yo miraba el pájaro atrapado en los cristales.

Crece el agua mientras más se la descubre.
De aquella fuente caía agua del cielo
Y quedaba todo hecho aire

que no podrán ya dividir ni apartar.
Cuál es el agua del estanque
o el aire que cayó del cielo.

XX

Puesto que con curiosidad y diligencia buscaba los hechos, oía cuanto no había visto. Cuando las cosas se me escondían saltaba de noche guiadas de mi ingenio. El lugar era favorecido para la malicia. La rueda de la memoria descansaba y tomaba aliento cada tarde, aguijón de sendas infinitas. La fama ha guardado en las memorias de Ponce unas famosas justas que en aquella ciudad se hacían. Allí pasaron cosas dignas de valor. Pensativa quedé y toda llena de congoja y pesadumbre me fui por el camino.

Una plaza con iglesia—catedral y el paseo de trances miraban la muchedumbre corrillera que llegaba cada día con anticipadas esperanzas trocando los caminos. Todas las mujeres se sacaban de dudas y al punto se hallaban dentro por la ancha puerta de lamentos. Aspero y desapacible lugar, al que entraban poco a poco mujeres amigas de novedades. Por las tinieblas la voz gangosa atormentaba las llamas internas:

Kyrie eleyson
Christe eleyson
Kyrie eleyson

El mujeril vocerío todo dedos y oídos maltrataba las cuentas negras, dientes con diente. Se atormentaban unas a otras con las miradas, sin dejarse arrancar el secreto hasta la noche. Maridos descuidados, honras inciertas eran desgranadas por las manos y las bocas. Gozaban el infierno ajeno de la carne atormentadas de no sufrirlo en carne propia. Infinitas varas de medir relucían en las tinieblas y se desplegaban como rayos.

En la iglesia en penumbra voces bien vestidas en lo alto, puño y cuello al calor. A cada palabra contestaba la turba de voces: Amén. Piedad, Señor, piedad. El de lo alto, que a la cuenta mandaba, decía:

Omnis homo mortalis.

—Aquí estamos, hermanas, rezando por el alma de Francisca Segarra de Valdivieso, que irá al cielo. Otros hay que perseverando en su mala vida, se aseguran de la divina misericordia. Pero en esta alma, la voluntad tuvo paz consigo y la convirtió en provecho espiritual. Mientras todos haciendo mal esperan en Dios, ella lo esperó. Tuvo entendimiento privado de la visión beatífica. Vio la brevedad de los deleites y la eternidad del alma.

Mentira breve que acabó cuanto duró el resposo. Luego supe que la corte de mujeres a chuchilladas rompió aquella noche la honra así sustentada. No se inquietaron al hacerlo. En sus manos y arbitrio estaba la de todo el mndo. Compuestas costumbres aquellas. Las oí de niña, desvanecida de miedo y de pena.

XXI

No pienso ya si hay glorias. Con ceño fruncido bajé aquel día al paseo. Con hurtos de sol y primavera, en el pueblo

37

las setenta casas de la plaza se abrían. Eduvige leía la pragmática, linda ocasión aquella para burlarla. Indicio breve de cambios la mañana. Su voz era débil sonido, pólvora oprimida su anciano cuerpo de ébano. Pavoroso ceño el del pueblo, que la salpicaba con rotas dicciones. Lumbre frenética de atropelladas voces.

Eduvige siguió con balbuciente lengua, en mal pronunciadas letras que salían del arcabuz de la garganta.

En la cuidad de Ponce, a los catorce días del mes de septiembre, ante mí, el infrescrito Escribano Real y Público, y testigos
Testigos, testigos de doblarle la cerviz en apacible gesto La rauca voz seguía

se da ya concede plena y gracios libertad a Eduvige Cornelia Cipriano del Carmen, de sesenta años, de la propiedad de doña Juliana Lucas-Maristany, tasada la Eduvige en ochenta pesos...Doy fe...

Giraba desigual el tiempo para todos. Punta altiva su encorvado cuerpo entre las mudas voces. Ella, nacida sombra del soberbio pueblo, aun con abiertos ojos no miraba las mansiones sombrías. Sus ojos se fijaban en sus manos y palpában sus piernas. Simulacros de libertad aquellos papeles firmados por nocturnas manos, jeroglíficos de ciego error.

Un ejército de sombras la seguía. La tardía o mal recobrada libertad no la engañaba. Voraz, el tiempo no borraría las huellas. Eduvige aún no sabía recobrarse a sí misma. Aquel día fue sola a la fuente. El cristalino portento fue obstáculo opaco que empañó el aire. En el estanque permanece cautiva. Eduvige desata las cadenas del sueño.

Prosigue, Paloma, tu cuento, y repite los sueños. Estos son fuerzas de la imaginación donde suelen representarse las cosas con tanta vehemencia, que se agarran de la memoria, de manera que quedan en ella, siendo mentiras, como si fueran verdades.

XXII

El ocio peregrinaba allí por los balcones. Las miradas corrían tras las noticias, fábulas de todos. La murmuración de celosías no dejaba sentido para el cansancio. Se turbaban los ojos imaginando placeres. Las ventanas ardían de ira bajo el calor, hurtando horas fugitivas al tiempo. El día desmentía su nombre disfrazado de sombras. Trasgos abreviados las palabras que penetraban por los resquicios de las puertas. Las calles y plazas estaban pobladas de figuras acechantes. Cada rostro paseaba rey de la calle, cintas, encaje y cadena de oro. Todo el pueblerino vocerío se medía por el grande empeño de vacilar secretos. No se sale—me dije—sino por la puerta del agua. Para sacarme de esta extraña imaginación muchos decían que les hablase desde lejos y les preguntase lo que quisiera.

Doña Fidela López de Peralta había procurado siempre llamarse señoría y entretenía memorias melancólicas. Su nombre no era una palabra breve, infinita muchedumbre de perfecciones sus canas que le permitían los consejos y las manos agujereadas, las oraciones. Visitaba poco las casas llanas. Los días aciagos entretenía la mentira y alimentaba las apariencias. No se espantaba de saber poco. Según su natural, revisaba todo el concurso de gente. Envainando sus gestos a las tres de la tarde incensaba la iglesia con sus faldas. Dirigía la procesión de sayas enlutadas, también la seguían las muchachas de la doctrina que llegaban a la plaza gritando su letanía, abreviando las velas para tener tiempo de sumirse en el paseo y hablar de mano. La iglesia era solo convite para las viejas que recibían con gusto el enviudar de las amigas y los entierros. Templo sin doctores, lleno de cuentas y cuchicheos.

El plañido de las campanas a voces era llanto autorizado. El pueblo las olía desde lejos. Las casas se despojaban entonces y desnudaban sus paredes. Sollozos y suspiros llenaban aposentos y lloraba a tientas y oscuras doña Fidela. Las demás mujeres remediaban con el lloro sus perdidas voces. Reloj anticipado, ella animaba a conformarse a la desdicha, mientras hacía llover del cielo virtudes y miserias.

Sólo una vez la vi entrar en mi casa. Ni en el camino ni en ella tenía atrevimiento para alzar los ojos al cielo, que me parecía que sobre sus párpados cargaba todo el peso de la deshonra y la pesadumbre del mundo.

Digo, en fin, sobre cuán, flacos cimientos levanté tan grandes quimeras.

AQUI YACE LOLA CALVO DE BARCELO,
QUE MURO POR CASAR. DESMAYOS
(ACABARON
SU VIDA DE DONCELLA ENCERRADA.)

Yo estuve encerrada mucho tiempo, pero viendo que la desgracia continuaba, determiné andar libre y salí por la ciudad, causando admiración y lástima a los que me conocían.

XXIII

A cada viento volvian las puertas su silencio. Atravesé la calle desierta, vestida de humildad. Aquellas aceras eran tierra extraña: vivir receloso el de los grandes. Cada celosía era un cuchillo silencioso y cada rayo de luz larga cola de dragones. Ostentación a título de ricos. Era atrevimiento levantar la voz. En embeleso, los pueblerinos ojos escondían sus atrevimientos y hablaban quedo. A solas consideraban cómo entrar con la luz del mediodía por las persianas.

Pocas horas se habían entrado por el día cuando poco y de mala gana los Lucas-Maristany abrían las puertas. Porque se oyese el ruido que hacía, yo daba gritos y hacía expirar en mis manos las piedras. Obligaba a la risa a volver por mí. Al mediodía limpiaba mi falda lo mejor que podía y aguardaba a que se abrieran. Entre mí decía ¡Alerta!, proponiéndome hacer nuevo oído a cuanto vislumbrara en el patio.

Confieso que es poca la nobleza que hay entre la gente principal. Las casas estaban pobladas de sombras y gastaban todo el día en aumentarse. En el confín de la calle veía correrse bultos que no podía tomar con la mano. Afligíame mucho por no poder nombrar las cosas. Desgracia grande en un palmo de cuerpo. De claro en claro llegaba la noche, al amanecer estaba yo apartada en aparente dulzura. A todos les hacía cortesía, haciendo culebras de una acera a otra. Al llegar a la calle, iba pisando tieso para disimular mi flaqueza.

Puestos en las ventanas los ojos, era de contemplar las trazas que me daba por hurtarle el secreto a la casa. Quedó su presencia tan impresa en mi alma, que no la podía apartar de mi memoria. Nunca logré, penetrarla, aún contemplo las puertas marchitas con embeleso.

Abran
yo no puedo estar por las calles.
Déjenme entrar.
Con los dedos crispados
aprieto la garganta del timbre.

XXIV

El clavo de la rueda de la fortuna giró y la esfera de su movimiento rompió el silencio. Con un grande suspiro se agitaron las sombras de melancolía. Aquellas tres oficiosas, digo, atrevidas hermanas, eran las piadosas medianeras del pueblo. Cuerpos opacos, compuestos triplicados en acecho. Filomena, Fidela, Carola, sombras fugaces en los resquicios de las puertas. Aguas y vientos dividían. Con ellas el alba le usurpó su púrpura a la aurora. Triforme pavor, aves nocturnas sin plumas aladas. Todo, en fin, ocupaban con sus cuentas. Los numerosos cristales del rosario se enturbiaban en sus dedos.

Digo, pues, que eran medianeras de sombras. Tendían corporales cadenas desde el cálculo pequeño de su sala. Embestían con armas soñolientas y hacían ceder la luz. Ellas traían los fantasmas que huían, multiformes, portentos de engaño. Estiraban los reflejos oscureciéndolos, fingiéndolos. Hasta la azogada luna de la fuente se hundía en aguas turbias y revueltas. Gobernaban olvidos, componían y descomponían las tardes. Reino de pesadumbre su casa, urdimbre de falsas verdades. Puerta de sombra, modelo de labertintos y centro de minotauros.

Y no puedo dejar de decir que tenían muchas finezas. Dicen que una vez ostentaron tres hermosos rostros. Los peligros y las tentaciones los voltearon al revés. Espejos convexos ahora, belleza rota remendada por oraciones. Todas ángulo, sin perspectiva ni igualdad. Sus huellas miraban hacia atrás y sus manos hilaban la camisa o mortaja de las famas. Cien candados de bronce corrían entonces. Ninguna puerta se abría en los huecos de sus quicios sin dar paso a un redoble de campanas. Hace ya tiempo fueron las amargas fuentes de mi llanto.

41

Habiéndoles preguntado sobre la forma de sus casas, respondieron que son bajas, de madera sin tejados inclinados, con una cornisa que lleva el agua al suelo. Viven en las habitaciones frontales. Además, dijeron que únicamente se relacionan con los miembros de su propia familia. Por mí supieron que su año tiene seiscientos días y que las distancias y la noción del espacio dependen totalmente del estado interior de sus almas. Ocurrió cuanto he dicho, pero mi cuerpo permanece en el mismo lugar en donde el viaje comenzó. El envés y revés quedaba segado en los balaústres de la casa. Los enigmas transparentes pasaban por sombras. En la noche el orden. El pueblerino en gris o negro todas las mañanas. Vieja superlativa aquella Filomena que paseaba todas las mañanas sin presunción de mocedad. Polilla en los huesos de sus manos torcidas. Enflautadora de sueños, amanecida de voces, portavoz de la huida del mundo, con acentos nuevos para celebrar el juicio y el infierno. Ilustre alteradora de balcones y celosías;

Descuidada y divertida, su sueño envejeció y murió incrédulo. La visión beatífica del rey de sotas fue también su posada, perseguida por mil balcones que le huían. Los desengaños le servían de espuelas a la legión de demonios que tenía en el cuerpo.

Llegó en esto el día y quedé sin pulso con la amargura de lo que miraba. La voz se me pegó en la garganta y pudo tanto el dolor, que no me dejó tomar aliento para proseguir camino. Determiné irme con el mismo silencio y recato que había venido.

XXV

Vuelvo a mi comenzado y nunca acabado cuento. En la historia peregrina los rostros son infinitos y unos se encadenan de otros y se eslabonan, formando un continuo movimiento.

El alma andaba ocupada en soñar. Colmos de perfecciones su pensamiento, sutileza alada que construía torres de viento. Sus espacios imaginarios—mentira plausible— andaban empinados. Entró al mundo con los ojos del alma cerrados, su esclarecida presencia era piedra de toque al desvelo. ¡Qué

42

tropel de sentimientos la embargaba! No daba tregua a su fiereza y con palabra blanda señoreaba su desamparo. Verdadera señora de sí misma, quedaba absorta, casi desnuda. Todos se conjuraban en perseguirla. Ella no respondía palabra, ni osaba, ni la oían. Más valía enmudecer con ella que segarla dormida. Paseaba con alados pies cada domingo y paraba en el estanque de los leones. Por los cuatro caños brotaba el agua de la fuente. La plaza es célebre por sus líquidos cristales que resbalan sobre el cansancio pueblerino. Para la gente de cuenta había sombras y bancos, extremada cortesía ganaba los rostros. Llegaba la tropa de paseantes y quedaban alterados. Notable vista Carolina Malaret, revolvía el mundo sin saber porqué. Era su natural, hablaba y no la entendían. Contaba historias vagas: Erase un rey...Mostraba su eficacia con el hilo de soplos ¡cosa lastimosa en aquel lugar y tiempo! Volvía inquietando mentiras y recuerdos. Se daba verdes de juventud y caía en encubierta trampa de flores. Al vuelo, volvía los ojos hacia adentro, Carolina Malaret, pereciendo su memoria con sonido de otras voces.

Nadie podía competir con Carolina Malaret. Se llevaba los ojos, el tiempo volvía al revés. Con su paso no dejaba cosa en su lugar ni tiempo. Con incauta candidez sacaba al mundo de sus quicios. Iba muy consolada y miraba siempre al mundo no como le suelen mirar todos, sino por la otra parte, haciéndose la desentendida. Sabía los atajos del sueño, siguiéndola no era fácil volver atrás y desenredarse.

Qué enjambre de moscas la seguía los domingos a la plaza. Maravillosas sutilezas de silencio. Con el tiempo perdió de todo punto el habla. Todo el interior se le revolvió y quedó llena de aire. Siempre tuve yo mala sospecha de que vio más dormida que vieron cuantos ojos tiene el cielo en sus estrellas. Un día creí no verla más, con que quedé muriendo.

La mueca engaño agitaba los rostros. El sol se ahuecaba en sombras, que estiraban los reflejos de la fuente. Atenta a su oficio de medir el tiempo, Carolina Malaret, con la brújula de su entendimiento, se hundía en sus aguas revueltas. Rostro tornadizo el suyo, donde la ilusión se quedaba ya a medio camino. Gobernaba sus olvidos en pensamientos invisibles.

43

La plaza era su reino de pesadumbre, allí descosía los recuerdos y se olvidaba de sí misma. Había desbordado el dolor. La fuente tornaba la luna de sus espejos al reflejarla. Simulacros de verdad los de la fuente de los leones. Allí urdía falsas verdades: Una vez, en 1837...la plaza no existía entonces, ni las mansiones vastas y melancólicas. Carolina Malaret enredaba los hilos de la verdad. Evocaciones inciertas aquellas. Fue en 1898, con los americanos...

The March

LAKE SAGARIS

S he started up out of her sleep, like a mother who has lost
her child. She rubbed her eyes with unaccustomed force
and looked around her, feeling the unusual silence of the
place. Where was she? Shreds of dreams and memory clung to
her and she had trouble knowing which was which.

She stared at the canvas walls, hastily put together, eyes
of light peering at her through the holes. Then she remembered
something. Tito! Where was he?

She scrambled up off the floor and only then did she
realize how stiff and bruised she felt. What had happened?
She went outside. The tent crouched with a hundred others,
grey, weatherbeaten, huddled together as if a wolf were stalking
the horizon.

A shadow of voices murmuring, the clatter of pots and
pans and the smell of beans for breakfast (the same odor which
had followed them from home to here, the big city, the capital,
the President's house...ah, that was it, the President). But
where was Tito? Her dark-eyed, skinny son, with two dimples
so deep it looked like his smile had been nailed on. Indeed,
his three-year-old eyes expressed an anguish that made his
smile unreal, irrelevant.

"Tito!" she cried. "Tito! Where are you? Come here." A
gust of empty wind darted past her, but nothing more, no
answer, no footsteps, no voices whispered in the dry canvas,
hot under the midday sun.

She saw her old shawl, now a clumsy tent door, and remembered trying to decide whether to take it or not. She heard

Chavela's voice calling her: "Rosamaría! Ven pu'h! Nos vamos ahora mismo," and she remembered grabbing Tito's hand and hurrying after her friend.

That was it, of course. That's why there was no one here. They had risen early to go downtown to see the President, to tell him everything, to ask for help.

'But I went with them,' she thought, confused. With little Tito beside me, his thin legs agile as a spider's even though he's only three years old.

She remembered the time he'd gone wandering and got locked behind the heavy wooden door where they parked the mine vehicles. Less than a year old and he'd pulled and crawled his way up the door. She had turned at the sound of his plaintive "ma—ma," only to see his head disappear abruptly as he lost his grip and fell.

She could hear him crying as she threw herself against the rough boards, trying to get to him. And then she was rolling on the ground, her son beside her, the security guard who had opened the door laughing down at them. His laughter was rain-fresh. She looked at her wandering son and she too began to laugh. A sudden smile chased the tears from Tito's face.

He's a tough one, she thought proudly, as hard and dark as the coal they tear from the mines, with the same fire glowering inside.

Perhaps this is a dream, she thought. Perhaps they had only just arrived and, exhausted from the long march she was sleeping, dreaming. But she remembered the morning. Where had they all gone? Where had they taken the morning?

She looked down the dusty road that stumbled uncertainly into the city and remembered Chavela: "Ya, Rosamaría. Ven acá. We're going to see the president. We're going to explain about the strike, the prices, the company store, how the children…"

While she listened to her friend's confident voice, she watched his thin legs flash in the sun as he kicked a stone down the hill, and ran after it.

Dreaming or waking she walks down the hill and with each step the city moves toward her, its paved streets hold her feet, the hot air burns her face, she sees again the people's

46

eyes, turned toward them, this raggle-taggle mob of women and children who've come to see the President, come to explain why the strike, why the men won't go back to work until the company—

"Tito," she calls. And searches among the dirty children playing on the cracked sidewalk. Tito, she calls again, unconsciously tracing the same route, following the morning, Chavela, her son's legs, the sturdy arms and backs of neighbors and friends, the white blouses clouded with dust, the dark hair streaked with grey and a hunger for justice hidden behind the wrinkled mouths, cared for by the rough hands, like a weak child, all the more loved because its time is so short.

Asleep, or awake, she follows the memory of movements down the main street toward the palace, remembers her husband's grey, gritty kiss, his eyes red from coal dust and lack of sleep, alive with something she'd never seen before. There was exhaustion, attraction, and something new, surprise, as if she were a stranger, this woman, this wife, who suddenly left the daily ticking of their life to go out and meet the President, to argue for justice for her husband, her son, for all the miners on strike. And Tito marched along beside her, or rode majestic on her broad shoulders. She remembered her husband watching her, that new expression on his face, on all the strikers' faces, their husbands, their brothers, their fathers, waiting at home for the women who left for the city.

And here she was, dreaming awake in the city, her hand full of the memory of Tito's hand, her eyes full of the memory of all those backs and steady arms, heads held high, marching to the palace gates, calling the President, calling and calling, a hundred voices, a hundred women's voices, the children laughing, a thousand voices crying out for their daily bread, not pleading, not begging, claiming the daily bread earned in the daily struggle in the mines. She had never been down a mine, but she knew it intimately. Her husband filled their house with it every night, and took it away with him when he went to work every morning.

But the road she was traveling stopped abruptly in a wooden barricade, guarded by soldiers.

"Where are you going?" one asked, stepping in front of her, his machine gun cradled in his arms.

"I want my son," she said. "We came by here. I remember."

He looked at her. A shadow crossed his face. He pushed her away.

"Move along, lady. The road to the palace is closed. You can't pass."

She had been at the end of the long line of women. Tito had wandered off; she remembered seeing him kick a stone and run and then a line of soldiers, and then the thunder of bullets as if the whole world had caved in. And she was running toward her son, and someone beside her fell and clutched her leg. Chavela grabbed her arm and dragged her away screaming, from the President, the shiny clean palace, the soldiers calmly firing. Chavela fell and she had run and run and run, forgetting everything except the time Tito fell off the wooden door, the security guard laughing, his gun a toy in friendly hands, Tito's dimples so deep, like two nails, his hands, the time Tito fell before the soldiers, his dimples obliterated by the sharp teeth of hungry bullets, chewing his face until it was nothing but blood and grey, spongy thoughts that might have been love or mother or one day the mine—

And she was running toward him, ducking under the barricade, past police cars, tanks, ambulances, somewhere here here her son, Chavela, she had to take them home, she had to tell the President, she had to tell the men on strike, the President—! the company—!

The machine gun fire.

And no more memories. No more dreams.

dos

The stories presented in the center of the book are el corazón de este libro, for all are about growing up. They describe not only the women who formed us, but also the ways in which we came to form our own mestiza identities. Often the cuentos force us to remember some of the most painful aspects of growing up Latina—the violence we internalize and then display against our children, the violence our men internalize and display against us.

In these stories, the battle for identity is waged on several fronts: with self, family, friends, and the outer world. Particularly for the U.S. Latina, the rules and values we were taught by mami are often in sharp contrast to the norms of the dominant society.

Los cuentos de nuestra infancia se hallan el centro del libro, porque son el corazón. No sólo hablan de las mujeres que nos moldearon, sino que también de cómo formamos nuestra identidad mestiza. A veces los cuentos nos obligan a recordar los aspectos más dolorosos de crecer latinas—la violencia que internalizamos y luego desplegamos contra nuestros hijos, la violencia que nuestros hombres internalizan y despliegan contra nosotras.

En estos cuentos la batalla por la identidad se libra en varios campos: consigo misma, con la familia, con amistades y con el mundo externo. Especialmente para la latina en los EEUU los valores que nos enseñó mami a menudo resaltan en agudo contraste con las normas de la sociedad que nos rodea.

Hunger's Scent

CENEN

L ittle wind blew that day. White fluffy clouds floated slowly across the turquoise skies as though weightless. From a distance, the pine trees with their pointy tops appeared to tickle the bottoms of the passing clouds. The trees swayed majestically in the gleaming sun, rooted in fertile soil and fed by fresh air and plentiful rainfall, they were home—this was the boundary to our camp.

Sunlight drenched the dry, dusty browndirt roads, fringed on each side by cut grass, uncut only around the edge of the forest, the lake, the public toilets and the wooden houses, areas mainly used only by the workers. Each house rested on four cinder blocks which were secured to each corner by a thin piece of wire. That was our camp's foundations— this, in hurricane territory.

Ninety houses stood in five or six rows of military-like formation. With one exception, all had two rooms. The different one stuck out like a soldier out of uniform. Those who had lived in the camp seasons before me said it had been enlarged by a Mexican to keep his twelve children together.

Each room was wide enough for two army surplus, metal-framed, mud-colored bunkbeds placed lengthwise across from each other. In each room, one bare lightbulb hung from a long electrical cord wound around the center beams of the two-by-four wooden frame which held up the zinc plank ceiling. For the use of the electricity, a dollar a week was subtracted from each worker's pay, regardless of how many workers lived in the same house. Three dollars a week was

taken from my mother and my fourteen and fifteen year old
brothers. When my thirteen year old brother and I picked
tomatoes one weekend, a dollar was taken from each of our
75¢-an-hour kid's pay; the adults earned $1.00. Unemploy-
ment insurance was collected from each of the 500 or more
weekly workers, though as migrant workers and/or children,
we couldn't collect unemployment insurance.

The houses' wooden windows were each held open by
half a broomstick. Water came from outdoor spigots. The
public toilets were an equivalent of two and-a-half city blocks
away. They sat in cinder block houses, in two rows of fifteen
which faced each other. There were no partitions from
commode to commode. The workers preferred the privacy of
the dense forest.

Each house had two doors. Mami and I stood near the
one where the hot plate was. It was an early summer morning.
She was standing with her back to me, attempting to make
breakfast.

"Mami, what's there to eat?" — I asked, though I already
knew. I was hoping for something more. As she turned towards
me I felt as though I could hear her forty-two year old bones
creaking. Her bloodshot eyes looked down and away from me.
Her tired face twisted, distorting itself as though uncomfort-
ably anticipating my reaction to her answer. She spun her
words in front of her like a spider's web shield which vindi-
cated her while at the same time, leaving my anger unjustified:

"Some of that bread from yesterday..." — she said. But
quickly added with an uneasy cheerfulness betrayed by a
crack in her suddenly louder voice — "I'm making some coffee
with powdered milk for Grandma. You can have some t—"

"THAT HARD BREAD! I'M HUNNGRY!" — We had been
eating from that bread for days. I never drank coffee and
she knew that.

"I want something to EEAT!"

"That's all there is." — She answered with meek finality.

"Then I don't want it!" —

I jumped out of the door to the ground just below.

Angry! Hungry! And not knowing where to go for food
I pounded my feet down the dirt road heading in the direction
of the artificial lake. Where the rows of houses ended, the

51

trees and tall grass began. The lake was not much further away. By the time I reached it my rage had given way to thinking of ways to find food. I remembered finding a snake skin earlier that year. Maybe I could find the snake this time. There were plenty of rocks to kill it with, I just hadn't thought of how to cook it yet.

With a rock in my right hand and a twig in the other, I screwed up my eyes to readjust them from the sun's summer brilliance to the shady, untreaded earth between the large tree roots, growing partially above ground. I overturned rocks and poked through layers of dried leaves which rolled away easily, revealing the wet, sticky decaying ones underneath. As I worked, I remember telling myself I was holding the rock too tight, and that if the snake showed I wouldn't be able to let go of the rock. I began to look up at the trees and started to imagine large ripe pears weighing down the tree branches. I stared up hoping to really see the fruit, but suddenly remembered there had been none in the past seasons:

I remembered it was the end of Fall when we first arrived at the camp; there were no fruits then. Nor were there any in the Winter that followed. It was my first Christmas at the camp. The camp owner had all of us line up to receive a set of clothes and a toy for each child. I wanted a white ball with red circles on it. But I was 12—"Too old" said the man behind the table with the neatly folded girls blouses. He waved me away, ridiculing my desire with a smile that told me, *I should accept the tightness of my blouse around my chest as a sign of my growing into other games.* At first my mother tried to pacify me by offering to buy me a ball— I knew she wouldn't so I tried to get her to help me get *this ball.* Finally she pushed me aside the same way his smile did. I didn't understand then that in this "grownup's hard-life environment" I needed to feel recognized as a child by the gift of that ball.

Though they didn't live in the camp, the whites were first in line to receive the Christmas gifs, as in the fields where they picked tomatoes from the very tops of the vines, therefore never having to bend. Nor did the Blacks live here either, but then, they weren't allowed to by the owner. The

Blacks were last in line, as in the fields, where they had to bend the lowest to lift the plants to pick everyone else's leavings. The Puertorricans and the Chicanos who did live here fought each other to see who would occupy the middle first...

Spring brought no fruits. But it did bring some happiness with its warmer temperatures after those chilly winter nights had seeped between the houses wooden planks. We didn't have enough warm clothes or blankets to protect ourselves from the cold. But Spring did bring its rainy season...and on one particularly rainy day, the driver of the school bus had decided to help us out of the rain by dropping off all the migrant workers' children last. The rain was pounding the bus' roof, the water streaming down onto the road. We were worried about the bus overturning each time it swerved on the slippery road. Knowing the distance some of us would have to walk to reach our homes, the bus driver had said she'd not leave us at the edge of the road, where foot paths would lead some of us toward camps long walks away. Those who got off at the first campsite stop, glad to have avoided sinking in the mud and wading through small pond-like puddles, wished to hell they had...

From the road to the path the bus ambled like a wobbling, overweight person. Its tires gave temporary company-design tread marks to the muddy earth. The pond-like puddles were displaced by the enormity of the passing bus' weight. Tree branches that had been accustomed to sharing their heights with only their own, and had hardly been touched by a human hand, had to part, bend, and even crack to the sides of this powerful bus. The children who lived beyond the path and behind the trees were happy to be dropped off right in front of their homes. But none of us were prepared for what we found. Many of the camp tents had been leveled to the mud and were being shaken, dropped and dragged off by the wind as though by a playful puppy. All of us quietly moved towards the windows closest to this natural disaster. Yet we averted our eyes from the kids whose chins were resting on their chests as they got off the bus, in a procession of silence unusual for children whose usual was getting off with much pushing and happiness. The other unusual thing was their walking on into this torrent of huge drops without protecting themselves from this wetness for a long time.

When finally, the school bus driver drove our group to the gates of our campsite, she offered to go up and down each row of houses to leave us as dry as possible in front of our doors. Some of the children, who lived way down towards the end of the rows, accepted her offer; that was the side of the camp the Chicanos were allowed to live in. Most of us who lived nearer refused and fled. I couldn't accept. Not because I thought the planks of my home had been washed away. But because the memory of her face reacting to the tent children's camp seemed to have said *How can they live like this?* I didn't want her disgust to define me too.

I waded through muddy puddles and took a shortcut between the houses, through the uncut grass now leveled by the rain. Just as I was reaching my home, thinking I avoided her, and pretending she didn't know I lived in one of the ninety wooden houses, the sound of her bus turning the corner, just up the road from me, made me look up right into her smiling face. But seeing the "caught" look on mine, her self-satisfaction turned to puzzlement. She seemed not to have realized why her help was so embarrassing to me.

Our family had more than most families in camp. It was our Social Security check — the little support our father had to die to give us. But this particular month someone had stolen it. So, forgetting all the other time and seasons, I walked the shore of the lake, willing to believe there should be fruits in these trees, for *what else could the snake eat?*

Eventually, I gave up searching for snakes or fruit. I had begun to focus on a smell. A smell faint at first. I started following it slowly up a dirt road, my neck carefully turning. My nose was hunting out the smell. The wooden houses began to reappear along the roadsides as I found myself walking back toward camp. Now I consciously admitted to myself that I was following the scent of food.

I followed the scent for a long while. At the same time I noticed the rustling of the tall grasses swaying, and an occasional twig breaking under the weight of small wild animals out on the hunt themselves. My head finally jerked

54

into the direction I was looking for. My eyes caught sight of a man with a plate in his hand. I rushed my walk to get closer. I stood at the road's edge, watching and waiting for him to call me. He didn't. I walked over to a rock diagonally across from him but still at the edge of the road. I didn't feel welcome and I didn't want to threaten him. I sat down to watch him eat. I knew him. He sat on a wooden bench by his front door. His chest was bare, pantlegs rolled up, legs spread apart, bare feet planted firmly on the ground. He balanced his white porcelain bowl in one hand a tablespoon in the other.

He took heaping spoonfuls of food, maneuvering each one carefully into his mouth. I could see his arm muscles move with each spoonful. My mouth opened along with his. My saliva ran along with his. Even though I was some 40 or 50 feet from his plate, I could identify the scent. It was crab meat topping a hill of white rice, probably soaking in crabmeat sauce. He had probably gone crab hunting the night before. My family and I were too new at being migrants or living in the country to know how to hunt for crabs. He ate slowly. Obviously, he was in no hurry.

After a while, an almost forever while, he called me over. I might have run, I don't remember. He asked if I wanted some. I said "Ahum!" real fast, nodding my head and opening my mouth all at once to one of his heaping spoonfuls. I think I closed my eyes as my mouth closed over the food. But before I knew it, I had spit it out. It was spicy hot. Just as fast I was on my knees picking up the food from the ground. Suddenly a thought flashed through my hunger, *He expects you to be embarrassed.* I dropped the food again and ran home crying, angry at myself for pretending to be embarrassed instead of eating the food.

55

Childhood

from Bitita's Journal

CAROLINA MARIA DE JESUS

Translated by Marilyn Hacker
with Ana Oliveira

The poor lived on public land: "The Patrimony."
There wasn't any water. Even if they sank wells, they still
had to cart the water. We lived on land that my grandfather
had bought from his master, a teacher who had a private
school. The price of the land was fifty mil-reus. Grandfather
used to say that he didn't want to die and leave his children
to the mercy of their stars.

Our little hut was covered with sapé. It had mud walls,
roofed with dry grass. Every year we had to change the grass
because it rotted, and we had to do it before the rains. My
mother used to pay ten mil-reis for a cartload of dry grass.
The floor was bare—beaten earth packed down from being
walked on.

There, I made my grand entrance into the world.

I knew my brother's father, but not my own. Did every
child have to have a father? My mother's father was Benedito
José da Silva. The last name was his former owner. He was a
tall and calm Black man. Resigned to his condition of a sold-
off slave. He didn't know how to read, but he was eloquent
when he spoke. He was the most handsome Black man I've
ever seen till today.

It was nice for me to hear my mother say, "Father!" And my grandfather answer her, "What is it, my daughter?" I envied my mother because she'd known both mother and father. Many times I thought of questioning her to find out who my father was. But I lacked courage. I felt it would be an affrontery. To me, the most important person was my mother and my grandfather. I used to hear the old women say that children ought to obey their parents and respect them.

One day, I heard from my mother that my father was from Araxa, and that his name was Joao Candido Veloso. And the name of my grandmother was Joana Veloso. My father played the guitar and didn't like to work. He had only one suit of clothes. When my mother washed his clothes he stayed in bed, naked. He waited for his clothes to dry to get dressed and go out.

I came to the conclusion that we didn't need to ask anything from anybody. With time, we get to know everything. When my mother spoke, I'd come closer to listen to her.

One day, my mother scolded me and said, "I don't like you!" I answered her, "If I am in the world it's through you! If you hadn't paid attention to my father, I wouldn't be here." My mother smiled and said, "What a clever girl! And she's only four years old!"

My aunt Claudimira commented, "She's impolite."

My mother would defend me, saying that I'd told the truth.

"She needs to be spanked. You don't know how to raise your children!"

They began to argue. I thought, "It's my mother who was insulted, and she isn't hurt." I realized that my mother was the most intelligent one.

"Smack her, Cota! Smack that negrinha! She's only four, but the bough is bent when it's green!"

"Whatever you *have* to be, you *are* already when you're born," my mother answered.

I was worried, thinking, "What does it mean, to be four? To be sick? To be a sweety?" I ran off when I heard my brother's voice calling me to come pick gabirobas.

What worried me were Saturdays. What a hullabaloo! Men and women getting ready to go to the ball. Is the ball

57

indispensable in people's lives? I asked my mother to take me to the ball. I wanted to see what it was, the ball, that made all the Black folk anxious. They talked about the ball more than a hundred times a day! The ball...it must be a very fine thing, because those who talked about it, smiled. But the ball was at night, and at night I was sleepy.

I envied the women. And I wanted to grow up to find a sweetheart.

One day I saw two women fighting over a man. They were pulling each other's hair and saying "He's mine, you miserable Bitch! Shameless! If I find out that you slept with him, I'll kill you!"

I was flabbergasted. Is a man that good? Why do women fight over them? Is a man, then, better than cocada, pe de moleque, fried potatoes with beef? Why is it that women want to get married...Is a man better than fried bananas with sugar and cinnamon? Is a man better than rice and black beans with chicken? When I grow up, will I be able to get a man for me? I want a fine-looking one!

My ideas changed from one minute to the next, like the clouds in the sky that made splendid shapes, because it wouldn't be graceful if the sky were always blue.

One day I asked my mother: "Mother, am I a person or an animal?"

"You're a person, my daughter!"

"What does it mean to be a person?"

My mother didn't answer.

At night I was looking at the sky. I stared at the stars and thought: "Do the stars talk? Do they go dancing on Saturday night? On Saturday, I'll watch and see if they're dancing. In the sky there must be women stars and men stars. Do the women stars fight over the men stars? Is the sky only what I can see of it?"

When I went to gather wood with my mother, I saw the sky and it had the same shape...

In the woods I saw a man chop down a tree. I was envious and decided to become a man, to be strong. I ran to my mother and begged her, "Mother, I want to become a man! I don't like being a woman! Please, Mother, make me turn into a man!"

"Go to bed. Tomorrow when you wake up, you'll be changed into a man already."

"Good! Good!" I said to myself, smiling. "When I become a man, I'll buy a hatchet to chop down a tree." Smiling and bursting with joy, I thought that I'd need to buy a razor to shave, and a strap to hold my trousers up. Buy a horse and saddle, a wide-brimmed hat, and a whip. I intended to be a proper man. I wouldn't drink pinga. I wouldn't steal, because I didn't like robbers.

I went to bed and fell asleep. When I woke up, I went to look for my mother, complaining. "I haven't turned into a man! You tricked me!" And I pulled up the dress so she could check.

I trailed after my mother everywhere, crying and demanding, "I want to become a man!" I went on about it all day long.

The neighbors became impatient and said, "Dona Cota, spank that negrinha! What an annoying girl. Monkey!"

My mother tolerated it and used to say: "When you see the rainbow, you pass under it, that will turn you into a man."

"I don't know what a rainbow is, Mother!"

"It's the old woman's arc..."

"Oh yes..." And my look turned to the sky. If that's so, I have to wait for when it rains and the rainbow appears.

I left off crying for some days. One night it rained. I got out of bed to see if the rainbow was visible. My mother followed me to see what I was doing. When she saw me staring at the sky, she asked me: "What are you looking for?"

"The rainbow, Mother."

"The rainbow doesn't come out at night."

My mother did not speak much. "Why do you want to become a man?"

"I want to have the strength that a man has. A man can chop down a tree with a hatchet. I want to have the courage that a man has. He walks in the woods and is not afraid of snakes. A man who works earns more money than a woman, and he gets rich and he can buy a fine house to live in."

My mother smiled and took me to bed.

But when she got tired of my questions she smacked me. My godmother was the one who defended me. She was white. When she bought herself a dress she bought another for me.

She combed my hair and kissed me. I thought I was important because my godmother was white.

Poor women had no free time to look after their homes. At six in the morning they had to be in their employers' houses to light the fire and start making breakfast. It was awful. Those who had mothers left their children with them. As maids they had to cook, wash, and iron. Meals had to be presented with sophistication, little baskets of tomatoes stuffed with mayonnaise, baskets of potatoes stuffed with minced ham and olives. The meals were served like this: first soup, then rice, black beans, meat, and salad. If there was fish, other plates and silverware were used. Finally, dessert and coffee. What a lot of plates and cutlery and serving dishes to be washed! The silverware had to be cleaned and polished. The kitchen tiles washed with fresh water and dried with dishcloths. The women didn't leave their work until eleven o'clock at night. They worked only in the kitchen. You'd often hear the Black women saying, "Oh Lord, how tired I am!"

They were allowed to take the leftover food home with them. Their children, whom they called negrinhos, were awake waiting for their mother to come home with delicious food from the rich people's houses. At dinner the cooks prepared more food to have leftovers. The food that the masters wouldn't eat in the evening the food they ate at midday.

A good cook earned thirty mil-reis a month. When the end of the month came and the cook received her wages, she felt like a hero. She patted herself on the back saying, "I can take it! It is not anyone that can cook for Doctor Souza!" What pride, what vanity, from being Doctor José da Cunha's cook, or President Franklin Viera's, or José Alfonso's!

Often, you'd hear the rich people say, "Do you know with whom you're speaking? I am the top dog!" And the arrogant Black women sometimes said, "Do you know with whom you're speaking? I am the President's cook!"

On Saturday night, the cooks went dancing. What torture on Sunday to prepare meals half-asleep! But after the midday meal, they were allowed to go out and take a stroll until four o'clock, and return to prepare dinner. And they were not tired.

The following Saturday, they'd dance again until six in the morning. On Sundays, they had to go to work at seven in the morning because their mistresses wanted to sleep until seven.

When the cooks were sleepy, they would wash their faces with cold water to wake themselves up. The only fear was to over-salt the food and for the mistress to find it out. There were many people to work but very few places to work.

The mistress was treated like a saint in her altar. If they were nervous, the servants had to say, "Yes, Madam!" If they were friendly they said "Yes, Madam."

The poor are begotten, born, raised, and must live always with patience only to endure the whims of the bosses of the world. Why only the rich men could say: "Do you know with whom you're talking?" to show their superiority.

If the bosses' son beat up the cook's son, the cook couldn't complain without risking her job. But if the cook had a daughter, poor negrinha! The bosses' son would use her for his sexual explorations. Girls who still thought only of dolls and nursery rhymes were violated by the sons of senhores Pereira, Moreira, Oliveira, and other "eiras" who came from beyond the ocean.

After nine months, the negrinha was the mother of a darkish or lightish mulatto. And the people would attribute the paternity: "It was probably So-and-so's son" or someone else's. But the Black mother, ignorant and uninstructed, couldn't reveal that her baby was Doctor X's or Professor Y's grandchild. Because the mother would lose her job. What a struggle for such a mother to raise such a child.

How many single mothers killed themselves, others died rachitic from so much weeping.

The Black father was voiceless. If he intended to complain, the bosses would cut them short: "Silence, lazy Negro! Vagabond!"

61

El Sueño Perdido

ALMA M. GÓMEZ

There's an old white woman sitting behind us now. She's wearing a dirty coat that's got plastic flowers on it, and her eyes move back and forth across her face like she's on the train watching for her stop to get off. The man sitting next to her is pretending to be dead. He was alive before she sat down beside him and started telling him about her husband who beat her, the son-of-a-bitch, she never had any children, they probably would have come to no good, and she worked all her life until she fell. The man holds a newspaper in his lap. He sits barely breathing.

We do what everyone else does. We wait and play a game. There is a constant story I ask mamí to tell me. I get something from it and ask her to tell me again and again. She begins the story in the same way.

I reached twenty in the last year of the war. Early in the year most of the young women in my town went to work in the shoe factory. I punched out holes. The shoe factory, located behind the river, was so huge that it took thirty minutes to walk from one end to the other and it hummed with the sounds of the black machines. The muchachas were not allowed to talk to one another.

One morning I received the first love letter of my life.

She pauses here, looks up to see if her number has been called, and continues—

It was from Juan. Juan had come to Nueva York before me to earn some money. He had had to pay for his first job. When he left he could not speak a word of English...I could not wait until I was home to read it. The envelope was a delicate blue and white, thin, and the note was written in neat letters that smacked of painstaking penmanship. He always sent me a money order. This time Juan was asking me to come to New York.

I finished the letter. I had to go and walk. I was afraid to tell my family, my mother did not like Juan. I walked that day. During the day you could walk down the street to the plaza and see no one but the old men. But at night the street was crowded.

My sister Julie was there. She worked in a tuxedo factory. I was scared on the plane. But I came to New York. I got married and we moved to Delancey.

I stop her. She's changed the order of the story. I want her to tell me about the flowers first. She goes back to the story. This time I close my eyes.

In those days the young women would oil their hair with sweet-smelling flower smells. You could pick the flowers off the trees. Red, yellow, white, big. You would place the flower in your hair. You knew who was married by where they placed their flower. As I was triqueña I loved the red flowers in my hair. Gardenias were for the fiestas.

En Nueva York it was hard to find the flowers. Contrary to my expectations everyday life showed not the slightest chance of beginning. Juan lost his job. Julie died. I had to work...making bras...until the children came.

A black man is called. The old woman is mumbling louder. Mamí hugs me to her brown raincoat. We stare at each other and after a few seconds she begins again. I raise and lower my head.

It's been fourteen years since I've been back...The life has changed...You've never been there. But nena don't worry, Si Dios quiere, one day we'll go back. I'll show you the flowers...

She doesn't finish. It's time. We are called to a desk. As we get up, I steal a glance at a group of chairs in the sun.

63

Some sort of soft drink has been spilled on a seat and throws back reflections. We leave the old woman waiting.

Growing

HELENA MARÍA VIRAMONTES

The two walked down First Street hand in reluctant hand. The smaller of the two wore a thick, red sweater with a desperately loose button swinging like a pendulum. She carried her crayons, swinging her arm while humming *Jesus loves little boys and girls* to the speeding echo of the Saturday morning traffic and was totally oblivious to her older sister's wrath. "My eye!" Naomi ground out the words from between her teeth. She turned to her youngest sister who seemed unconcerned and quite delighted at the prospect of another adventure. "Chaperone," she said with great distain. "My EYE!" Lucía was chosen by Apá to be Naomi's chaperone and this infuriated her so much that she dragged her along impatiently, pulling and jerking at almost every step. She was 14, almost going on 15 and she thought the idea of having to be watched by a young snot like Lucía was insulting to her maturity. She flicked her hair over her shoulder. "Goddamnit," she said finally, making sure that the words were low enough so that neither God nor Lucía would hear them.

There seemed to be no way out of this custom either. Her arguments were always the same and always turned into pleas. This morning was no different. Amá, Naomi said, exasperated but determined not to back out of this one, Amá, América is different. Here girls don't need chaperones. Mothers trust their daughters. As usual Amá turned to the kitchen

65

sink or the ice box, shrugged her shoulders and said: You
have to ask your father. Naomi's nostrils flexed in fury as
she said, But Amá, it's so embarrassing. I'm too old for that;
I am an adult. And as usual, Apá felt different and in his
house, she had absolutely no other choice but to drag Lucía
to a sock hop or church carnival or anywhere Apá was sure
she would be found around boys. Lucía came along as a spy,
a gnat, a pain in the neck.

Well, Naomi debated with herself; it wasn't Lucía's fault,
really. She suddenly felt sympathy for the humming little girl
who scrambled to keep up with her as they crossed the freeway
overpass. She stopped and tugged Lucía's shorts up, and
although her shoelaces were tied, Naomi retied them. No, it
wasn't her fault after all, Naomi thought, and she patted her
sister's soft light brown and almost blondish hair, it was Apá's.
She slowed her pace as they continued their journey to Fierro's
house. It was Apá who refused to trust her and she could not
understand what she had done to make him so distrustful.
Tú eres mujer, he thundered, and that was the end of any
argument, any question, and the matter was closed because
he said those three words as if they were a condemnation from
the heavens and so she couldn't be trusted. Naomi tightened
her grasp with the thought, shaking her head in disbelief.

"Really," she said out loud.

"Wait up. Wait," Lucía said, rushing behind her. "Well
would you hurry. Would you?" Naomi reconsidered: Lucía
did have some fault in the matter after all, and she became
irritated at once at Lucía's smile and the way her chaperone
had of taking and holding her hand. As they passed El Gallo,
Lucía began fussing, grabbing onto her older sister's waist for
reassurance and hung onto it.

"Stop it. Would you stop it?" She unglued her sister's
grasp and continued pulling her along. "What's wrong with
you?" she asked Lucía. I'll tell you what's wrong with you,
she thought, as they waited at the corner of an intersection
for the light to change: You have a big mouth. That's it.
If it wasn't for Lucía's willingness to provide information,
she would not have been grounded for three months. Three
months, 12 Saturday nights, and two church bazaars later,
Naomi still hadn't forgiven her youngest sister. When they

crossed the street, a homely young man with a face full of acne honked at her tight purple petal pushers. The two were startled by the honk.

"Go to hell," she yelled at the man in the blue and white chevy. She indignantly continued her walk.

"Don't be mad, baby," he said, his car crawling across the street, then speeding off leaving tracks on the pavement, "You make me ache," he yelled, and he was gone.

"GO TO HELL, Goddamn you!" she screamed at the top of her lungs forgetting for a moment that Lucía told everything to Apá. What a big mouth her youngest sister had, for christsakes. Three months.

Naomi stewed in anger when she thought of the Salesian Carnival and how she first made eye contact with a Letterman Senior whose eyes, she remembered with a soft smile, sparkled like crystals of brown sugar. She sighed as she recalled the excitement she experienced when she first became aware that he was following them from booth to booth. Joe's hair was greased back to a perfect sculptured ducktail and his dimples were deep. When he finally handed her a stuffed rabbit he had won pitching dimes, she knew she wanted him.

As they continued walking, Lucía waved to the Fruit Man. He slipped his teeth off and again, she was bewildered. "Would you hurry up!" Naomi ordered Lucía as she had the night at the Carnival. Joe walked beside them and he took out a whole roll of tickets, trying to convince her to leave her youngest sister on the ferris wheel. "You could watch her from behind the gym," he had told her, and his eyes smiled pleasure. "Come on," he said, "have a little fun." They waited in the ferris wheel line of people. Finally:

"Stay on the ride," she instructed Lucía, making sure her sweater was buttoned. "And when it stops again, just give the man another ticket, okay?" Lucía said okay, excited at the prospect of highs and lows and her stomach wheezing in between. After Naomi saw her go up for the first time, she waved to her, then slipped away into the darkness and joined the other hungry couples behind the gym. Occasionally, she would open her eyes to see the lights of the ferris wheel spinning in the air with dizzy speed.

When Naomi returned to the ferris wheel, her hair undone, her lips still tingling from his newly stubbled cheeks, Lucía walked off and vomited. Lucía vomited the popcorn, a hot dog, some chocolate raisins, and a candied apple, and all Naomi knew was that she was definitely in trouble.

"It was the ferris wheel," Lucía said to Apá. "The wheel going like this over and over again." She circled her arms in the air and vomited again at the thought of it.

"Where was your sister?" Apá had asked, his voice rising.

"I don't know." Lucía replied, and Naomi knew she had just committed a major offense, and that Joe would never wait until her prison sentence was completed.

"Owww," Lucía said. "You're pulling too hard."

"You're a slow poke, that's why," Naomi snarled back. They crossed the street and passed the rows of junk yards and the shells of cars which looked like abandoned skull heads. They passed Señora Nuñez's neat, wooden house and Naomi saw her peeking through the curtains of her window. They passed the "TU y YO," the one-room dirt pit of a liquor store where the men bought their beers and sat outside on the curb drinking quietly. When they reached Fourth Street, Naomi spotted the neighborhood kids playing stickball with a broomstick and a ball. Naomi recognized them right away and Tina waved to her from the pitcher's mound.

"Wanna play?" Lourdes yelled from center field. "Come on, have some fun."

"Can't." Naomi replied. "I can't." Kids, kids, she thought. My, my. It wasn't more than a few years ago that she played baseball with Eloy and the rest of them. But she was in high school now, too old now, and it was unbecoming of her. She was an adult.

"I'm tired," Lucía said. "I wanna ice cream."

"You got money?"

"No."

"Then shut up."

Lucía sat on the curb, hot and tired, and she began removing her sweater. Naomi decided to sit down next to her for a few minutes and watch the game. Anyway, she wasn't really in that much of a hurry to get to Fierro's. A few minutes wouldn't make much difference to someone who spent most of his time listening to the radio.

She counted them by names. They were all there. Fifteen of them and their ages varied just as much as their clothes. Pants, skirts, shorts were always too big and had to be tugged up constantly, and shirt sleeves rolled and unrolled, or socks mismatched with shoes that didn't fit. But the way they dressed presented no obstacle for scoring or yelling foul and she enjoyed the zealous abandonment with which they played. She knew that the only decision these kids possibly made was what to play next, and she wished to be younger.

Chano's team was up. The teams were oddly numbered. Chano had nine on his team because everybody wanted to be in a winning team. It was an unwritten law of stickball that anyone who wanted to play joined whatever team they preferred. Tina's team had the family faithful 6. Of course numbers determined nothing. Naomi remembered once playing with Eloy and three of her cousins against ten kids, and still winning by three points.

Chano was at bat and everybody fanned out far and wide. He was a power hitter and Tina's team prepared for him. They could't afford a homcrun now because Piri was on second, legs apart, waiting to rush home and score a crucial point. And Piri wanted to score it at all costs. It was important for him because his father sat outside the liquor store with a couple of his uncles and a couple of malt liquors watching the game.

"Steal the base!" his father yelled, "Run, menso!" But Piri hesitated. He was too afraid to take the risk. Tina pitched and Chano swung, missed, strike one.

"Batter, batter, swing!" Naomi yelled from the curb. She stood up to watch the action better.

"I wanna ice cream," Lucía said.

"Come on, Chano!" Piri yelled, bending his knees and resting his hands on them like a true baseball player. He spat, clapped his hands. "Come on."

"Ah, shut up, sissy." This came from Lourdes, Tina's younger sister. Naomi smiled at the rivals. "Can't you see you're making the pitcher nervous?" and she pushed him hard between the shoulder blades, then returned to her position in the outfield, holding her hand over her eyes to shield them from the sun. "Strike the batter out," she screamed at the top of her lungs. "Come on, strike the menso out!" Tina delivered another pitch, but not before going through the motions of a professional preparing for the perfect pitch. Naomi knew she was a much better pitcher than Tina. Strike two. Maybe not, and Lourdes let out such a taunting grito of joy that Piri's father called her a dog.

Chano was angry now, nervous and upset. He put his bat down, spat in his hands and rubbed them together, wiped the sides of his jeans, kicked the dirt for perfect footing.

"Get on with the game!" Naomi shouted impatiently. Chano swung a couple of times to test his swing. He swung so hard he caused Juan, Tina's brother and devoted catcher, to jump back.

"Hey baboso, watch out," he said. "You almost hit my coco." And he pointed to his forehead.

"Well, don't be so stupid," Chano replied, positioning himself once again. "Next time back off when I come to bat."

"Baboso," Juan repeated.

"Say it to my face," Chano said, breaking his stand and turning to Juan "say it again so I could break this bat over your head."

"Ah, come on, Kiki," the shortstop yelled, "I gotta go home pretty soon."

"Let up," Tina demanded.

"Shut up marrana," Piri said, turning to his father to make sure he heard. "Tinasana, cola de marrana, Tinasana, cola de marrana." Tina became so infuriated that she threw the ball directly to his stomach. Piri folded over in pain.

"No! No!" Sylvia yelled. "Don't get off the base or she'll tag you out!"

"It's a trick!" Miguel yelled from behind home plate.

"That's what you get!" This came from Lourdes. Piri did not move, and for a moment Naomi felt sorry for him, but giggled at the scene anyway.

"I heard the ice cream man." Lucía said.

"You're all right, Tina," Naomi yelled, laughing, "You're A-O-K." And with that compliment, Tina bowed, proud of her performance until everyone began shouting, "STOP WASTING TIME!" Tina was prepared. She pitched and Chano made the connection quick, hard, the ball rising high and flying over her head, Piri's, Lourdes', Naomi's and Lucía's, and landed inside the Chinese Cemetery.

"DON'T JUST STAND THERE!" Tina screamed at Lourdes, "Go get it, stupid!" After Lourdes broke out of her trance, she ran to the tall, chain-link fence which surrounded the cemetery, jumped on the fence and crawled up like a scrambling spider, her dress tearing with a rip roar.

"We saw your calzones, we saw your calzones," Lucía sang.

"Go! Lourdes, go!" Naomi jumped up and down in excitement, feeling like a player who although benched in the sidelines, was dying to get out there and help her team win. The kids blended into one huge noise, like an untuned orchestra, screaming and shouting Get the Ball, Run in Piri, Go Lourdes, Go throw the ball Chano pick up your feet throw the ballrunrunrunrunthrow the ball. "THROW the ball to me!!" Naomi waved and waved her arms. For that moment she forgot all about 'growing up,' her period, her breasts that bounced with glee. All she wanted was an out on home base. To hell with being benched. "Throw it to me," she yelled.

In the meantime, Lourdes searched frantically for the ball, tip-toeing across the graves saying Excuse me, please excuse me, excuse me, until she found the ball peacefully buried behind a huge gray marble stone, and she yelled to no one in particular, CATCH IT, SOMEONE CATCH IT! She threw the ball up and over the fence and it landed near Lucía. Lucía was about to reach for the ball when Naomi picked it off the ground and threw it straight to Tina. Tina caught the ball, dropped it, picked it up, and was about to throw the ball to Juan at homeplate, when she realized that Juan had picked up the homeplate and ran, zig-zagging across the street while Piri and Chano ran after him. Chano was a much faster runner, but Piri insisted that he be the first to touch the base.

"I gotta touch it first," he kept repeating between pantings, "I gotta."

The kids on both teams grew wild with anger and encouragement. Seeing an opportunity, Tina ran as fast as her stocky legs could take her. Because Chano slowed down to let Piri touch the base first, Tina was able to reach him, and with one quick blow, she thundered OUT! She threw one last desperate throw to Juan so that he could tag Piri out, but she threw it so hard that it struck Piri right in the back of his head, and the blow forced him to stumble just within reach of Juan and homeplate.

"You're out!!" Tina said, out of breath. "O-U-T, out."

"No fair!" Piri immediately screamed. "NO FAIR!!" He stomped his feet in rage like Rumpelestiltskin. "You marrana, you marrana."

"Don't be such a baby," Piri's father said. "Take it like a man," he said as he opened another malt liquor with a can opener. But Piri continued stomping and screaming until his shouts were buried by the honk of an oncoming car and the kids obediently opened up like the red sea to let the car pass.

Naomi felt like a victor. She had helped, once again. Delighted, she giggled, laughed, laughed harder, suppressed her laughter into chuckles, then laughed again. Lucía sat quietly, to her surprise, and her eyes were heavy with sleep. She wiped them, looked at Naomi. "Vamos" Naomi said, offering her hand. By the end of the block, she lifted Lucía and laid her head on her shoulder. As Lucía fell asleep, Naomi wondered why things were always so complicated when you became older. Funny how the old want to be young and the young want to be old. Now that she was older, her obligations became heavier both at home and at school. There were too many demands on her, and no one showed her how to fulfill them, and wasn't it crazy? She cradled Lucía gently, kissed her cheek. They were almost at Fierro's now, and reading to him was just one more thing she dreaded doing, and one more thing she had no control over: it was another one of Apá's thunderous commands.

When she was Lucía's age, she hunted for lizards and played stickball with her cousins until her body began to bleed at 12, and Eloy saw her in a different light. Under the house, he sucked her swelling nipples and became jealous. He no longer wanted to throw rocks at the cars on the freeway with her and she began to act different because everyone began treating her different and wasn't it crazy? She could no longer be herself and her father could no longer trust her because

72

she was a woman. Fierro's gate hung on a hinge and she was almost afraid it would fall off when she opened it. She felt Lucía's warm, deep, breath on her neck and it tickled her momentarily. Enjoy, she whispered to Lucía, enjoy being a young girl, because you will never enjoy being a woman.

Memories of Her

AMINA SUSAN ALI

In the photograph she is younger and darker than I remember her. She is smiling and leaning against a palm
tree, wearing a two-piece bathing suit with a scarf tied around
her head. That was before I knew her. When I knew her she
wore dresses, teased hair and red lipstick.

She was always complaining because I was "fresh." I
couldn't understand why fresh meant bad. The milk carton
said the milk was fresh and that meant it was good, but my
being fresh meant a smack on the mouth. She used to tell me
I was supposed to obey and if I didn't want to I had something
evil in me, and if it got too evil she was going to have to
take me to a place where they would pour holy water on me and
burn incense.

The thought of her admitting how bad I was to another
person embarrassed me so much that I would be quiet for a day
or two, eat everything she fed me, even broccoli, wouldn't
scream when she didn't have enough coffee to pour a little
into my Donald Duck cup, and above all, I would never ask,
"Where's Daddy?"

When we were around other people I was supposed to
smile and act right. "Acting Right" meant not talking too
much but not being too quiet either, not spilling or breaking
anything, and for God's sake, not being or getting dirty. I
never seemed to strike the right balance with her because
afterwards she would say I had hurt her feelings because I
hadn't wanted to talk to her friend, aunt, sister-in-law or
cousin, or because I had said the wrong thing, or because I

had asked a question about something that wasn't supposed to exist. Soon I learned to endure these visits by asking to turn on the T.V. and then falling asleep in front of it.

She taught me at a very early age the rules of behavior I would have to follow if I wanted to survive in the real world. Rule Number One: Don't expect too much. "Too much" meant what you wanted. Too much meant the sky. That's why I wasn't allowed on the roof. But on days when she was at work and I was on hooky leave, I would open the Frankenstein door, shudder at the loud scraping noise it made and, after waiting a few seconds to see if anyone was coming, sit on the tar and look up at that blue that went on endlessly, that succeeded in getting away from the neighborhood. Like the sea. The first time I went to the beach I remember running up to her to shake her hand, because she, unlike anyone else I knew personally, had been to Europe and back.

I'd look up from the tired, slumping roof at the sparrows circling around and around, and my eyes would follow the one or two that would fly in the opposite direction, or just go off on their own way. Those were the ones that made me lose faith in the desirability of being human over other forms of life.

Human life, as far as I could see, sure was a drag. It was being proper and acting right and not having too much to tell in confession. But no matter what I did or did not do, or say or did not say, there was always something that I was doing or saying wrong. I couldn't go to science camp when a teacher urged me to because that would encourage my nasty habit of collecting bugs, rocks, and reptiles. Why didn't I prefer the companionship of pink plastic rollers, Simplicity patterns and pots and pans? Why did I hang out in the park all alone till it was almost dark, and sometimes even when it was already dark? What was I doing there? Did I expect anyone to believe that I was just watching the trees and the lake and the questionable things that swam around in it? Why couldn't I be like Carmen, who tweezed her eyebrows, shaved her legs and won twist contests at age 10?

But I couldn't care less about Carmen. Or her kind. I was totally embroiled in my first and only love, Joan of Arc. I learned all about Joan of Arc on TV in a movie they showed one day when I was playing hooky from junior high school. With that short hair and armor, jumping on her horse, leading her troops to battle—I knew this was for me. It sure beat being a secretary or waitress, and the Catholic Church even made her a saint. But who was I going to lead, and for what cause? There weren't any wars going on, at least not in my neighborhood, and I wasn't allowed to go on the West Side. Nonetheless, I cut my own hair, slept on the floor because I heard that's how saints had visions, and waited for my voices. In the meantime, I practiced being misunderstood.

My home became the perfect training ground for martyrdom. Contrary to popular belief, the Spanish Inquisition commenced the first time a Puerto Rican girl came home five minutes late. It was torture first, questioning later. Confessions were meaningless because no matter what you said, it didn't mean shit.

"I'm your mother!"—smack! "Don't you forget that."

Did I really have to be reminded?

Papi y el Otro

Luz Selenia Vásquez

Siempre me han fascinado los caballitos. Puedo estar horas contemplando los caballos elegantes pintados de colores subiendo y bajando y volteando en círculos eternos. La música me llena de una emoción desconocida por muchos, por aquéllos que no tienen tiempo para "cosas tan triviales." A mí siempre me han encantado. Me gusta contemplar a los padres que aguantan a sus niñitas con sus caritas asustadas. Me hacen recordar a mi propio Papi, a mi cara asustada y a mi fe en los brazos que me aguantaban para que nunca me cayera. Recuerdo el retrato que tenemos en casa, el retrato de mi Papi y yo. Yo trepada en el caballo llorando y Papi aguantándome, tratando de hacerme reír. Qué lástima que me haya caído del caballito, que Papi se haya ido, que Mami no tenga tiempo ni inclinación para llevarnos a mí y a mis hermanos a los caballitos y qué lástima que para mí los caballitos se han acabado.

Mi Papi era un poquito loco dice la gente. Durante cierta época no hablamos más que de la locura de mi padre. Les digo ahora que Papi no era loco, es que había dos personas: Papi y el Otro. No era fácil distinguir a uno del otro. Creo que ni Mami podia hacerlo. Tampoco entendía realmente que ella vivía con dos hombres. Había que concerlos bien para poder distinguirlos y más fácil era para Mami maltratar a Papi que al Otro, o torturar a Papi hasta que surgía el Otro. Yo sí podía distinguir entre ambos y confieso que quería muchísimo a Papi pero el Otro me daba miedo.

Papi era el hombre bajo y calvo, el que estuvo yendo a la misma factoría en Brooklyn por más de veinte años. Papi hablaba lo que otros llamaban "Broken English" y nosotros hacíamos burla de sus intentos frustrados de gritarnos en inglés. Sonreía a veces y cantaba por la mañana mi Papi. Antes de irnos para la escuela, nos limpiaba los zapatos y cantaba canciones que él mismo componía.

El Otro se parecía un tanto a Papi. Casi la misma estatura y la misma cantidad de pelo pero sus facciones eran algo torcidas y su voz era ronca y llena de dolor. El Otro no llegaba por mas que de noche. Gustaba del escondite que le proporcionaba la oscuridad; no cantaba, sino que conversaba mucho de Hitler y de bombas y de matanzas. El Otro había estado en Corea. Pasó allí tres meses en un hoyo grande con una Biblia y otro puertorriqueño que murió. No creo que haya leído la Biblia en aquellos tiempos porque luego blasfemó bastante y se jactó de ser muy buen amigo del diablo. Le fascinaban los cuchillos y gustaba de andar por la casa con uno en la mano. Le divertía ponernos el cuchillo al cuello y moverlo un poquito, no para cortar, sino para mostrarnos que sería capaz de herirnos cualquier dia. Por esa razón llego la noche en que mi hermanito tuvo que esconder los cuchillos con que jugaba el Otro y nunca sacarlos hasta la mañana cuando se levantaba Papi. Papi los empleaba en cortar pan.

Creo, sin embargo, que Mami odiaba más a Papi que al Otro. Bueno, en realidad odiaba a ambos, pero su odio hacia el Otro sabiendo que el resto de la familia también lo odiaba, era un odio de lo más franco. En cambio, el odio hacia Papi era más discreto, y a la vez más venenoso. Mami odiaba a Papi porque el todavía la amaba, porque él la encontró y la quiso cuando ella acababa de cumplir trece años, y a los veinte y ocho todavía la quería. Lo odiaba también porque era jibaro, porque habia ido a las escuela solamente hasta sexto grado, porque hablaba "Broken English". Ella se había criado aquí y hablaba inglés perfectamente. Odiaba la diferencia de diez años que había entre ellos, odiaba su deseo de embarazarla año tras año y más que nada odiaba cada intento suyo de tocarla de acariciarla. Creo que de paso, Mami se odiaba a sí misma porque durante various años Papi era el mundo entero y luego se convirtió en otra repugnancia más en su vida.

Recuerdo la última vez en que tuve que tratar con el Otro. Era miércoles y Papi estaba con nosotros. Mami siempre llegaba tarde del trabajo y a Papi le tocaba cocinar. Cantaba con el radio aquel bolero de cuando conoció a Mami.

"Era que estabas preciosa
Con el color sencillo y sin igual...
Era que eras novia mía
Y que yo te sentía nerviosa entre mis
brazos suspirar..."

Nos hallábamos muy felices. Mami entró maldiciendo, y Papi empezó a cambiar. Ella dijo que no tenia hambre y se acostó como a las siete de la noche dejándonos en la mesa con Papi.

Después él anduvo bien agitado por el apartamento. Decidió finalmente irse a dormir y yo entré al baño para ducharme. Mis hermanos se acostaron temprano también, y fue esa alteración de nuestro horario normal lo que hizo que mi hermano se olvidara de esconder los cuchillos.

La cosa empezó cuando salí del baño. Me sentía relajada y lista para dormir cuando oí un grito y unas palabras de Mami:

"Anita call the..."

Su voz sonó como si su boca estuviera tapada por una mano. Pensé que en realidad nadie había hablado, que tan solo había imaginado aquello. Pero al entrar a mi cuarto llegó Mami corriendo:

"Get dressed fast, we're leaving."

Mientras ella se dirigía al cuarto de mis hermanos, vi a Papi caminar hacia la cocina. Me paralicé al oír que allá, una gaveta se abría y brotaba el ruido de los cuchillos.

Teníamos que pasar por la cocina para abandonar la casa y allí obstruyéndonos el paso, nos tocamos con el Otro. Sus ojos brillaban cuando empezó a reír.

"Nadie va a salir vivo de esta casa esta noche. Váyanse otra vez para sus camas y nada les va a pasar."

Quedó parado frente a nosotros con un cuchillo que brillaba. Empecé a llorar y a rogar, porque en otros momentos eso bastaba para que el Otro volviera a ser Papi.

"Papi, please, por favor, no hagas esto. Papi, please, for me, por mí, déjanos," le dije.

Pero mis lágrimas no cambiaron nada, el Otro seguía allí. Entonces Mami dijo: "Alright if nobody is going to leave this house, then I'll get someone to come in."

Cuando Mami trató de coger el teléfono para llamar a la policía, el Otro arrancó el teléfono de la pared. Le dijo el Otro a Mami: "Voy a matarlos a todos, pero voy a matar a los niños primero, desde el más pequeño hasta la mayor. Después te voy a matar a ti, pero quiero que tú veas cuando mueran tus hijos. Quiero que seas testigo."

El Otro estaba tan preocupado con Mami que no prestaba atención ni a mí ni a mis hermanos. Empecé a moverme hacia la puerta, a la vez que les indicaba que me siguieran. Ellos estaban tan asustados que no podían moverse. El Otro decía:

"Y después que estén muertos, voy a hacer lo mismo que hicimos en Core con esos condenados chinos. Voy a cortarles las cabezas y guindarlos de un árbol."

Me hallaba cerca de la puerta cuando él viró la cabeza y me vio. Extendió su mano para agarrarme y yo solté un grito que espantó al Otro. Corrí hasta la vecina en busca de socorro.

Después que yo salí el Otro se confundió y aprovechándose de su confusión pudieron salir mi mama y mis hermanos. Luego

80

de telefonear a la policía, regresamos a nuestro apartamento. Se podía oír el radio. Estaba todo oscuro con la excepción de la cocina de donde venía la música del radio. Papi, sentado a la mesa, lloraba. Tenía los brazos llenos de sangre porque el Otro se había cortado las muñecas. Me detuve para ver a mi Papi llorar mientras la sangre corría. La policía llamo a la ambulancia y se lo llevaron.

No sé quién ganó la batalla, Papi o el Otro. Esa misma noche recogimos lo nuestro y nos fuimos. No fue una despedida triste. Ya el Otro nos había sacado el rencor. Pero cada vez que alcanzo a ver los caballitos recuerdo a Papi ¿Qué será de él?

Teenage Zombie

Amina Susan Ali

My younger sister, Millie, had curly black hair that she
refused to cut for as long as we lived with our mother
in a railroad apartment on Ludlow Street. We grew up in the
kitchen, in front of the stove cooking rice and beans and Spam,
at the window hanging up and taking down laundry, and
around the kitchen table with various visitors and relatives
on summer nights, sucking on ice cubes because there was
never enough money to buy soda for everyone.

Millie looked a lot like me—she had the same eyes and
the same smile—but she was darker. She was also darker than
Mami and Papi. When Mami lost her temper she called Millie
a nigger. Millie set her hair on empty soda cans to make it
look straight. When it rained, she wouldn't go out if she could
help it, and she rarely went swimming.

When we were home alone we'd put the radio on full
blast and dance on the furniture. The best spot was on top
of the couch because you could see yourself in the big mirror
on the living room wall. One time we gave a show and invited
the kids from the neighborhood. For an opening act, Miguel
from next door did a magic act. He showed the audience a
baseball card and said he was going to make it disappear. Then
he told everyone to close their eyes, but everybody started
booing him. Carmen threw her M&M's at him and then some
of the other kids started throwing popcorn up in the air, so
we had to make him stop. He was five years old.

Then Millie and I came on. I had tied celery and lettuce
leaves in my hair and wore a white sheet wrapped around

me and tied around my waist and across my chest with a piece of rope, like someone from ancient Greece. Millie wore my pink ballet leotard and a lace curtain around her shoulders. We danced to a Tito Rodríguez record. It was too bad the record player kept stopping and starting, but everybody liked it anyway.

When Millie turned thirteen she started going to a little church two blocks from our house. From the outside it just looked like a metal door, so I had passed it many times without noticing it. Soon Millie stopped smoking and playing hooky. She stayed away from the kids on the block, no longer stopping to listen to rock & roll on the transistor radios on weekend nights. Though we were all baptized Catholics Mami didn't object to Millie's new interest. In fact, she seemed relieved that Millie wasn't heading in the direction of the other girls in the neighborhood.

One Sunday Frankie, one of the guys from the block, and I were sitting in Washington Square Park. It was summer, it was 1967 and I was sixteen. We were sitting on a bench near the chess players, when this guy came over and sat next to us, not too close, but close enough, and started reading this book, *Catcher in the Rye*. Nobody said anything for a long time, then all of a sudden Frankie said, "Why are you so quiet, Angie?" Then the guy who was sitting next to us put the book down and said, "That's not what you should say!" Then he got down on his *knees*, right in front of me, and said, "Spill your guts to me and I'm yours forever!"

I just looked at him. I didn't know what to say. He stood up and said, "O.K., I guess that doesn't work either." He stuck out his hand. "Hi. My name's Jim." Frankie and I introduced ourselves and he started talking to us just like somebody off the block. It turned out that he was living a few blocks from us. The three of us spent the rest of the day together. I was surprised that he didn't feel uncomfortable, not knowing whether or not Frankie was my boyfriend. But Jim didn't think that way. He had run away from Michigan and thought New York was a great place. As it turned out, he had seen more of the city that summer than I had seen in my whole life. The reason Frankie and I were in the park talking that day was that Frankie had wanted to go out with Millie. Millie knew this but because Frank was Black she didn't want anything to do with him. I remember the afternoon she came home and told me that Frankie liked her. She was furious. She kept repeating, "Is he color blind? Doesn't he have eyes?" I felt like asking her, "Do you?" because she was almost as dark as he was. But because we were Puerto Rican, she didn't think so. I was trying to explain this to Frankie without hurting his feelings.

As I said before, Millie had started going to this church. She brought Mami to church with her, then she brought me. It was a pretty nice church. They had an organ, two guitars, a guy who played saxophone, a drummer, and a lot of the sisters played tambourines. All the services were held in Spanish. We started going on Sunday mornings, then to the Young People's meetings on Wednesday nights, but the best meetings were on Sunday nights. Everybody came to church then, even the little kids and babies. Piles of diapers were laid in the aisles and formula and juice bottles rested on the floor inside the pews. I liked to watch the minister walk up and down the platform, up and down, up and down, back and forth, then all of a sudden he'd jump, then he'd be walking back and forth again, constantly preaching, then he'd start talking a little faster and a little louder, then he'd repeat something over and over again, then bang his Bible on the pulpit, and somebody would yell Hallelujah and somebody else would yell something else and then practically the whole church would be yelling and shouting and carrying on, then after a little while they'd quiet down, and the minister would pick up where he left off and go right on preaching. They'd carry on like that for hours.

I liked the church and kept going to services. Once, a group of us from the Young People's Society visited an English-speaking church. Their service was a lot quieter than ours. Millie seemed to like it there. They had clean white pews and a red carpet, instead of tired brown wood pews and floors and old pictures of Jesus like our church. Soon after Millie started making excuses as to why she didn't want to go to the Spanish church. She said her Spanish wasn't that good and she couldn't understand much of what was going on. My

Spanish wasn't so good either but I had both an English and Spanish bible, and every night I'd read something from the Spanish bible, then re-read the parts I didn't understand in English. I told Millie that she should have done the same but she didn't seem to want to try. She said she had enough trouble reading English.

After a while she started going to the English-speaking church by herself regularly, and eventually joined. Then I noticed that she got annoyed every time I spoke to her in Spanish. She'd ask, "Can't you speak English? What's wrong with you?" Pretty soon after she would only associate with her friends from the American church, as if they were more holy than anyone else.

A couple of months later, she was preparing for her SATs. She mentioned that some of the girls in her class told her that they could guess on some of the vocabulary because they knew Spanish. And then Millie, my sister, said, "But that doesn't help me because I'm not Spanish. Not I can't *speak* Spanish, but I'm not Spanish." So I said, "What are you, then, Millie?" She said, "I'm American." So I said, "Yeah, sure, you're Puerto Rican." She said there was no such thing. Puerto Rico wasn't a country, so how could anybody be Puerto Rican? I said I didn't know anything about all that, all I knew was that there was something called American and I was not it. She said that was the wrong way to think and that God made us all the same. I said, if we're all the same, why did the Americans have white pews and a red carpet in their church while we had broken-down wood pews and old floors? She said she didn't know what I was talking about, she didn't care what her church looked like, and that there was no such thing as a Puerto Rican, she was not one, and she did not speak Spanish.

I was also trying to explain all this to Frankie that Sunday afternoon, but soon lost my ambition after meeting Jim.

Jim and I got to be really good friends. He was eighteen years old and read a lot. He had sandy colored hair and was the first American who spoke to me with some purpose other than to tell me what to do. He listened to what I said instead of putting his eyes on me and his ears someplace else. He wore sneakers all the time and carried paperback books and newspapers wherever he went. He wore T-shirts and jeans and his hair was always dripping into his face.

I knew I really liked him, but he wasn't of the faith, he was of the world. I wasn't supposed to have a boyfriend who wasn't a Christian. And as far as my mother was concerned, I wasn't supposed to have a boyfriend, period. Boys only got girls in trouble, she had taught us, the proof being the other girls in the neighborhood who all had babies by the time they were sixteen. And then there were the stories about our father, how he was like every other man who couldn't be counted on. It seemed the only men who could ever meet with her approval were somewhere far away or very rich.

Every night that summer we'd meet in front of his building except for Sundays and Wednesdays, when I went to church. We'd go for a walk, or go get pizza, or go to the park. I couldn't bring him home because of my mother, and I had to be indoors by 9:30 because she got home from the restaurant where she worked at a quarter to ten, so that put a limit on the amount of time we spent together. Sometimes we'd hold hands or else he'd put his arm around me, which started getting me worried about meeting somebody from church in the street, so I would manage to find an excuse, like complaining about the heat, to put a quick end to *that*.

One night we didn't have any money between us and really didn't know what to do. It was about ninety degrees and I was bored and angry because I had been in the house all day and ended up having an argument with my mother over doing the ironing. When I met Jim outside he suggested that we go to his house, and I agreed. I felt I had stepped into a foreign country. The apartment was filled with psychedelic posters, rock albums, and furniture I had seen in the street. What would my mother think, I thought, what would the people at church think if they knew I had a friend like this?

I sat at the kitchen table, my usual post at home. Jim said a few things to me and I answered, not hearing what I was saying, but feeling the sounds in my head. He put his arms on my shoulders, bent over and kissed my face a few times. I closed my eyes—I wanted to so much—then quickly opened them looking at the floor and just managing to say,

"No, I can't, that's all." I heard him half-laugh, half-gasp, like, this was one of my jokes, right? So he said, "Come on, Angie, we're only human, God will understand," trying to make a joke out of it.

I stood up and ran out of the apartment, down the dark stairs and into the night. When I got home Millie was there, folding laundry and singing to herself in an expressionless voice. She wore a white slip and had her hair set on soda cans.

"Where were you?" she asked. "I thought you'd be home for dinner. Did you eat?"

"No, I'm not very hungry. I went someplace with a friend and got lost on my way home."

It was too hot to try to make sense out of everything, so I started to get ready for bed. I never spoke to Jim again.

La Veintiuna

Luz María Umpierre

Decidió levantarse del sillon pues el olor a carne frita le invitaba a la cocina. Se detuvo en el dintel. Adentro, una mujer de estatura pequeña, de pelo blanco recogido en forma de dona, canturreaba mientras movía las ollas.

—Ay, turululu, ay, turulete, el que no tiene boca no bebe leche.

—Titi—interpeló la niña—dame un bihte con arroh y salsita.

¡Muchacha! Tú debe tenel fiebre, pidiendo comida. Voy a selvilte ante de que te arrepienta.

Miró a su tía detenidamente mientras le servía. Sus ojos se parecían a los de la virgen que ella tenía en su cuarto, pero los ojos de la virgen eran como los de una americana y titi los tenía prietos.

La tía Lala se movía incansablemente, parecía un pulpo por todas la cosas que cambiaba, movía o arreglaba en un momento.

—Mi'ja, ¿quiere leche o quiere agua?

La niña se limitó a sonreír.

¡Bribona! Tú lo que quiere eh refrehco. Cuando acabeh te doy pá que compreh uno en el cafetín. Pero te lo tiene que comel tó, dejal el plato limpio.

La niña aceptó con un marcado movimiento de la cabeza. Devoró los pedacitos de carne y mixtura. Cuando hubo terminado, llevó el plato a la cocina.

¡Ay, qué güeno! ¡Si no voy a tenel que fregal el plato! Toma, vete a compral el refrehco. Ten mucho cuida'o; vete pol la orillita.

La niña salió de la casa corriendo hacia el cafetín que quedaba tres casas hacia arriba.

—¡Don Julio, don Julio! Déme una cola chanpán.

—Ay, si es la nena de Umpiérre. Enseguiíta te la doi.

Don Julio tenía el pelo blanco como la tía Lala y usaba espejuelos igual que su padre.

—Ascaracaracatisquistascatisquis tascaracatas. Ascaracaracatisquis tasca tisquis ascaracaracatis. As caracaracatisquis tas ca tisquis ascaracacatis.

La vellonera dejaba oír un merengue de moda y la niña se viró a mirarla. Parecía una alcancía gigantesca.

—Aquí tiene mi'ja.

—Gracia.

—Dále recuerdo a Don Edualdo.

Al salir oyó el clink de la caja registradora. Se llevó la botella blanca llena de aquel líquido oscuro a la boca y bebió mientras caminaba el corto trayecto a la casa. La saliva, como hilitos de telaraña, se le quedaba colgando de los labios cada vez que apartaba la botella de la boca. Era dulce la cola chanpán, no como la coca cola que no tenía tanta azúcar.

Al llegar a la casa ocupó nuevamente el sillón, agarró entre sus dedos el guano de la almohada y comenzó a mecerse.

—Kincallerooo. Kincalleroooo. Tu tut tu tut. El que me deba que me pague y el que no que me regale.

La calle seguía con su espectáculo de circo mientras ella se mecía y se mecía hasta dormirse con el bobo en la boca y la almohada entre los dedos. Baba y mocos. Sentada en la baranda suciamente azulosa, amacigaba la almohada de guano entre sus dedos y chupaba el bobo, lo mordía, lo llenaba de baba.

La escena se repetía diariamente cuando el sol se situaba perpendicularmente sobre los techos y la gente. Frente a la niña la calle llena de luz, los carros abalanzandose la gente de prisa hacia el trabajo o la escuela.

—Tack, tack, tack—los tacones sobre la acera hirviente.

Mi pana, la maehtra me dijo que me largara del...

—¿De veras que te costó quince chavos?

—¡Voa yegal talde!

Los ojos caídos de la niña mamaban con la retina aquel diario

89

trajín. Le gustaba sentarse ahí a esa hora; su tía dormía la siesta y ella podía estar sola.

Juan Vaca había pasado con su olor a ron cañita, su chaquetón sucio colgándole hasta los tobillos, su corbata al cuello desnudo, su sombrero prápra. Acompañándolo iba Farruca con las tetas fuera de la blusa color de su carne negra.

—Jalda arriva va cantando el Populal.... Mira, eh la hija de don Umpierre. ¿Cómo está mi niña? ¿No tiene una lemosneta?

Subieron de prisa hacia la parada de gúagúas. Allí era bueno pedir a esta hora en la cual la gente del barrio regresaba al trabajo después del almuerzo.

—Paico. Tilín, Tilín, Tilín. Paiiico. Cho co la te, Cocoi piña.

La niña mascaba el bobo y la goma se sentía blanda entre sus dientes.

—Asta que no me bañe no me comprarán un mantecado en palito.

—Cuando venga Rafi noh ehcondemo en el baño, llenamo la bañera de agua y nadamo pa'bajo y de lao y lao como Talzán.

Pensando en esta cosas su dedo índice se enroscaba en el pelo y hacía sortijas con él.

En el aire una peste a orín de gatos. Dino, el gato gacho, estira la pata contra el poste del frente y se mea. A lo lejos el timbre de la Central High School anuncia el comienzo de las clases de la tarde. Hasta las tres no se verá un alma por la calle. La calle queda desierta y la niña en el balcón del 609 sigue mamando.

Las moscas llenan el mantel de la casa sin mano que las espante. La niña sigue acariciendo el guano. La calle es una gran chorrera vacía.

El aire caliente le da en la cara y la adormila. Quiere irse a la cama-cuna, pero su Tití Carmen no está para dormir con ella. Tití llega horita con dulces y su pelo rojo; pelo rojo y chicle de bomba. Mientras tanto, el sol pica y el sudor le corre pelo abajo.

—Papo, Rafi y Cuqui vienen a la treh.

Con sus uniformes azul marino y gris de escuela pública, distintos al de la niña de la baranda.

—Tití no llega con loh chicle. Cuando yo me baño ella

90

me pone jugo de limón en el pelo.
Su pelo es ahora una masa de agua de sal y cabello encrespado.
La vellonera del kiosco suena:
—Batancuintuntulai, conectando con bontelain, dice la planchadora que si no hay lana no va pa'llá.
A lo lejos el timbre de la Central. Son las tres.

Conversaciones con mi Nana: Juani en tres tiempos

MYRIAM DÍAZ-DIOCARETZ

Querida Juani:

Formas parte de la cartografía de mi vida. Te veo ahora llegar por primera vez a nuestra casa, con tus trenzas largas y tranquilas, como ébano esculpido, y tus grandes ojos de ciervito asustado. Tu silencio y desconfianza inicial revelaban que las historias ancestrales no son leyenda de sobremesa: son pies que sangran, son puertas de adobe derrumbadas, son frustraciones en los rostros de greda milenaria, son manos que quisieran ver cortadas. Como una recién nacida aprendiste a hablar nuestro idioma; lo aprendimos tú y yo casi al mismo tiempo:

    Mai mai peñi   Hola Buenos días
    Mai mai   Buenos días

    Y me soltaste la mano
    clin-clin-clin
    sonaron las monedas
    en el tarro
    del organillo.

Hiciste una cruz
con tu índice en los labios

    (como ese día en misa

92

cuando te dije
demasiado fuerte:
¡Nanita, los calzones
me aprietan!)

Le diste un bocado
a la lorita
y ésta se puso a cantar:

Yo quiero un canto que
me diga qué hacer
con un problema que
debo resolver

yo quiero un libro que
me enseñe a meditar
será la isla donde
hallaré mi libertad

hay mucha gente que
piensa como yo
con mis hermanos y hermanas
de dolor

ya no se atreven a dudar
ya no se atreven a jugar

por miedo a interrumpir
la larga siesta del señor

Te despediste de la organillera, diciendo:
"diez años que trabajo,
diez años que vengo
a conversar con la virgen
que más de un milagro me dio".
Entonces,
me guiñaste un ojo,
y en tu mano de nuevo sentí tu suave calor de domingo.

Tu voz fue mi voz—Mai mai peñi Mai Mai. Y muchas

veces vi que tus ojos de ciervo no se cierran. Ibas cabizbaja buscando respuestas en la mesa de tus sueños. Entonces pensaba, me digo ahora: comenzaste a tejer a escondidas en tu cuarto, y yo, a escondidas, a juntar mis juguetes. Y tú amasaste tu pan. Y llegó tu Marcelita con sus ojos de aceituna. Y juntamos las palmas de las manos.

Decías de Bach: música de muertos   ruido de los solos   música de cirios   luz de vela larga   corazón de ataúd. A los diez tu chiquita desengrasando los platos que no usó cantaba con desafinado orgullo: *"Y te voy a enseñar a querer   como nunca has querido... Si tú   mueres primero es mi promesa... si yo muero primero...* De la cueca decías: música de cientos   vida zapateada   pájaros volando   sal en la comida plata en el baúl. Bach. Cueca. Bolero. Bach música de muertos.

Decías. Y entonces ambas queríamos

Ser románticas como mi abuela, detener la tormenta en el invierno, y no dejarla ir hasta que esto se ahuyente. Suspirar ante una foto frente a la ventana y salir luego al balcón a recoger los pensamientos.
Ser romántica pero no como aquél que al nadar muy bajo, siendo pez
se convirtió en pescado.
Nada me dijo ella, mi Juani, cansada, pensé, porque era día de lavado.
Más tarde se cerró la noche en agua.

Habla, Nana, habla...
Mai mai peñi Mai Mai

(Del libro inédito *Conversaciones con mi Nana*)

94

La virgen en el desierto

MARIANA ROMO-CARMONA

L a señora había muerto sin decir casi una palabra a nadie, porque todo lo habíamos sabido a través de su hijo. Ella de vez en cuando, dirigía una palabra o dos a mi mamá, o tal vez se quejaba, casi no se podía oír con el ruido del camión. Pero ahora se puede oír todo demasiado bien, y mientras yo pretendo conciliar el sueño en mi dormitorio, los sollozos del muchacho que no ha dormido en cuatro noches no vienen. Está callado en la cocina con mamá, que siempre sabe qué decir. Yo no, yo no sé ni qué pensar, ni si debo dormirme o quedarme despierta, solo quiero que llore el muchacho delgado que no ha dormido en cuatro noches.

La señora tenía el pelo largo en un moño, y mamá la tenía apoyada en sus brazos para que respirara mejor. A veces creo que le decía algo, aunque con el ruido del camión, no se oía mucho. Todos pensábamos y eso era lo único que se oía con el ruido del camión. Todavía siento esa vibración del vehículo viajando solo por la pampa oscura por kilómetros y kilómetros de vuelta a la ciudad. A veces el milico joven nos contaba una historia y el gringo que manejaba se reía con una risa ancha, pero ése no era yanqui, era holandés, aunque igual tenía acento y pelo rubio. El milico hablaba de su novia que tenía ojos pardos, y la señora sonreía aunque estaba enferma. Mamá me dijo que cantara un rato y yo canté "Niña en tus trenzas de noche", la canción favorita de mamá porque se trataba de una campesina chilena del sur, no del desierto amarillo al mediodía y rojizo al atardecer, con facciones in-

95

distinguibles bajo la luna y la niebla.

A mí, que tengo doce años, me gusta el desierto y la altura porque me siento ligera, pero a mamá le da "puna" y se siente mal. Una vez cuando fui al desierto con mamá, pasamos por la falda de la montaña en un pueblo llamado Caspana, donde el camino era tan estrecho que apenas cabía el jeep, y mamá me contó con orgullo que los Indios de Caspana habían construido ese camino de piedra con sus propias manos. Claro que como yo estaba mirando el lado de la montaña, donde el camino parecía como cortado con un cuchillo, se me ocurrió preguntar qué sucedía si venía otro vehículo saliendo del pueblo—¿tendríamos que retroceder? Nadie contestó, pero mamá dijo "ay, niñita."

Llegamos a Caspana a conversar con el profesor de la escuela, y él nos convidó a tomar desayuno, y me acuerdo de lo bueno que estuvo ese desayuno mientras trato de dormir y no se oye nada más que la ausencia de sollozos que deberían oírse. Pensé en el desayuno, en la montaña florida y con hielo al mismo tiempo, en la piscina de piedra de Toconao en que no pude nadar y me dió tanta pena, pero de nuevo el camión en la pampa oscura y la señora en brazos de mamá mientras yo cantaba... "Niña en tus trenzas de noche, ay, luceros de rocío, traes la risa mojada cantando al borde del río."

En Caspana el río pasaba al lado de la montaña por una quebrada muy honda y yo quedé emocionada porque nunca había visto una quebrada. Salí a jugar con los niños del profesor y yo les dije que en el sur había visto cataratas y ellos se rieron de mí, dos muchachitos menores que yo. Nos pusimos a saltar por las rocas y a escalar las paredes de la quebrada, yo buscando unas florecitas silvestres con tallo delgadito. Uno de los chicos dijo que había truchas en el río, y al mirar para abajo me resbalé en el hielo y casi me caí al fondo de la quebrada. Yo ni grité de puro susto, pero los muchachos aullaron y saltaron en busca de una rama para ayudarme, pero yo trepé de nuevo por la roca hasta que llegué a la orilla y nos alejamos de allí.

En Caspana, como en casi todos los pueblos del desierto, había una escuelita con paredes de piedra y piso de tierra. Todas las casas son así, pero en Toconao son de piedra blanca, como la piscina linda donde no pude nadar. En Toconao seguí los acueductos de piedra que usaban para regar, saltando con un pie dentro y otro afuera porque estaban secos en el verano, y llegué a una huerta de perales hermosos, altísimos y cargados de fruta. La huerta era grande y los perales seguían en hilera por la arena. Hacia el este del pequeño valle me vi rodeada de paredes de piedra tan inmensas, que tenían cascaditas de agua, ramitas y helechos saliendo de la piedra misma. Era todo tan lindo que apenas me contenía de gusto, y fui corriendo a decirle a mamá cuando me tropecé con un animal muerto que parecía un jabalí. Ese hallazgo también me emocionó, porque nunca había visto un jabalí como los que hay en las selvas, pero mamá dijo que no era jabalí, que apenas era un cerdo viejo.

Todo está quieto, y cuando cierro los ojos, veo la piscina de piedra en Toconao con el agua cristalina y profunda que salía de una vertiente del río Loa y se convertía en una piscina en el desierto.

Tan quieto el muchacho que no ha dormido por cuatro noches, cuidando a su mamá, hasta que nosotras llegamos a Peine en el camión. Ahora trató de dormir, pero la señora había estado enferma de hace harto tiempo, y los del hospital le habían preguntado a qué partido político pertencía. Los del hospital son unos bestias, eso dijo mamá.

Hoy en el desierto fuimos a los pueblos del interior buscando objetos de arte para la feria de Calama. La gente es amable y calmada, morena y con pecas como las mías, y hablan despacio y con una pregunta al final de las frases. Mamá les pregunta acerca de su arte, los tejidos y jarros decorados de greda café y roja. En Toconao, un joven llamado Emilio hizo una réplica de greda de la iglesia de su pueblo. Era muy linda y hasta tenía campanitas de verdad. Había una señora de trenzas larguísimas que tejía telas multicolores sentada en el suelo usando los dedos de las manos y los pies. Doña Guillermina había estado en la cárcel porque no tenía certificado de nacimiento. Ella no podía probar a las autoridades que era chilena y que no había cruzado el desierto desde Bolivia. Pero cuando se trataba de votar en las elecciones, a las autoridades les deba ceguera con los certificados, eso decía mamá. En Caspana, el profesor nos contó cómo habían venido los jefes de los tres partidos políticos a decir discursos y a convencer al pueblo que votaran por su candidato para presidente. El pueblo escuchaba respetuosamente. El jefe quedaba complacido y ofrecía un gran afiche de un candidato pálido y serio. El profesor nos mostró dónde estaban los afiches colgados, uno al lado del otro, como si todos fueran iguales.

En Caspana el sol brillaba y había un silencio suave en el aire. Del lado de la quebrada se veía el pueblo encrustado en la montaña, las casas a desnivel que parecían haber crecido así, una a una a través de largo tiempo. Detrás de las casas se veían las terrazas sembradas, apenas verdeando y bajando gradualmente hasta donde se abría el canal de irrigación. Más allá de las casas y los escalones de tierra rojiza y café, se extendía el desierto.

Bajo un cielo azulísimo donde la antigüedad flotaba por épocas, ahí había nacido la gente de sol. En cada pueblo se sentía el tiempo que no corre, que solo se desliza con el viento. Pero sí había cambios. La madre de Emilio nos contó historias de los tiempos pasados, antes de que ella naciera, cuando las lluvias venían fielmente a regar los perales, a mojar los campos, y las llamas y alpacas pacían libres en el pasto abundante.

En cada pueblo nos daba la bienvenida la esposa del profesor, después visitábamos la iglesia, y a mí como tengo doce años, siempre me mandaban a jugar con alguien mientras mamá conversaba y organizaba la feria de arte.

Cuando fuimos a Chiu Chiu visitamos la iglesia construida por los jesuitas en 1510. Yo no me quise quedar porque me asustó la apariencia de tumba que tenía, con paredes bajas de piedra amarilla y corredores estrechos. En la sacristía había toda clase de paños morados y encajes, santos antiquísimos y una virgen de casi un metro con ropa de terciopelo y cara de porcelana, ojos de vidrio grises y una corona de oro. Yo había oído de los santos que los jesuitas usaban para convertir a los Indios. Eran así, con pelo de veras y ojos de vidrio que vertían lágrimas por agujeritos y los curas lo declaraban milagro. Yo me salí de la iglesia y me quedé esperando afuera al sol tibio de esa tarde. Alrededor del jeep se había reunido un grupo de gente, y conversamos acerca de la Feria. Algunos jóvenes decidieron ir a Calama en dos semanas cuando la Feria comenzaba, y mamá les invitó a nuestra casa. Una señora nos presentó a las tejedoras y las artesanas que hacían jarros de greda, y después nos regaló un pan fresco que comimos en el camino. Yo estaba feliz, viajando con mamá, y siempre aprendiendo cosas nuevas. Allá en la pampa que es tan grande, no hay razón para estar triste, con el sol y el viento suave. Ahora sí estoy triste, pero entonces no lo sabía.

Pero el viaje de hoy fue el más largo. En Toconao apenas nos detuvimos una media hora para recoger la iglesia de Emilio y ponerla cuidadosamente en el camión, envuelta con frazadas de lana de llama. A la hermanita de Emilio la mandaron a jugar conmigo y salimos corriendo, porque ella dijo que me iba a mostrar la piscina. Salimos por un sendero y de repente, allí estaba, como un ojo abierto entre la roca lisa que se extendía alrededor. En las orillas de la piscina se quebraba a veces la piedra para dejar crecer plantas trepadoras, algunas crecían hasta debajo del agua. Las dos nos tendimos en la orilla a mirar el fondo de la piscina donde se veía todo tipo de piedrecitas, plantas y peces azulados. Yo nunca había visto algo tan maravilloso. La niña parecía comprender porque nos quedamos quietas, y ni siquiera nos dijimos los nombres. El agua se veía soleada y clara, viva, llena de color. Era casi imposible no sumergirse y bucear por ese reino fértil que se veía desde la superficie, nadar con los brazos abiertos de orilla a orilla de piedra blanca y amarilla entibiada por el sol del desierto. La niña y yo nos sonreímos y yo quise volver a jugar con ella y a nadar en la piscina. Al volvernos, me acerqué a la vertiente y bebí el agua fría y deliciosa.

99

Antes de salir de Toconao, el milico joven le tuvo que echar bencina al camión con una manguera. Cada vez que chupaba la manguera y la ponía en el camión, la bencina se devolvía al barrilito y no salía nada.

Yo quise ayudar, pero él me dijo gracias de todas maneras. El holandés, que resultó ser misionario del Salvation Army, comenzó a dirigir la maniobra de la bencina. Mamá conversaba con una señora que tejía capuchitas de lana. De repente la bencina empezó a subir del barrilito y el milico se tragó una buena porción y tuvo que toser y escupir detrás del camión, pero no quiso que nadie se ocupara de él.

Nos dirigimos a Peine, que es el pueblo más lejano, casi al lado de la cordillera de los Andes. El camino era largo y yo me dormí hasta que llegamos. En Peine nos esperaba el concilio del pueblo con una variedad de contribuciones para la Feria: mantas tricolores, frazadas gruesas de lana de llama que daban gusto tocar, cordones tejidos de lana de alpaca que habían sido trenzados con un diseño de lana café y blanca. Los cordones eran tan fuertes como sogas, y se usaban para ponerles riendas a los animales. Toda la gente escribía orgullosamente su nombre en una lista que tenía mamá, donde se indicaba a quién pertenecía cada objeto y cuánto dinero recibiría en caso que se vendiera en la Feria.

En casa del profesor de Peine nos sirvieron una comida deliciosa. La señora del profesor era muy tímida y no conversaba, pero me acuerdo de ella porque era muy linda, alta y morena, con manos pequeñas y sonrisa de ángel. Un joven se sentó en uno de los bancos de madera y tocó la guitarra.
Había sido un día tan largo en el desierto, que yo casi no me acordaba de mi casa. Me hubiera quedado allí para siempre.

Antes de irnos, un señor vino a conversar con mamá al lado del camión. Entonces supe que llevaríamos pasajeros a Calama, una señora que venía enferma con uno de sus hijos. El muchacho y ella se sentaron en el asiento de atrás junto a mamá y conversaron suavemente.

La noche en el desierto es traicionera, dicen, porque oscurece de repente y la temperatura baja mucho. Cuando el camión se echó a andar camino a la ciudad, ya comenzaba a oscurecer. Yo no me ocupé de nada más. Me acurruqué en el primer asiento con una frazada de lana de llama, mirando por la ventanilla al camino. Todavía tengo la impresión de estar en el camino, zumbando a través del desierto, hora tras hora, y yo recordando lo que había hecho durante el día, y mi amiguita de la piscina que me había pedido que volviera. Yo había dicho que sí, pero no sabía su nombre ni ella el mío. Todos estaban quietos en el camión. El milico joven se sentía mal por haberse tragado la bencina, así es que se había tendido a lo largo de un asiento. El muchacho estaba mirando a su madre que estaba al lado de la mía. Fui hablar con mamá y la señora tosió un poco. Mamá le tomó la mano y ella se calmó. Su hijo nos contó que hacía días que trataban de ir al hospital, pero no había nadie que los llevara. No había autos en Peine porque queda tan lejos de la ciudad. Había pasado un camión militar la semana pasada, pero les habían dicho que no podían transportar a civiles. La señora asintió lentamente. También había pasado un jeep hace dos días, pero los tipos que manejaban dijeron que estaban haciendo campaña política y no podían desviarse. Hacía ya cuatro días que la señora no podía respirar bien.

Ya estaba oscuro y hacía frío. Mamá me dijo que cantara algo bonito y canté una canción popular que a mí me gustaba, pero no sonaba bien con el ruido del camión y todo. El milico se animó y pidió que cantara un tango, pero yo no sabía tangos, así es que él cantó un bolero y después le dio náusea con lo de la bencina y se tuvo que tender de nuevo. Yo canté "Niña en tus trenzas de noche" y me puse a pensar en las palabras de las canciones, en los minerales del desierto, y tantas cosas que ni me di cuenta cuándo el camión partió por otro camino lleno de hoyos y más estrecho. Ibamos camino a San Pedro de Atacama porque la señora se había agravado y teníamos que llegar a la clínica donde seguramente habría un doctor, o por lo menos, la medicina que necesitaba. Me acuerdo de cuando fuimos a San Pedro por primera vez. San Pedro es uno de los pueblos más conocidos, tal vez por el museo, o tal vez porque solo queda a dos horas de Calama. Pero también, mamá me había contado que San Pedro fue el primer pueblo que encontraron los españoles cuando cruzaron el desierto. Pedro de Valdivia ordenó que se construyera una iglesia, después que tomó el pueblo, lo incendio y mató a doce de los jefes.

Nosotros fuimos a ver el museo arqueológico y a conversar con el cura belga que había fundado el museo. Él era tan simpático que no parecía cura y sabía mucho de los Indios de Atacama. Vimos momias en cántaros de greda inmensos, y collares de turquesa pulida, y tablitas de rapé, y flechas de piedra negra. Yo quise ser arqueóloga para descubrir tumbas y aprender la historia del desierto.

Antes de llegar a San Pedro hay que pasar por entre dos montañas de pura sal. De ahí se saca la sal de roca con dinamita, pero no se hacen excavaciones como en Chuquicamata en las minas de cobre. Después de las montañas hay un valle de dunas de arena que llaman "El Valle de la Luna". Durante el día, todo se ve normal, como cualquier otro desierto. Pero esta noche, cuando vi las montañas de sal, había una luz blanquisca, o tal vez era la niebla, y al pasar por el valle, todo había cambiado de tal manera que realmente podía ser un valle de la luna. Me quedé pensando en el cambio sorprendente de la pampa. Acaso era la atmósfera de sal que producía los fantasmas, porque siempre se contaban historias de las ánimas de la gente que se pierden en la pampa y vagan eternamente por esos lugares. Por eso se ven en el camino, llenos de polvo, pequeños altares con una virgen y una inscripción para conmemorar a los viajeros perdidos.

De vuelta en San Pedro nos dirigimos derecho a la clínica. Ya era casi medianoche y el frío calaba hasta los huesos. Mamá y el holandés entraron corriendo a hablar con las enfermeras y a buscar al doctor, pero no había doctor esa noche y no había manera de encontrar uno. Por el pasillo de baldosa fría trajeron una camilla para la señora y la llevaron a una pieza de emergencia para darle oxígeno. Al muchacho no le hablaron, aunque se trataba de su madre. Nos quedamos esperando en el pasillo mientras mamá fue a llamar a Calama para que estuvieran listos para atender a la señora en el hospital. El milico me dijo en voz bajita que el doctor estaba en la ciudad, y yo le pregunté por qué no tenían un doctor Indio para que estuviera siempre en la clínica, y el dijo "Eso mismo". Yo dije que iba a rezar a la Virgen.

Ahora todo está quicto y no quiero cerrar los ojos en la oscuridad. En la mañana mamá me dirá con voz grave que la señora falleció anoche. Yo voy a querer hacerle muchas preguntas, pero no voy a poder porque me da mucha pena.

Mirando por la ventanilla de atrás, yo veía cómo el camión ganaba distancia minuto a minuto. Susurrando las palabras yo rogaba a la Virgen que salvara a la señora, que acortara el camino, que hiciera respirar a la señora que estaba en brazos de mamá y dormía a ratitos. Pero no rezaba a la virgen de los jesuitas, sino a una virgen que yo había inventado, una virgen viva y morena que salía de la piscina linda de Toconao, una virgen llena de luz que se desparramaba por todo el desierto.

En el camino se veían sombras negras que parecían dobleses de género, y cada vez que pasábamos por uno, yo rogaba con toda mi alma que la Virgen usara el doblés para acortar el camino. Apenas moviendo los labios yo repetía, "que se acorte, que se acorte" como una fórmula mágica, tratando de encontrar toda la fé que yo tenía hasta que realmente se acababa la distancia y ya se veían las luces de Calama. En el asiento de atrás, mamá también decía "Fuerza, señora, ya vamos llegando," Se agrandaban las luces, y de vez en cuando una casa chiquita, y un camión, y un bus, y otra casa y otra y yo feliz rezando secretamente hasta que llegamos al hospital y salieron unos enfermeros con una camilla a buscar a la señora. Yo me despedí, hasta luego señora, que se sienta mejor, y todos seguimos detrás de la camilla y tuvimos que esperar de nuevo en el pasillo. Allí nos quedamos, el holandés, el muchacho, el milico y yo, mirando las baldosas amarillas hasta que vimos pasar a un doctor y una enfermera y después nada más por largo rato. Finalmente salió mamá y le dijo al muchacho que había que ponerse en contacto con su tía en cuanto llegáramos a nuestra casa, y que su mamá estaría mejor en la mañana. El muchacho dió las gracias y nos subimos al camión de nuevo. Entonces, mamá le dijo bajito al holandés que todavía no la habían atendido, que le preguntaron a qué partido pertenecía y mamá se enojó mucho.

Ahora ya deben ser las cuatro de la mañana y hace mucho tiempo que sonó el teléfono con la llamada del hospital. Todo está quieto y cada vez que cierro los ojos veo el camino en sombras que se acorta y se acorta pero, ay, ya la señora se ha muerto sin decir casi una palabra a nadie.

Amanda

Roberta Fernández

Transformation was definitely her specialty, and out of georgettes, piques, poie de soie, organzas, shantungs and laces she made exquisite gowns adorned with delicate opaline beadwork which she carefully touched up with the thinnest silvers of irridescent cording that one could find. At that time I was so captivated by Amanda's creations that often before I fell asleep I would conjure up visions of her workroom where luminous whirls of lentejuelas de conchanacar would be dancing about, softly brushing against the swaying fabrics in various shapes and stages of completion. Then amidst the colorful threads and telas de tornasol shimmering in a reassuring rhythm, she would get smaller and smaller until she was only the tiniest of grey dots among the colors and lights and slowly, slowly, the uninterrupted gentle droning of the magical Singer and her mocking whispering voice would both vanish into a silent solid darkness.

By day whenever I had the opportunity I loved to sit next to her machine observing her hands guiding the movement of the fabrics. I was so moved by what I saw that she soon grew to intimidate me and I almost never originated conversation. Therefore, our only communication for long stretches of time was my obvious fascination with the changes that transpired before my watchful eyes. Finally she would look up at me through her gold-rimmed glasses and ask, "¿Te gusta, muchacha?"

In response to my nod she would proceed to tell me familiar details about the women who would be showing off her fin-

105

ished costumes at the Black and White Ball or some other such event. Rambling on with the reassurance of someone who has given considerable thought to everything she says, Amanda would then mesmerize me even further with her provocative chismes about men and women who had come to our area many years ago. Then as she tied a thread here and added a touch there I would feel compelled to ask her a question or two as my flimsy contribution to our lengthy conversation.

With most people I chatted freely but with Amanda I seldom talked since I had the distinct feeling that in addition to other apprehensions I had about her by the time I was five or six, she felt total indifference towards me. "¡Qué preguntona!" I was positive she would be saying to herself even as I persisted with another question. When she stopped talking to concentrate fully on what she was doing I would gaze directly at her, admiring how beautiful she looked. Waves of defeat would overtake me, for the self-containment which she projected behind her austere appearance made me think that she would never take notice of me, while I loved everything about her.

I would follow the shape of her head from the central part of her dark auburn hair pulled down over her ears to the curves of the chongo which she wore at the nape of her long neck. The grey shirtwaist with the narrow skirt and elbow-length sleeves she wore day in and day out, everywhere she went, made her seem even taller than she was. The front had tiny stitched-down vertical pleats and a narrow deep pocket in which she sometimes tucked her eyeglasses. She always seemed to have a yellow measuring tape hanging around her neck and a row of straight pins with big plastic heads down the front edge of her neckline. Like the rest of the relatives she seemed reassuringly permanent in the uniform she had created for herself.

Her day lasted from seven in the morning until nine in the evening. During this time she could dash off in a matter of two or three days an elaborate wedding dress or a classically simple evening gown for someone's coming-out party which Artemisa would then embroider. Her disposition did not require her to concentrate on any one outfit from start to finish and this allowed her to work on many at once. It also meant that she had dresses everywhere, hanging from the edge of the doors, on a wall-to-wall bar suspended near the ceiling and on three or four tables where they would be carefully laid out. Once or twice Amanda managed to make a bride late to her own wedding, when at the last minute she had to sew-in the zipper by hand while the bride was already in the dress. Somehow people didn't seem to mind these occasional slip-ups, for they kept coming back, again and again, from Saltillo and Monterrey, from San Antonio and Corpus Christi, and a few even from far-off Dallas and Houston. Those mid-Texan socialites enjoyed practicing their very singular Spanish with Amanda, and she used to chuckle over her little joke, never once letting on that she really did speak perfect English.

As far as her other designs went, her basic dress pattern might be a direct copy from *Vogue* magazine or it could stem from someone's dearest fantasy. From then on the creation was Amanda's and everyone of her clients trusted the final look to her own discretion. The svelte Club Campestre set from Monterrey and Nuevo Laredo would take her to Audrey Hepburn and Grace Kelly movies to point out the outfits that they wanted, just as their mothers had done with Joan Crawford and Katherine Hepburn movies. Judging from their expressions as they pirouetted before their image in their commissioned artwork she never failed their expectations, except perhaps for that occasional zipper-less bride. She certainly never disappointed me as I sat in solemn and curious attention, peering into her face as I searched for some trace of how she had acquired her special powers.

For there was another aspect to Amanda which only we seemed to whisper about, in very low tones, and that was that Amanda was dabbling in herbs. Although none of us considered her a real hechicera we always had reservations about drinking or eating anything she gave us, and whereas no one ever saw the proverbial muñequitos we fully suspected that she had them hidden somewhere, undoubtedly decked out in the exact replicas of those who had ever crossed her in any way.

Among her few real friends were two ancianas who came to visit her by night, much to everyone's consternation, for those two only needed one quick stolen look to convince you that they were more than amateurs. Librada and Soledad were toothless, old women swarthed in black or brown from head to-

107

toe and they carried their morral filled with hierbas and potions slung over their shoulders just as brujas did in my books. They had a stare that seemed to go right through you, and you knew that no thought was secret from them if you let them look even once into your eyes.

One day in the year when it rained more than in the previous four years and the puddles swelled up with more bubbles than usual I found myself sitting alone in the screened-in porch admiring the sound of the fat rain-drops on the roof when suddenly I looked up to find Librada standing there in her dark brown rebozo, softly knocking on the door.

"La señora le manda un recado a su mamá," she said while my heart thumped so loudly that its noise scared me even further. I managed to tell her to wait there, by the door, while I went to call my mother. By the time that mother came, Librada was already inside, sitting on the couch, and since the message was that Amanda wanted mother to call one of her customers to relay a message, I was left alone with the old woman while mother went to make the call. I sat on the floor pretending to work on a jig-saw puzzle while I really observed Librada's every move. Suddenly she broke the silence asking me how old I was and when my eighth birthday would be. Before I could phrase any words, mother was back with a note for Amanda, and Librada was on her way. Sensing my tension mother suggested that we go into the kitchen to make some good hot chocolate and to talk about what had just happened.

After I drank my cup, I came back to the porch, picked up one of my *Jack and Jill's* and lay down on the couch. As I rearranged a cushion my left arm slid on a viscous greenish-grey substance and I let out a screech which had mother at my side in two seconds. Angry at her for having taken so long to come to my aid, I was wiping my arm on the dress and screaming, "Mire lo que hizo la bruja." She very, very slowly took off my dress and told me to go into the shower and to soap myself well. In the meantime she cleaned up the mess with newspapers and burned them outside by the old brick pond. As soon as I came out of the shower she puffed me up all over with her lavender-fragranced bath powder and for the rest of the afternoon we tried to figure out what the strange episode had meant. Nothing of great importance happened to anyone in the family during the following wet days and mother insisted we forget the incident.

Only I didn't forget it for a long time. On my next visit to Amanda's I described in detail what had happened. She dismissed the entire episode as though it weren't important, shrugging, "Pobre Librada. ¿Por qué le echas la culpa de tal cosa?" With that I went back to my silent observation, now suspecting that she too was part of a complex plot that I couldn't figure out. Yet, instead of making me run, incidents like these drew me more to her, for I distinctly sensed that she was my only link to other exciting possibilities which were not part of the every-day world of the others. What they could be I wasn't sure of but I was so convinced of the hidden powers in that house that I always wore my scapular and made the sign of the cross before I stepped inside.

After the rains stopped and the moon began to change colors I began to imagine a dramatic and eery outfit which I hoped Amanda would create for me. Without discussing it with my sisters I made it more and more sinister and finally when the toads stopping croaking I built up enough nerve to ask her about it.

"Oye, Amanda, ¿me podrías hacer el traje más hermoso de todo el mundo? ¿Uno como el que una bruja le diera a su hija favorita? ¡Que sea tan horrible que a todos les encante!"

"¿Y para qué diablos quieres tal cosa?" she asked me in surprise.

"Nomás lo quiero de secreto. No creas que voy a asustar a los vecinos."

"Pues, mire usted, chulita, estoy tan ocupada que no puedo decirle ni sí ni no. Uno de estos días, cuando Dios me dé tiempo quizás lo pueda considerar, pero hasta entonces yo no ando haciendo promesas a nadie."

And then I waited. Dog days came and went, and finally when the lechuza flew elsewhere I gave up on my request, brooding over my having asked for something which I should have known would not be coming. Therefore the afternoon that Artemisa dropped off a note saying that la señora wanted to see me that night because she had a surprise for me, I cooly said that I'd be there only if my mother said that I could go.

All the time that I waited to be let in I was very aware that I had left my scapular at home. I knew this time that something very special was about to happen to me, since I could see even from out there that Amanda had finally made me my very special outfit. Mounted on a little-girl dress-dummy a swaying black satin cape was awaiting my touch. It was ankle length with braided frogs cradling tiny buttons down to the knee. On the inside of the neckline was a black fur trim. "Es de gato," she confessed, and it tickled my neck as she buttoned the cape on me. The puffy sleeves fitted very tightly around the wrist, and on the upper side of each wristband was attached a cat's paw which hung down to the knuckles, on top of each hand. Below the collar on the left side of the cape was a small stuffed heart in burgundy-colored velveteen and, beneath the heart, were tear-shaped red translucent beads.

As she pulled the rounded ballooning hood on my head, rows of stitched-down pleats made it fit close to the head. Black chicken feathers framed my face, almost down to my eyes. Between the appliqués of feathers were strung tiny bones which gently touched my cheeks. The bones came from the sparrows which the cats had killed out in the garden, she reassured me. She then suggested that I walk around the room so that she could get a good look at me.

As I moved, the cat's paws rubbed against my hands and the bones of the sparrows bounced like what I imagined snow-flakes would feel like on my face. Then she put a necklace over my head which reached to my waist. It too was made of bones of sparrows strung on the finest glittering black thread, with little cascabeles inserted here and there. I raised my arms and danced around the room, and the little bells sounded sweet and clear in the silence. As I glided about the room I noticed in the mirror that Librada was sitting in the next room, laughing under her breath. Without thinking I walked up to her and asked what she thought of my cape.

"Hijita, pareces algo del otro mundo. Mira que hasta me acabo de persignar. Me da miedo nomás en pensar del montón que te vas a llevar contigo al infierno. ¡Qué Dios nos libre!"

As I looked at Librada for the first time, I felt that the room was not big enough to hold all the emotion inside of me. So I put my arms around Amanda and kissed her two, three, four times, then dramatically announced that I was going to show this most beautiful of all creations to my mother. I rushed outside hoping not to see anyone in the street and since luck was to be my companion for a brief while, I made it home without encountering a soul. Pausing outside the door of the kitchen where I could hear voices I took a deep breath, knocked as loudly as I could and in one simultaneous swoop, opened the door and stood inside, arms outstretched as feathers, bones and cascabeles fluttered in unison with my heart.

After the initial silence my sisters started to cry almost hysterically, and while my father turned to comfort them, my mother came towards me with a face that I had never seen on her before. She took a deep breath and quietly said that I must never wear that outfit again. Since her expression frightened me somewhat, I took off the cape, mumbling under my breath over and over how certain people couldn't see special powers no matter how much they might be staring them in the face.

I held the bruja cape in my hands, looking at the tiny holes pieced through the bones of the sparrows, then felt the points of the nails on the cat's paws. As I fingered the beads under the heart I knew that on that very special night when the green lights of the linternas were flickering much brighter than usual, on that calm transparent night of nights I would sleep in my wonderous witch's daughter's cape.

Sometime after the Júdases were all aflame and spirals of light were flying everywhere I slowly opened my eyes on a full moon shining on my face. Instinctively my hand reached to my neck and I rubbed the back of my fingers gently against the cat's fur. I should go outside I thought. Then I slipped off the bed and tipped-toed to the back door in search of that which was not inside.

For a long time I sat on a lawn chair, rocking myself against its back, all the while gazing at the moon and at the familiar surroundings which glowed so luminously within the vast universe, while out there in the darkness the constant chirping of the crickets and the chicharras reiterated the reassuring permanence of everything around me. None of us is allowed to relish in powers like that for long though, and the vision of transcendence exploded in a scream as two hands grabbed me

111

at the shoulders, then shook me back and forth. "What are you doing out here? Didn't I tell you to take off that awful thing?"

Once again I looked at my mother in defiance but immediately sensed that she was apprehensive rather than angry and I knew that it was hopeless to argue with her. Carefully I undid the tiny rounded black buttons from the soft braided loops and took off the cape for what I felt would be the last time.

Years passed, much faster than before, and I had little time left for dark brown-lavender puddles and white lechuzas in the night. Nor did I see my cape after that lovely-but-so-sad, once-in-a-lifetime experience of perfection in the universe. In fact, I often wondered if I had not invented that episode as I invented many others in those endless days of exciting and unrestrained possibilities.

Actually the memory of the cape was something I tried to flick away on those occasions when the past assumed the unpleasantness of an uninvited but persistent guest; yet, no matter how much I tried, the instrusions continued. They were especially bothersome one rainy Sunday afternoon when all the clocks had stopped working one after another as though they too had wanted to participate in the tedium of the moment. So as not to remain still I mustered all the energy that I could and decided to pass the hours by poking around in the boxes and old trunks in the storeroom.

Nothing of interest seemed to be the order of the afternoon when suddenly I came upon something wrapped in yellowed tissue paper. As I unwrapped the package I uttered a sigh of surprise on discovering that inside was the source of the disturbances I had been trying to avoid. I cried as I fingered all the details on the little cape, for it was as precious as it had been on the one day I had worn it many years ago. Only the fur had stiffened somewhat from the dryness in the trunk.

Once again I marvelled at Amanda's gifts. The little black cape was so obviously an expression of genuine love that it seemed a shame it had been hidden for all those years. I carefully lifted the cape out of the trunk wondering why my mother had not burned it as she had threatened, yet knowing full well

112

why she had not.

From then on I placed the little cape among my collection of few but very special possessions which accompanied me everywhere I went. I even had a stuffed dummy made upon which I would arrange the cape in a central spot in every home I made. Over the years the still-crisp little cape ripened in meaning, for I could not imagine anyone ever again taking the time to create anything as personal for me as Amanda had done when our worlds had coincided for a brief and joyous period in those splendid days of luscious white gardenias. When the end came I could hardly bear it. It happened many years ago when the suitcase containing the little cape got lost en route on my first trip west. No one could understand why the loss of something as quaint as a black cape with chicken feathers, bones of sparrows and cat's paws could cause anyone to carry on in such a manner. Their lack of sympathy only increased my own awareness of what was gone, and for months after I first came to these foggy coastal shores I would wake up to lentejuelas de conchanacar whirling about in the darkness, just as they had done so long ago in that magical room in Amanda's house.

Back home Amanda will soon be eighty, and although I haven't seen her in years, lately I have been dreaming once again about the enchantment which her hands gave to everything they touched, especially when I was very tiny and to celebrate our birthdays, my father, she and I had a joint birthday party lasting three consecutive days, during which he would make a skeletal frame for a kite out of bamboo sticks to which Amanda would attach very thin layers of marquisette with angel cords which my father would then hold on to, while I floated about on the kite above the shrubs and bushes and it was all such fun. I cannot recall the exact year when those celebrations stopped, nor what we did with all those talismanic presents but I must remember to sort through all the trunks and boxes in my mother's storeroom the next time that I am home.

I Never Told
My Children Stories

ROSARIO MORALES

I never told my children stories. I said I couldn't make things
up. "Go ask your father. He makes things up all the time."
Now me—I like the truth. I figured if I ever wrote any stories,
they'd be true stories, things that happened to me, the real
stuff of life, not all that airy invention.

Of course, that was before I realized how much of my
truth was embroidered. No, not embroidered exactly—just
remembered in special ways. Before I began thinking of
people's truths as the stories they tell about themselves. Oh
well, I might as well get personal. Before *I* began seeing
my truth as the story *I* tell to let you know what I think *I'm*
all about, to clue you in on what I think is *really* happening:
how I'm pretty lucky, and about the rotten childhood I had,
or how mean people have been to me. You know, these stories
are like stage directions in a play, telling you how to do the
character:

> *Zoreida*   She sees herself as upright and values her
> integrity. She dramatizes her life, everything
> that happens to her, tragic mostly but comic
> too. Play her large but with restraint as if
> all that energy, all that drama that is her life
> must be strenuously held in if it's not to
> explode all over everybody.

See? Drama. It's my sense of drama that really made me

see the fiction in the telling of my life. Girl! I'm really into those dramatic values, whatever those things are. Heighten a little here, smooth there. Those are irrelevant details and detract from the main point. And oh my! My sense of timing! That's what made me see I could tell stories, too. 'Cause if that's what a story is, honey, I'm for it, I'm with it, I'm your woman and here we go!

Of course, now that I'm here and real conscious that I'm going to dramatize and tell a story I'm all self-conscious and shy. It's one thing to do it naturally, it's another to sit down in cold blood and dramatize. Go ahead Zoreida, dramatize! Yeah! Perform! "Zoreida, go kiss titi María. Show them your new shoes. Show them how much you've grown. Show them how well you play the piano. Do the piece you did for me yesterday. Do a tap dance, Zoreida! Stand on your head Zoreida! Jump out of the window Zoreida! Fuck it! Why can't they leave little girls alone. You'd think all we were were wind-up toys you pulled out of the drawer and set on the floor to amuse the relatives. Nah. I won't perform on command. I won't. I just get angry thinking about it.

"Act one, scene two." My sister said that. Oh boy—I just remembered her getting at me with those words. You have to hear the sneer in them to understand them though: try it again: real exaggerated, the way only an 8 year old can sneer, "*Act one, scene two.*" She'd do it whenever I got worked up about something. Mean bitch. It was like feeling anything at all was acting. I guess that's why it took me so long to see about how I dramatized. If I admitted it, it was like admitting to my sister that all my feelings were a big act put on just to impress her. Well, fuck her too.

I probably had to exaggerate to get heard. My sister just sneered and my mother was being the tragic heroine of a novela—*mi vida es como una novela,* she used to say.

A novela is a puertorican soap opera and shit! They beat your stuff hollow for drama. I mean they really let themselves go. And they all talk a fancy kind of Spanish all hissing with esses and syllables like a Spanish Shakespeare or something. Not that my mother talked that way. No, it's just that every-thing that happened to her was part of this novela. That there were mustachioed evil men plotting to do her wrong and

115

shifty-eyed women jealously trying to trip her up and really heavy things befell her and she foiled them all and rose white-breasted and triumphant out of heaps of ashes again and again. Why, just going to the grocer was fraught! She dressed up for it like for a first night—catch her running across the street in her bata and a naked face! And if he gave her a special price, her smile hinted at ancient liaisons and secret passions.

No wonder I was into telling the truth, trying to tell the strict truth, and who me? tell stories?

Now that I told you about my mother and my sister, I should tell you about my father. And how he fit into all this—but I don't know! It's still hard for me to get a perspective on him. He's *too* real. Most of that is my mother's doing. She dramatized him to hell-and-gone and I drank it all in. I believed every word and if there were villains in my mother's life, my father was top villain, a sort of Moriarty to her Holmes, the evil genius who was plotting to do her in, kill her.

I don't know how many times she'd tell us that he would kill her, mostly when me and my sister said—"leave him, divorce him." She'd say—heavy voice, scared face, eyes darting sideways—"He'd shoot me!"

Why just the other day I realized for the first time that my mother was over 70 and she never did get killed! What a gyp!

Not that I wanted her dead. Far from it. I took it on myself to keep her alive. No, it's just that I spent my childhood—my life—being terrorized for no good reason. It's just the novela taking over again. "Mi vida es como una novela." My life is like a soap opera. Nah. It doesn't sound right in English, it sounds comic. It hasn't got the pizzaz, the dramatic power, the believability of the Spanish: eyes slightly upward, hand on breast, "como una novela."

Shit, it was *my* life that was like a novela. Nite after nite waking up in a dark room to voices shouting and screaming. My father hitting out, my mother poking and probing with her sharp words, her sharp tongue, like a picador with a bull—getting back at him by enraging him some more—my father's heavy hand, heavy feet—my sister rushing in like a terrier, yapping, yapping, sticking herself in the middle,

116

butting my father, pushing the temperature up, upping the ante, raising the stakes and me—I stand still, I stand there holding myself in, as if I could still my mother's tongue by going mute, as if I could stay my father's hand by standing paralyzed, as if I could cool them all down by freezing myself to death. As if I could cool them all down by freezing myself to death!

Funny I didn't turn out one of those cardboard-faced, eventoned no-feeling prudes, ain't it? Funny I didn't freeze.

Just the contrary. Heck, I think I was jealous. I had no room in that family, no scope for my talents. But the minute I left home and moved in with Jacob...pow! I was my mother in a novela, my father in a fit, my sister in her sneer!

Poor Jacob. I'd picked him out because he was not like any of them. No temperament, no demands. Quiet, gentle, loving—sweet really, a sweet guy. God knows why he picked me. Maybe he saw the potential for a bit of T.N.T. and matches in his damped-down emotional life. I sure hope so. 'Cause he sure got some.

I mean, here I spend twenty years of my life with three escapees from a bad melodrama, I go in search of sanity and love in a mad world, I find it. And then what do I go and do? I re-form the repertory company and put on my own show.

Really I was shocked and ashamed. I was pretty naive at nineteen, well, all thru my twenties. Naive as all shit. I I thought all I had to do to change the way my life had been was to SAY. Say things like "I'm not going to live in a tragicomedy any more." Or, "I'm never going to hit my children." Or, "I'm not going to be scared and in pain when I give birth." Oh dear. It's sad really. Somebody should've told me. Not that I'd a listened. The kind of people that told me it was harder than all that were the same folks who told me not to try and change anything, ever. "Go fight City Hall" that's what my neighbor, Olga, used to say about most anything. That was what most of everybody I knew, met and grew up with used to think: "Go fight City Hall." And in New York City, City Hall was the Rock of Gibraltar, Mount Everest and the Atlantic Ocean all rolled into one. Immovable. Go fight City Hall.

Well, I showed them! The next thing I did was take on

117

City Hall, Washington, D.C., the C.I.A., the F.B.I. and the City's Finest, all in one go. I joined the Communist Party! No, that doesn't come across right. Not enough shock value. Not here, not now, in 1982. No. I've gotta set the stage first.

OK. It's 1949, see? World War II ended four years ago. Truman had dropped a couple of A-bombs on two Japanese cities in 1945. He announced the cold war in 1946. The Unamerican Activities Committee started the McCarthy era in 1947. Congress passed anti-red laws with jail sentences for anyone just *thinking* about wanting to overthrow the U.S. government in 1948 or 9 or so. They revamped the old concentration camps that held the Japanese during the war and thought of building a couple more in nice desolate dry places of the country for when they rounded up the reds and pinks and rose-colored. The leaders of the C.P. were on trial or in hiding, the members were tearing up their membership cards every day! *Women's Day* ran stories about Russian invasions of the U.S. and Russian teachers taking over our schools and closing our children's wide-open little minds. People were being pursued in the streets, hounded out of their jobs, denounced by their neighbors. And what does Conchita's little girl go and do, esa niña loca? What does Ramoncito's little girl go and do? She becomes a red, joins the Communist Party, takes on city hall.

How's that for chutzpah? How's that for up yours, baby, for what the books I read call *epatez les bourgeois.* If that didn't epatez them, I don't see what would have. Living in sin only got a tsk-tsk out of 'em.

But it wasn't all like that. Cause some part of me just went all sort of comfy and at home being in that embattled minority. Some part of me is never comfortable unless I'm doing that kind of uncomfortable thing. I think it's the part of me that stood still as a statue when my family fought, the part of me that swore I'd never hit my children, that cries over all the massacres in the history books, all the deaths behind the anthropology textbooks, or in the newspaper and on the radio. The hatred of pain and injustice. The hatred of pain and injustice of that brown-eyed skinny puertorican girl gets stirred up, and then...bang! There I am, in the front lines again.

There's nothing I want more than that, than the end to so much unnecessary pain. I wanted it then, I want it now, and I'll die wanting it. I wish I could die having it but that doesn't look too likely. You know, it's hard for me to take the end of the world seriously. I guess 'cause I grew up *here* and in the thirties, not in Europe where people were getting fed to ovens or in Asia where hundreds of thousands got incinerated at one go, but *Here* where you could hear about it but not experience it, where you could think it could all be stopped. But I take the end of that kind of horror real serious. I go and work it the way I set out to sew a quilt, snip by snip, stitch by stitch, a lot of boring repetitious labor but with the vision of the end product clear in my mind: glorious pattern and color and warmth and comfort. Glorious comfort to last many, many lifetimes.

That's what being a communist, a socialist has meant to me, being a feminist, a radical, a so-called trouble maker. And if I could epatez a few bourgeois while I was at it, so much the better.

Well, I seem to have changed the subject pretty effectively, I was stuck on showing you how I went from a good, quiet well-behaved girl to a stormy bad-tempered young woman who wasn't expecting the new role. And how dramatizing a lot is like making up a story, sort of. That reminds me that there was a time when I did some real acting. I mean, regular plays, on stage kind of acting. High school. I was part of the drama club and the radio club. I remember in the radio club there was an all woman production and I had most of the parts—well, face it, I was the only one with a deep voice and everyone else sounded like a kid or a bird, all high and chirpy. My voice is low and mellow and on the air sounded just lovely. I liked that a lot of course.

But I used to hate my voice when I was little. The teacher didn't even have to lift her head to look to know it was me talking. "Zoreida!" she'd say "Zoe-reh-dar! Stop talking!" Ugh. I used to hate my name, too. I stood out so, was so different. "Ooooh," grownups would say in their fakey fake make-believe-interested voices, "oooooh, what an *IN-teresting* name! Where are you from, little girl?" "From right here, you bitch!" No, that wasn't what I really said. I was a good little girl, remember. I'd say "Puerto Rico" and watch the oh-oh sort of look creep up over their faces before they tightened up their "how-nice" look. It still happens, you know. All sorts of people you kinda hoped wouldn't turn out like that. They get a kind of flat look in their eyes, not the interested, excited look they'd get if I said "Spain!" or "Argentina!" or something else exotic and far-away and not associated in their ratty little minds with dark skin or cockroaches and knives.

There was a whole big part of my life, my teens mostly, when I wanted to forget I was puertorican. I used to look in the mirror front face and try to look like Hedy Lamarr 'cause if I looked side-face I could see my oh-so-foreign cheekbones and shaped head, I tried to feel 100% American which of course meant white and anglo, not Indian—red Indian, you know, the real 100 percenters. But there was my name. No getting away from it. Zoreida Alvarez, right at the front of the alphabet so it'd get called right off and everyone would turn and look at me. Zohrehdar. Elvrez. Pretty ugly-sounding, said that way. Jeez, no wonder I hated it.

It was years before I really got to like it and I guess to like myself too. Jacob helped. He really dug Puerto Rico and puertoricans and plátanos and arroz con pollo and learned some Spanish words off my father first thing. It sure helped to get my family over getting pissed that I'd moved in with him. I mean, it was Jacob I was living in sin with, not some títere off the streets, that nice jewish boy who loved fried eggs con plátanos maduros fritos y aguacate and knew how to say sinvergüenza and canalla and coño and all sorts of other puertorican insults and bad words. My father especially. It reconciled him—I think that's the word. My mother didn't need much reconciling. She'd handed me over to a GOOD MAN, not one of her villains, a man who wouldn't beat me, abuse me, kill me. The man in the white hat on the white horse, that one. And when she got into the horror of her existence in a low husky, full-of-suffering voice, she would pause, raise her eyes to heaven and look thankful to God and the Virgin Mary and half-a-dozen saints and say, "Gracias a Dios, mi hijita tiene un hombre bueno que la cuide." And then down with the eyes, back to the tale of woe. Take care of me? Stuff! *I* did the taking care of. Trust nobody to see that though. That kind of thing is real invisible, especially in the fifties. That kind of work wasn't even *there*, except just you stop doing it and boy, you'd get noticed all right. Not just shopping and cooking and dishwashing and laundry and beds and floors and bathrooms but feelings and, you know...mothering. No wonder I had scope for temperament. I had a shitload of work I hadn't counted on especially as we'd contracted to a free union, an *arrangement* between equals. We didn't get married to avoid all that artificial stuff and the herr-leader complex for the guy, and the sweet-little-woman stuff for me. We were young communists and enlightened and knew about male chauvinism and the household slavery of women and Engels on the family. But I came away with 90% of the housework and 95% of the emotional mending and ironing any old how.

But I was telling you about acting when I got into all this about how I was in plays in high school and college. It's strange really. I was so shy it was painful. Not just for me, I'm sure. You've seen people like that, so shy it's painful to watch. But from real little I liked being on stage. I was the carrot in the grade school play on good nutrition and remember reciting a piece about Cordell Hull for assembly, except what I remember was not raising my voice or his picture high enough. Learnt my lesson. I can project with the best of them now.

In high school I did some scenes from Shakespeare. *As You Like It*, I think it was. I was fair Rosalind in a long dress and my rhinestones being diamonds around my neck and a well born high haughty posture to my head. Yum. That was fun. In college we did a play about nuns and I wanted the lead so bad it hurt but I missed out and became the old nun instead. I did men's parts a lot, you better believe it, with my voice in an all girls school? I liked hitching up my pants' legs when I sat. Standing masculine-like, thrusting my hips forward, hands in my pockets.

But I was still shy and it cost me a lot to get up there on the first night with a whole lot of people in front. I usually was sick that night or right after. I'd catch bad colds or get the runs. It's strange really.

Of course, now I know better. It makes a kind of sense: I know I needed to make people notice me, and if you're shy and a good girl to boot, it's hard to get any attention in real life. Getting up on stage though and getting your lines handed to you and with someone there to direct and correct you — "No, stand a little further forward. Look at him as if he were a worm, that's right." See, that was easier! And attention by the barrel load.

Course when I left school and moved in with Jacob and became a communist I had other things to do and I didn't act any more, not for years and years and years. Of course I had the attention of the F.B.I., the Puerto Rican Secret Service, the cops and all sorts of vigilant anti-red citizens. But that's not the same. And of course I got to enact dramatic scenes over a scorched pot or a broken teapot but that's not the same. No, I missed the stage. There's a kind of clean feeling about proper acting, a clean good feeling when you do it right and what you get is applause and admiration not suspicion, not jail sentences, not anger and sulks which is what I got, mostly, for being a red or badtempered. No. I missed that. Didn't know I missed it but I did.

When I look back — you know — all that reading I did for the children? That was acting. I didn't tell them stories but I read them other people's stories, acted them out. I loved it, kept it up till they were quite grown up and I was reading them proper novels. I had a ball. That's what I miss about their growing up and going away. One thing anyway. Yeah.

But I'm glad they're launched and out there and O.K. I guess I'm glad *I'm* here and launched and O.K., too! 'Cause I am, you know. I am.

tres

The final section depicts Latinas trying to break up out of the limits our culture has set for us. The most severe restriction placed upon the Latina is in relation to sexuality. This is the subject of most of these stories—the sexual politics of the Latina seeking to control her destiny.

La mujer latina is a living breathing contradiction. When our people deny us a place in our family we feel they are not our people. But, to be removed from our people is a pain nearly too great to bear.

This is our private dialogue with each other.

La sección final enfoca a la latina que intenta romper con los límites impuestos por nuestra cultura, el más severo de los cuales, define y restringe nuestra sexualidad. Este es el tema de la mayoría de estos cuentos: la política sexual de la latina que trata de controlar su destino.

La mujer latina es una contradicción viviente. Cuando nuestra gente nos niega nuestro lugar en la familia sentimos que no son nuestra gente. Pero estar lejos de nuestra gente es un dolor difícil de soportar.

Este es el diálogo privado entre nosotras.

We Women Suffer More Than Men

CÍCERA FERNÁNDEZ DE OLIVEIRA
Translation by Linda Shockey

We suffer more than anyone else, because, look: if you work outside, you get home and you can't rest—you work outside and then you do the household duties. When you get together with a man, everything revolves around him. He goes out to have a stroll, to fool around in the street, but we come home from work, we make lunch, do this, do that, go to the laundry and afterwards hang around waiting for the children. It's us who suffer—men never suffer. That's why I say it's worse for women. Take me, for example—my life is extremely hard. I don't know if it's the same for all women, but my life has always been and is now full of suffering, and I think I'm still going to suffer some more because of this grandchild that's on the way.

What happiness did I have with my husband? I worked outside the house so as to bring up the children. Sunday comes, and there he is, going out to enjoy himself with another woman leaving me alone in the house. I had my own money, but I didn't go out alone, out of consideration for him. Because back then I thought that if I were, for example...if he went out alone and so did I, then I'd lose my morals.

Some men say that women have everything at home—they don't need anything else. But no, a woman needs her husband at home, too. Just room and board can't make a woman happy. The man should go out with her on Sundays, go with her to

124

the movies, a party, the beach. I know so many women who stay at home, poor things, just to take care of the children. He fixes himself up, puts on some after-shave, goes out, never takes the poor woman along. You think a woman like that is happy? No way! Apart from living imprisoned in the house doing housework, she can't even go out alone because most of the time her husband won't let her. Why do you think I'm separated from my husband? For the same reason, of course. Now, I'm never, never again in life life going to trust a man. Never again! After we separated, he put the blame on me, saying I'd slept with other men. *He* was unfaithful, then he accused *me* of the same thing. When he left home, I had a seven-month belly...how could I fool around with a man in this condition?

When he went away they said to him, "You're going away? Leaving your wife there, your wonderful wife, a respectable woman, hard-working, who worked so to help you, and you're going to leave her for someone else? Don't do that!" The fellow who told me this said that my husband was rude and said that I'd deceived him.

On Sundays my husband filled the house with friends, male friends. That horde of men there in the house—sometimes it seemed they were going to take the meat right out of my pan to make a snack. Sometimes we even went without meat to eat. I can't count the number of times he sent some friend to fetch meat right out of my kitchen. Is that what you expect a man to do? I think he did all that because he wanted me to be unfaithful. But he would have died wishing, because all the time I lived with him I never was. Then, after a year and six months of separation, I fixed myself up with another man. I'm not going to say I didn't, because I wasn't paralytic.

I was 21 years old—was I going to stay single? My mother asked me to stay single, waiting for him:

"Your husband went away with someone else, but he'll be back. You wait for him."

But once he'd left, life got pretty difficult for me. My child—the one who died at eight months—was born, like I said before. I wanted running water in my house, and I went to ask the mayor promising to vote for him. He put it in, free. I was the only one on the street with water, and I gave it away to everyone. Very early in the morning there was a long line of clay pots—women with children on their hips, poor things. At the end of the month, I didn't want any money, but they came to pay me—one would give five cruzeiros, another one two or three. I told them to keep it to buy bread for their kids, because the water was put in because of my votes—if they wanted, they could vote for the same mayor.

My husband didn't let me go to political meetings, and he wouldn't go with me, either—he didn't like them. It was when we separated that I began to promise votes. I was husbandless, my life was free. I ran through the streets shouting at voting time. I shouted so much that I was hoarse in the evening after a meeting. That's how I managed to get shoes, dress—there was a time when I managed to get three pairs of sandals for Jacilene. I asked for something from every candidate—from my own because I voted for him, and from the others even though I didn't. I went from one party to the other, scrounging.

One time I went to a sugar factory to ask for sugar. I brought back a lot that the guy gave me because he was a city councilman. He also gave me brown sugar and sugar cane. I had to show him my voting card and say I was going to vote for him. Sometimes I voted, sometimes I didn't. But I did things that way because I enjoyed running around at voting time. I'd come back from work and I'd go to one of their houses, to another, asking for things. When my bathroom fell down, I went to ask because it was voting time, and the doctor gave me, at that time, 120 cruzeiros. I put in my bathroom, my "fixture," as they say there, not "bathroom" like here.

We voted for the Social Democratic Party (PSD) or for the Brazilian Workers' Party (PTB). My mother didn't want us to vote for the National Democratic Union (UDN). She said it was for rich people, for factory owners. In those days, the workers voted for the PTB: For Getúlio Vargas. When he was running, my mother wouldn't let anyone vote for José Américo. She said it was the party of the poor people, that they were the ones who created INPS (Social Security and national health insurance). And Dr. Eraldo, who was deputy, is terrific—I can go there and whenever he sees me, he gives me a big hug. He's very rich—he was the one who paid for my mother's operation and who helped me to put in water when I bought the house.

The rich people's party always gives the most money, but we vote for the other one, just because we like it. I worked in a group that cheered for Eraldo Gadelha in the meetings. They gave us a dress, a sort of uniform. Everyone went behind him with a flag, cheering, in the meetings and parades. I still remember today my poor mother...she'd miss a meal for Dr. Eraldo. He was very good to us, he was, and he still is. My father never aligned himself with a party, but my mother insisted that we had to vote for the one she liked.

Our family counted for 150 votes, including the in-laws. This was after the family had grown. Only one uncle revolted and went to another party. I think the UDN. When he went over, everyone was furious with him. The whole family lives in Santa Rita...we go to visit a relative, a brother, a friend at voting time and say, "Who are you going to vote for?" "Oh, I'm voting for our party, the workers' party." It's the party of the poor. I have an uncle who was a candidate for city councilman, but he wasn't elected.

I think that men are better at running politics. I think that's because men are better than women. I trust a male doctor, for example—I like to consult a man better than a woman. I think it's nicer when a man's in charge. I trust myself on some matters, on others no. If I'm nervous I do silly things. But I wouldn't want to be a man; I'd want to be born a woman. Because I am a woman, but I do both things—I do the work that a man does. I work outside, I take care of the house, I do the shopping, I have all the responsibility. The money we have at home is mine, without needing a man. The job of a woman is to take care of the house, and men are supposed to work outside.

I waited a year and six months to have another man. That was when I found Elinaldo's father, another no-good bum. But if it were up to my mother and brothers, I'd still be waiting— everyone was against it. They were mad at me. Some wanted to kill me, others wanted to beat me up, my father cursed me. But it was all very lovely for me in the beginning. I even swooned when I began to date him. The first night we went to sleep together, I fainted. I think it was from passion, from emotion. It had been a year since I'd been close to a man, and afterwards, I was pregnant with Elinaldo. I had to face the music then—I couldn't hide the romance any more, I took a lot of medicine to see if my period would come. Afterwards, people began to scare me, saying if I took a lot of medicines the child would be born crippled, so I stopped.

I didn't go to his house and he didn't come to mine. We went to a motel. We went far away. When I was three months gone, I was enormous, hiding my belly, and tongues began to wag: "Cícera is fat." He worked in the factory with me—he was my foreman, and I was a weaver. One day I said to him, "You know something? It's all going to come out in the open and I'm going to let it. I'm going to tell everyone that we're involved. I know that when my family finds out they're going to want to kill you or me, but no problem. No one tells me what to do—I work to support myself. The child will be born all the same."

When Sunday came, I called him to eat at my house, and he came. When he arrived, oh, but didn't my neighbors, married women, think I was disgracing the street! They were from the time of my husband—we lived there on Rio Branco St. for nine years. But I thought that, dammit, the house was mine, and I was the one in charge. I opened the door, turned on the record player, and listened to records, I bought beer, put the table in the living room—a formica table with four chairs, functional style, like was in fashion then. I put beef and chicken on the table and we had a wild spree.

In the North, the door is divided—there's the upper door and the lower door. I closed the lower one and opened the upper. After everyone was watching, I decided to open the whole thing. We toasted with beer. After lunch, I say, "Now you go on home. I'm going to tell everyone that I'm expecting your child." "You're not going to do that!" "I am, and my mother's not going to be the first to know."

I was the only one at home, because Jacilene was at my mother's house and the girl who helped out around the house had taken Jacinto to his father's house to spend Sunday.

He left and I revealed all to the neighbors. I said I liked Dedé: "It's been a year I've been waiting for Antonio; my mother wants me to wait, but I'm not going to any more." But you're crazy...everyone's going to say you were already seeing him when Antonio left."

I say no, because Dedé was a buddy of my husband and they had always been together in my house. One time I threw him out, but my conscience is clean before Jesus that I never ran around on my husband with anyone. I kicked him out because he was an alleycat and came to lure my husband away from home to fool around and he'd come back the next day. I really hated Dedé. One time, on a Sunday, I told him Antonio was still sleeping. But he heard from the bedroom and said, "I'm going out...no woman's going to control me!" It almost seems a punishment to like him after all that, but I still like him today.

My mother thought it would shame the family for me to find another man, because everyone's married. I'm married, too, but without a husband because he left me for another When my mother found out it was Dedé I was in love with it was even worse because Dedés quite dark. But his hair's not frizzy—it's like mine. She knew he'd been to see me and had eaten at my house.

"Give me your blessing, mother," I said. But she wouldn't. I went to the farm, I thought to look at my plants—coconut, mango, jackfruit. But she went to break off a stick and beat me...I could only stop her by grabbing her hand. But I got quite a beating. She wanted me to spend my whole life waiting for my husband. (At home, my mother's the one who does the whipping.) She thinks a man who runs off with another woman is going to leave her, because his real woman is the one at home. It's only the woman who causes shame, never the man.

I said, "it's not going to help, you beating me, because it's already been a year since he left." "But everyone's going to say you did wrong by him." "It's a lie, I swear on my honor before God that I never deceived my husband. I hated that man, I kicked him out of the house twice." "I'll never give you my blessing again, you're not my daughter any more, now that you've wrecked the morals of the family. What are the others' husbands going to think? They're going to say all the girls are bad, like you, that they're all going to sleep around." "No Mother, I'm not making anyone say that. Here in my house I'm the boss, because it's mine. Have I come to your place to even ask for a matchstick after my husband left me? It's more than a year that I'm separated, and I've never gone to my mother's house to ask for even a cup of coffee, nor to my brother's either. I've never begged a cup of coffee to give the children or a liter of milk; I stayed with the babies—I'm bringing up the one that was born after I separated right now. Did I ever come to you to take care of them? Did I ask anything of my father? Did anyone come to pay the light bill, the taxes on my house? Then I'm the boss in my life, because I work to support myself. I'm already 21 years old, I'm legally an adult; I can do as I please."

But none of this helped. She went off and spoke with my father. "I'll never give you my blessing either," he said. "God has it with him up in heaven, where he is." And he also never blessed me again, not even when I went to market with an enormous belly. "Give me your blessing, father." I said to him, "maybe I'll die with this baby." But he wouldn't. I came back wanting to cry, but I didnt cry in front of him. When I got home with that grief from my father cursing me, I cried.

I was close to having the baby and I knew that God pardoned sinners on Good Friday and that my mother, who was very Catholic, would have to pardon me. I arrived there at supper time with Jacilene all fixed up—Jacinto was already there. I wanted to go right in rather than talking in the street. But there was a talking parrot who said "People!" whenever someone arrived. So my mother looked at me and when she heard me say, "Your blessing, Mother," she said only one thing: "I've already eaten today."

I looked at my father—everyone was at the table: "Your blessing, father." He answered, "I've broken my fast, but you've come on Good Friday, so God bless you." Then my mother remembered: "So it is—God bless you."

I ate and went away. On Sunday I thought, "I'm going to have a chat with Papa." But it was Easter Sunday; he wouldn't see me. I thought there was no problem because my father sold tobacco in the market at that time—I could still go there the following Sunday. At any rate, I went to my mother's house to see her reaction. When I arrived, she hugged Jacinto and Jacilene, crying, and said, "Yes, my children, I'm your grand-mother, but your mother isn't my daughter any more." I was stricken by sorrow, grabbed the children, and left.

I met my brother at my house—he'd gone to visit my

parents for Easter. He said, "You know what I came here for? "What?" "I came to kill you." "Then kill me, my friend, you're killing a woman and your sister." "You shouldn't have done that. You should have waited for Antonio; I know he's still coming back. He knows you're expecting a child. If I were your husband, I'd come back from Rio to cut your belly open and rip out that child in there." "My friend, you are married, aren't you?" "I am." "Don't you have two children?" "Yes." "Well, I'm married too, and I have two children and now the third won't be my husband's. What difference does it make? My life is mine, I'm in charge." My brother threatened to come in the house. "If you come in here, you die. I'm the boss here, you go take charge of your wife, your house, and your children." Today he's my best friend...then he went away...didn't do anything to me. When I was getting ready for bed, my other brother arrived. He knocked on the door. "Who's there?" I asked. "It's me, come to give you a whipping."

"Whipping, nothing," I said, "I'm not opening the door for you." "Let me see which man you have in there with you." The man I have here is my son. There's me, Arlete, and baby Jacilene. If you were a real man, you'd break down the door. You're my brother, but we don't understand each other very well." "Damn you...I want nothing to do with you." And he left.

Afterwards, two other brothers came. The only one who didn't interfere was the one from Rio. He has more education, still today he doesn't meddle in my life. He's there and I'm here. But the others you couldn't stop!

They arrived the following Sunday. I offered coffee, but no one wanted it; I asked them to come in, no one would. "If you're pregnant we've come to kill you, to beat you up and leave you stretched out on the ground. We like Antonio who was your husband, not that black guy."

I answered, "Look, now it's the black guy who's my husband. I love him, but I'm not going to live with him because I don't want to. He'll live in his house, and I'll live in mine. Sometimes I go to his place, sometimes he comes to mine. Get one thing straight: no one but me controls my life."

I knew that would be the end of it. My sisters came past and pretended to think I was an animal. My married sisters. They thought that when a woman makes a mistake like that, when she's lost her husband and finds another man, if a married woman talks to her, it will be said that they're the same kind. Just ignorance. Neither my married friends or my godmother would pay any attention to me.

I didn't want to have any more children after the one I was expecting; I decided to have a tubal ligation. The doctor arranged for me to go into the hospital after I'd finished nine months, and he did all the exams for the Caesarian.

Soon after this business with my brothers and sisters, one day I was in the factory covered with oil, hair full of cotton fluff—a weaver is always messy—I feel that unpleasant little pain; the sign came. I went to the boss's desk to ask for permission to go to the doctor. When I got there, I reminded the doctor that he wanted to do the operation, but he examined me and said, "The child's already being born!" He was born normal, but I was angry, thinking, "I'm really stuck now... I'm going to have 20 children."

I went home. Elinaldo's father was crazy about the boy. When I got home, none of my family came to visit or ever showed up. No one. When my mother happened to meet my neighbors, they would ask, "Aren't you going to see your grandson?" "What grandson?! That ugly black baby?" But he wasn't black and he wasn't ugly. I was sad...I didn't have cousin or aunt or mother or sister or brother. No one.

After 25 days, I started to bleed a lot. I went back to the hospital and had a curettage. The doctor sent me home, saying, "If you're not better tomorrow, come back." Fat chance! Almost dying, without anyone to take care of me—only that girl who took care of the kids—I couldn't even get up, couldn't speak. The only one who came to the house was the baby's father. It was him who took me to the hospital already dying. I was completely bloodless, couldn't survive any more. When I got there, I wasn't myself. I was a dead woman...I didn't exist for myself any more. The doctor there asked me, Cícera, do you still intend to have the litigation? Because your problem isn't gong to be easy. You're going to have to cut the tubes."

I say, "Cut the tubes, take out everything, do what you like." That's what he did, took out the fallopian tubes.

My mother went to the hospital to see me. They say she cried because she was losing her daughter, who was damned.

But I didn't see her; I was dying. I didn't have anaesthesia; I was doing very badly, really dying. She came, my father came, all my brothers and sisters came to see me. I began to recognize people three days after the operation. I got better, I even got out of bed. My doctor showed me my fallopian tubes, I was satisfied, and all was well with me again.

I went back to work. For two years we lived very well, Dedé and I. He adored me and I adored him. He was a good worker, always helped raise Elinaldo. When I came here, I left the boy with a very good woman, so good that I was only able to bring him home with me when she died. I still like him, but I'm one of those terrible people—when I don't want them any more, I don't want them at all. And...you know, a woman who is betrayed—when we don't know for sure, we can take it; but when we know, I think it's cowardice to know he has another woman on the street and still stay with him. It makes me sick, I can't talk to him. Well, I do talk, but it doesn't work for him to be my husband. Because to hear "My darling..." Ugh. I can't stand it, I'll never be able to because look, my legal husband betrayed me, he left. That other one now betrayed me with my own daughter, I told him to get out. I hate the two of them; right now I don't hate Elinaldo's father because he betrayed me, but he didn't do it in front of my eyes. I found out because there was another woman expecting his child. But I wasn't absolutely sure—they told me about it and afterwards I confirmed it. Now, this last betrayal was really tough, with my own daughter...this was really—it came from hell, not from heaven. God doesn't even know this betrayal exists.

I don't know whether my mother would have accepted that, she never said. But she always said she was sure that my father was a wonderful husband. My grandfather, a widower, married five more times. He said that he stayed active because he was a real man. When he took his third wife, we went to peek through a crack in the door and the bed fell down with both of them in it and we laughed ourselves sick. The next day he saw the feet, our footprints, and went inside and measured our feet to see if those footprints were ours. When he wasn't looking, we went out and messed up the footprints, because our mother would've shot us if she found out. When he got married the last time, at 75, he died on the honeymoon. I lived in Rio then.

But I'd put my hand in the fire for my father—he never ran around on my mother. My brothers are trustworthy, too... they only go out with their wives. They're taking after my father. The woman who marries them is happy. The only one who wasn't happy with her husband was me, but I don't regret it; I don't feel any lack of happiness without a husband. I don't miss a sngle one of those husbands, not my legal husband, not Dedé, and definitely not the third. I can talk to him, but to me he's a dead man. I had three husbands, but the worst traitor was Messias, the last one, and he's going to be the last for good and all—no man's coming into my house ever again. Not to be my husband, anyway; a friend can come in and I won't say no. But to be my husband, never again... I'm going to live alone, I don't want any more men. I might feel like having a man from time to time—I'm still not paralytic. "Ah, let's go out for a beer, enjoy ourselves, something like that." "Sure, let's go." I'll come back to my own house later on. Because...I've already worked it out...I was screwed over three times, no way I'm going to get involved in a fourth, unless it's a rich old man who gives me everything. But he stays in his house and I in mine. Then I'd be interested but not in him, in his money. Anyway, I've lost interest. I've suffered too much at the hands of men.

About that time the Paraíban factory laid off all its workers and closed down, I'm not sure why. Many of my friends were living on charity; I always helpcd. I made a deal with an uncle who had a farm: I set up a stall in the market and sold potatoes, manioc, everything he grew. But I left it all for Rio; Elinaldo was two years old—I sold everything, the scales, my stall, and with the money I paid for my father's retirement... the part he still owed. When I'd been here in Rio for three years, he began to receive the money from INPS and he wrote me that he was very happy, that I was the only daughter for him, that he adored me. "—On that day you gave me the greatest happiness of my life..." he said.

That brother of mine in Rio never gave my father a garlic skin...I stayed in Rio a long time without being able to visit my home, and I nearly cry when they play that song about remembering your birthplace:

I remember the place where I grew up
My beloved birthplace I cannot forget
But today I find myself far away
My breast feels pain constantly yet.
I remember that house with the pretty curtains
Those children who I loved so
Time went by, plans changed
I left my youth there long ago.
I remember those roads where at evening
Boys would sing their songs
Now there's no more singing
In its place only troubles and wrongs.
I remember the old dam with clean, sweet water
It's gone, too, it's been let go
And those walls seized by the water
Are today a source of sorrow.
I remember the big house that was my school
I would tune my violin and play
But with all the years that I've been gone
I find it all different today.
I remember that house next to the road
That was my cradle, my hearth, my home
There I was raised with laughter and love
And in that little place Papa died.
Instead of laughter I have only a cross
Sadly, a symbol of one who died.
God has called my beloved father
He journeyed in a balloon of sleep
In that house of laughter and beauty
Today, instead of its master, lives sadness.

Sin luz

CHERRÍE MORAGA

When Carmelita was fourteen, they married her to a stranger. He remained so for some time, until his death when she felt she knew him perfectly. His face green and stiff in his anger, his thin lips stretched into a kind of cry she hadn't heard him utter in years, not since the early days when he would spit the sound between her legs, his thigh bones shuttering to a close.

"¿Ya?" she would ask, sin vergüenza. "Are you done, Viejo?"

She never hated him in sex. She didn't take it to heart. All this crying and jerking she knew had nothing to do, really, with the child growing inside her. El llanto era una señal, nada más.

The sound released the child in her.

That's who she'd think of on those occasions when he lifted her nightgown in sleep. His cry as he peed inside her was like a child's and the first time she heard it on the night of their boda, she knew she was going to be pregnant.

At that moment, as it would happen so many times later, when Viejo was done and too tired to move very fast, she kept him there a little longer. His thing all small and flabby, curling like a little pink and grey worm into the hair below her panza. Lifting her hand up from behind her head where he had held it and wrapping it around his back, she whispered, "Espera, un ratito, Viejo. Espera."

Then she let her mind wander and drawing the cool evening air into her mouth, holding it inside her, she imagined it like a pin of light, penetrating her rib cage, piercing her heart where the love would begin, enflaming her belly where the baby would grow.

In this way, she could always count on when the babies would come and that they would be healthy because of the light. All five, except Robertito, where no light had shown. that was the night when Viejo made her feel something. Pulling at her nightgown, she felt his cold hands running up the sides of her as she lay with her back to him. "¿Qué quieres?" she asked. He kept tugging at her gown, trying to get it up over her hips. "No Viejo. Estoy cansada... ¡Por favor! ¡Viejo! It was not like him to wake her like this so late in the night, but he had been out drinking. ¿Quién sabe dónde estaba? He could have been anywhere, seeing anything. Not that there was much to do in town. "Vaca Ca-ca town," the kids used to chant. Nothing but a cow town.

Carmelita tried to turn over toward him, but her esposo's hand against her back prevented her. Suddenly she felt his thing stiff against her nalgas.

"¡Quítate, Viejo! ¿Estás loco?"

"¡Cállate!" And pushing her onto her stomach, she felt him spread her nalgas with both hands as he twisted himself into her. It was so dry she thought *he must want to tear me open*. First, there was the pain, then the pulling inward, then a brief opening and release of pain. With each pounding into her, her thighs spread further apart. With each grunt from the old man, her pelvic bone hammered the bed, moving deeper into the spring and board of the mattress. He kept on until finally she began to be wide enough for him, the pain turning into a cold slick numbing.

Then the feeling overtook her. Like a spasm that grew from the corners of her hip bones and poured itself in hot flashes into the pool of her stomach. Like the light, but not the light.

Her mind silent.

The mouth between her legs. Lips swelling to a scream, tightening to a close in darkness.

And so without the light, Robertito died. At seven months, Esperanza, su comadre, came to the house to wipe up the last drop of sangre that would have made up their son.

from
The Gloria Stories

ROCKY GÁMEZ

Every child aspires to be something when she grows up. Sometimes these aspirations are totally ridiculous, but coming from the mind of a child they are forgiven and given enough time, they are forgotten. These are normal little dreams from which life draws its substance. Everyone has aspired to be something at one time or another; most of us have aspired to be *many* things. I remember wanting to be an acolyte so badly I would go around bobbing in front of every icon I came across whether they were in churches or private houses. When this aspiration was forgotten, I wanted to be a kamakazi pilot so I could nosedive into the church that never allowed girls to serve at the altar. After that I made a big transition. I wanted to be a nurse, then a doctor, then a burlesque dancer, and finally I chose to be a school-teacher. Everything else was soon forgiven and forgotten.

My friend Gloria, however, never went beyond aspiring to be one thing, and one thing only. She wanted to be a man. Long after I had left for college to learn the intricacies of being an educator, my youngest sister would write to me long frightening letters in which she would say that she had seen Gloria barreling down the street in an old Plymouth honking at all the girls walking down the street. One letter said that she had spotted her in the darkness of a theater making out with another girl. Another letter said that she had seen Gloria coming out of a cantina with her arms hooked around two whores. But the most disturbing one was when she said that she had seen Gloria at a 7-11 store, with a butch haircut and what appeared to be dark powder on the sides of her face to imitate a beard.

I quickly sat down and wrote her a letter expressing my concern and questioning her sanity. A week later I received a fat letter from her. It read:

Dear Rocky,

Here I am, taking my pencil in my hand to say hello and hoping that you are in the best of health, both physically and mentally. As for me, I am fine, thanks to Almighty God.

The weather in the Valley is the shits. As you have probably read or heard on the radio we had a hurricane named Camille, a real killer that left many people homeless. Our house is still standing, but the Valley looks like Venice without gondolas. As a result of the flooded streets, I can't go anywhere. My poor car is under water. But that's all right. I think the good Lord sent us a killer storm so that I would sit home and think seriously about my life, which I have been doing for the last three days.

You are right, my most dearest friend, I am not getting any younger. It is time that I should start thinking about what to do with my life. Since you left for school, I have been seeing a girl named Rosita, and I have already asked her to marry me. It's not right to go around screwing without the Lord's blessings. As soon as I can drive my car I'm going to see what I can do about this.

Your sister is right, I have been going around with some whores, but now that I have met Rosita, all that is going to change. I want to be a husband worthy of her respect, and when we have children, I don't want them to think that their father was a no good drunk.

You may think I'm crazy for talking about being a father, but seriously Rocky, I think I can. I never talked to you about anything so personal as what I'm going to say, but take it from me, it's true. Every time I do you-know-what, I come just like a man. I know you are laughing right now, but Rocky, it is God's honest truth. If you don't believe me, I'll show you someday. Anyhow it won't be long until you come home for Christmas. I'll show you and I promise you will not laugh and call me an idiot like you always do.

In the meantime since you are now close to the University library you can go and check it out for yourself. A woman can become a father if nature has given her enough come to penetrate inside a woman. I bet you didn't know that. Which goes to prove that you don't have to go to college to learn everything.

That shadow on my face that your sister saw was not charcoal or anything that I rubbed on my face to make it look like beard. It is the real thing. Women can grow beards, too, if they shave their faces every day to encourage it. I really don't give a damn if you or your sister think it looks ridiculous. I like it, and so does Rosita. She thinks I'm beginning to look a lot like Sal Mineo, do you know who he is?

Well, Rocky, I think I'll close for now. Don't be too surprised to find Rosita pregnant when you come in Christmas. I'll have a whole case of Lone Star for me and a case of Pearl for you. Til then I remain your best friend in the world.

Love, Gloria

I didn't go home that Christmas. A friend of mine and I were involved in a serious automobile accident a little before the holidays and I had to remain in the hospital. While I was in traction with almost every bone in my body shattered, one of the nurses brought me another letter from Gloria. I couldn't even open the envelope to read it, and since I thought I was on the brink of death, I didn't care at all when the nurse said she would read it to me. If this letter contained any information that would shock the nurse, it wouldn't matter anyway. Death is beautiful insofar as it brings absolution, and once you draw your last breath, every pecadillo is forgiven.

"Yes," I nodded to the matronly nurse, "you may read my letter."

The stern-looking woman found a comfortable spot at the foot of my bed and, adjusting her glasses over her enormous nose, began to read.

Dear Rocky,
Here I am taking my pencil in my hand to say hello, hop-
ing you are in the best of health, both physically and mentally.
As for me, I am fine thanks to Almighty God.
    The nurse paused to look at me and smiled in a motherly
way. "Oh, that sounds like a very sweet person!"
    I nodded.
    The weather in the Valley is the shits. It has been raining
since Thanksgiving and here it is almost the end of December
and it's still raining. Instead of growing a prick I think I'm
going to grow a tail, like a tadpole. Ha, ha, ha!

    The matronly nurse blushed a little and cleared her
throat. "Graphic, isn't she?"

    I nodded again.

    Well, Rocky, not much news around this asshole of a
town except that Rosita and I got married. Yes, you heard
right, I got married. We were married in St. Margaret's Church,
but it wasn't the type of wedding you are probably imagining.
Rosita did not wear white, and I did not wear a tuxedo like
I would have wanted to.

    The nurse's brow crinkled into two deep furrows. She
picked up the envelope and turned it over to read the return
address and then returned to the letter with the most confused
look I have ever seen in anybody's face.

Let me explain. Since I wrote you last, I went to talk to the
priest in my parish and confessed to him what I was. In the
beginning he was very sympathetic and he said that no matter
what I was, I was still a child of God. He encouraged me to
come to mass every Sunday and even gave me a box of
envelopes so that I could enclose my weekly tithe money.
But then when I asked him if I could marry Rosita in his
church, he practically threw me out.
    The nurse shook her head slowly and pinched her face
tightly. I wanted to tell her not to read anymore, but my
jaws were wired so tight I couldn't emit a comprehensible

sound. She mistook my effort for a moan and continued reading and getting redder and redder.

He told me that I was not only an abomination in the eyes of God, but a lunatic in the eyes of Man. Can you believe that? First I am a child of God, then when I want to do what the church commands in Her seventh sacrament, I'm an abomination. I tell you, Rocky, the older I get, the more confused I become.

But anyway, let me go on. This did not discourage me in the least. I said to myself, Gloria, don't let anybody tell you that even if you're queer, you are not a child of God. You are! And you got enough right to get married in church and have your Holy Father sanctify whatever form of love you wish to choose.

The nurse took out a small white hanky from her pocket and dabbed her forehead and upper lip.

So, as I walked home having been made to feel like a turd, or whatever it is abomination means, I came upon a brilliant idea. And here's what happened. A young man that works in the same slaughter house that I do invited me to his wedding. Rosita and I went to the religious ceremony which was held in your hometown, and we sat as close to the altar rail as we possibly could, close enough where we could hear the priest. We pretended that she and I were the bride and groom kneeling at the rail. When the time came to repeat the marriage vows, we both did, in our minds, of course, where nobody could hear us and be shocked. We did exactly as my friend and his bride did, except kiss, but I even slipped a ring on Rosita's finger and in my mind said, "With this ring, I wed thee."

Everything was like the real thing, Rocky, except that we were not dressed for the occasion. But we both looked nice. Rosita wore a beautiful lavender dress made out of dotted swiss material. Cost me $5.98 at J.C. Penny. I didn't want to spend that much money on myself because Lord knows how long it will be until I wear a dress again. I went over to one of your sisters' house, the fat one, and asked if I could *borrow a skirt. She was so happy to know that I was going to go to church and she let me go through her closet and choose anything I wanted. I chose something simple to wear. It was a black skirt with a cute little poodle on the side. She went so far as to curl my hair and make it pretty. Next time you see me, you'll agree that I do look like Sal Mineo.*

The nurse folded the letter quietly and stuffed it back inside the envelope, and without a word disappeared from the room, leaving nothing behind but the echoing sound of her running footsteps.

After my release from the hospital, I went back to the Valley to recuperate from the injuries received in the accident. Gloria was very happy that I was not returning to the University for the second semester. Although I wasn't exactly in any condition to keep up with her active life, I could at least serve as a listening post in that brief period of happiness she had with Rosita.

I say brief because a few months after they got married, Rosita announced to Gloria that she was pregnant. Gloria took her to the doctor right away, and when the pregnancy was confirmed, they came barreling down the street in their brand new car to let me be the first to know the good news.

Gloria honked the horn outside and I came limping out of the house. I had not met Rosita until that day. She was a sweet-looking little person with light brown hair, who smiled a lot. A little dippy in her manner of conversing, but for Gloria, who wasn't exactly the epitome of brilliance, she was alright.

Gloria was all smiles that day. Her dark brown face was radiant with happiness. She was even smoking a cigar and holding it between her teeth on the corner of her mouth.

"Didn't I tell you in one of my letters that it could be done?" She smiled. "We're going to have a baby!"

"Oh, come on, Gloria, cut it out!" I laughed.

"You think I'm kidding?"

"I *know* you're kidding!"

She reached across Rosita who was sitting in the passenger seat of the car and grabbed my hand and laid it on Rosita's stomach. "There's the proof!"

"Oh, shit, Gloria, I don't believe you!"

Rosita turned and looked at me, but she wasn't smiling. "Why don't you believe her?" she wanted to know.

"Because it's biologically impossible. It's...absurd."

"Are you trying to say that it's crazy for me to have a baby?"

I shook my head. "No, that's not what I meant."

Rosita got defensive. I moved away from the car and leaned on my crutches, not knowing how to respond to this woman because I didn't even know her at all. She began trying to feed me all this garbage about woman's vaginal secretions being as potent as the ejaculations of a male and being quite capable of producing a child. I backed off immediately, letting her talk all she wanted. When she finished talking, and she thought she had fully convinced me, Gloria smiled triumphantly and asked, "What do you got to say now, Rocky?"

I shook my head slowly. "I don't know. I just don't know. Your woman is either crazy or a damn good liar. In either case, she scares the hell out of me."

"Watch you language, Rocky," Gloria snapped. "You're talking to my wife."

I apologized and made an excuse to go back into the house. But somehow Gloria knew that I had limped away with something in my mind. She went and took Rosita home, and in less than an hour, she was back again, honking outside. She had a six-pack of beer with her.

"Alright, Rocky, now that we're alone, tell me what's on your mind.'

I shrugged my shoulders. "What can I tell you? You're already convinced that she's pregnant."

"She is!" Gloria explained. "Dr. Long told me so."

Yes, but that's not what I'm trying to tell you."

"What are you trying to tell me?"

"Will you wait until I go inside the house and get my biology book. There's a section in it on human reproduction that I'd like to explain to you."

"Well, alright, but you better convince me or I'll knock you off your crutches. I didn't appreciate you calling Rosita a liar."

After I explained to Gloria why it was biologically impossible that she could have impregnated Rosita, she thought for a long silent moment and drank most of the beer she had brought. When I saw a long tear streaming down her face, I wanted to use one of my crutches to hit myself. But then, I said to myself, "What are friends for if not to tell us when we're being idiots."

Gloria turned on the engine to her car. "Okay, Rocky, git outta my car! I should've known better than come killing my ass to tell you something nice in my life. Ever since I met you, you've done nothing but screw up my life. Get out. The way I feel right now I could easily ram up one of them crutches up your skinny ass, but I'd rather go home and kill that fucking Rosa."

"Oh, Gloria, don't do that! You'll go to jail. Making babies is not the most important thing in the world. What's important is the trying. And just think how much fun that is as opposed to going to the electric chair."

"Git outta the car *now!*"

I did.

Day After Day

MILAGROS PÉREZ HUTH

DAY AFTER DAY

The first part of this scene takes place in an alley with no exit. An unpaved street. Houses joined, tied to one another, all with the same exterior. The whole village has a look of total cleanliness and quiet monotony. The streets are deserted. It is one-dimensional, something is missing. In front of each house there is a garbage can. It is the beginning of another day. A door opens and a woman steps out with a broom in hand, sweeping the dust in front of her house. Soon she is joined by two, then three women. They are all wearing aprons. Now the street starts coming alive. Some of the women go in and out of their houses, others go to the market or the nearest grocery store. They are all housewives with identical duties. The nearest neighbor waves. The others continue sweeping or cleaning their windows.

First Woman: Good Morning (continues cleaning)

Second Woman: Hi, How are you? (since she is going shopping she does not let herself be stopped by the chatter.)

All the women are cleaning their houses, their children in school, husbands working. The morning is spent in frantic household activity. They all want to finish cleaning early so

147

they can rest in the early afternoon. The form of rest is to get caught up with the mending and the newest gossip. Now they look for one another.

First Woman: This is a tragedy, María. From here to the corner, from the corner to here, day after day, the same until death. I am fed up with the kids, I am fed up with cooking. Goddamn, Always the same.

María: So What are you cooking? I am making rice and beans and some little piece of meat.

First Woman: That's the problem, "what should I cook today" and its only 8:00 in the morning, and the first thing that came into my mind was "what am I going to cook today" and then I decided to forget it until I got to the market. I would think about it then. I wasn't going to let myself get intimidated. I had other things to do, like cleaning the house in case somebody should come in. I live in terror that someone should come and find my house dirty. I get a headache over stuff like that. Once I felt so strong I started to clean the ceiling and I couldn't stop cleaning, kept on and on. After some brandy I mopped the floor dusted and put out the garbage. But nobody came, they only come when my house is dirty. Then I get a ringing in my ears and I say "someone is talking about me" and I know what they are saying, they are saying, they are saying my house is dirty. What weariness for women cleaning their houses, always cleaning, so that others do not think bad about them. And such noises their voices make. "Luisito get out of here before you get dirty, I will hit you if you get dirty. Don't get dirty Luisito, go ahead and play son, and no one better hit you, if they hit you, you hit them." I have a headache now, my body hurts, I wish I could go to bed. After dinner then I will go to bed. I wish it was all done so I could go to sleep.

María: I hear you woman, I hear you.

First Woman: María, did you hear about the scandal those idiots started over their children. Even my nerves were affected by their screaming. Elena said to Carmen "you dirty filthy whore, whore, whore, worse than a whore" and Carmen said "who has told you I was a whore, tell me so I can rip their tongues out." "Your mother is the filthy dog of a whore." There were two men working in the street and they ran over so they could see what was going on. They stood in front of the house and laughed at the foolishness of the women. "Jerks, that's what those women are. What tigers, what mothers." But they should know that Elena is very clean. Her house shines like a mirror. She's always cleaning, from the minute she gets up and doesn't stop until everything shines. Delicately, slowly, she cleans, every day, always cleaning, day after day the same shit.

This little street is a cemetery, we are buried here. I want to go to work and get away from all this shit. *"But Lucía, there is no work."* You don't understand I have to do something. I am going crazy here. Everything always the same. I tell you all this stuff, the house the kids, the same thing every day. It makes me sick, sick, sick. I don't like to scream and I find myself screaming at the children unjustly. I am telling you, woman, I even hit them for no reason and then I feel sick. There are days when everything stinks, my life, my husband, my children, my home, my friends, everything I love and hold dear. Is that possible? *"I hear you woman. I hear you in my soul."* That's why there are days when I lock myself in the house. I don't want to see or talk to anyone because if I do I think I would explode. This is the damn cross we have to bear. That is why god put us on this earth. I love my husband. He doesn't have much. He works like a bull, tearing the earth with his hands so that we can eat, but something is wrong because I am sick of this. It has to change. I am a mother, a wife; but mother like Elena, clean like her I don't want to be. I want to be a woman with the ability to do for the world, for my self, to be of some consequence. In this alley with no exit my soul is rotting.

María: "I hear you woman. I hear you in my soul."

149

It seems that Carmen's cat was found poisoned to death on the morning of Tuesday, March 13th. The date is really unimportant. She was found two houses away in Isabel's patio. I am told that it was horrible to see. She clawed at the ground, there were hairs all over the spot, her eyes were bloodied and foam was coming out of her mouth. It was a sight. I had just come back from Sevilla. I went there to see an old friend from my years as a college student and would-be freedom fighter. It was good, she was glad to see us. The sun was shining all the day we were there, on Sunday after lunch we went to see some ruins from the Roman period in Spain.

I was all rested up when we came back home. But tensions were kind of high, five of the women in the immediate area had hit the lottery. Every morning the man who sells the lottery ticket can be seen coming out of one of their houses. They buy the same ticket every day because sooner or later it should come out. Anyhow, everyone was pretty happy. But one woman won more than the others, because she buys several tickets at one time. How many nobody knows. She won't tell, and guards them with intense secrecy. I know this and I won't ask, why should I? Some things are very personal. When an 82-year-old woman who has known the need of bread and has gone hungry for the lack of it decides to put her money on the lottery instead of the bread, you just better not ask how much she won. This is what happened. Somebody asked and the lady turned into a tiger. Some 82-year-old ladies don't seem to be afraid of anything any more. It seems she was fed up. The gossips had almost quadrupled the winnings. After all the excitement started to quiet down, Carmen's cat was found. She was angry but well under control. She knew who did it. She would wait until the culprit approached her. Cunning, she knew who did it and she would wait. It was Rosa, the fisherman's wife. A big woman with a big mouth, also afraid of cat shit on her flowers or any other place on her patio. She told me one day she was going to poison the cat if Carmen didn't keep it at home. I never paid no mind, because she talks a lot mostly out of compulsion.

Well today it seems she came over to see Carmen and Carmen told her she was never to talk to her again. She said, "put it in your mind that you poisoned me just like you poisoned my cat." Rosa reacted by denying all and creating quite a scandal. Rosa got up in the middle of the street and said, "I knew I would be blamed, because all the fucking bitches in here hate me, but I swear on the health of my child that it wasn't me, and 70 cats ain't worth her health," and she holler something sacriligious about the souls of the dead relatives of some of her neighbors. All the time bordering on hysteria as she defended herself.

I opened my door and so did everyone else. It was all the women of course, the men were all working. It was very exciting for all to see and the women immediately took sides. Carmen is an old woman who's not too well liked at the other end of the street because they said she is nosy, they said, "it was only an old cat" and Rosa went down there seeking comfort. On this end Rosa is the villain and a good one she is. After Rosa made a fool of herself, what a mouth on her, she had it coming. We looked at each other, trying so hard to communicate with our eyes because we wanted to stay clean. Carmen was cool throughout the whole thing as she had accomplished what she wanted. She walked away to get her lunch ready, she told me later she ate very well after all that.

LUCIA

Somedays I daydream about a vacuum cleaner that would suck in all the dirt and make my house spic and span. I am sure that 3/4 of my conscious time is spent on idiotic fantasies. I happened to be a good person but I am unsatisfied or something. Something has been bugging me for a couple of years. The whole thing started after I realized that it wasn't easy to be a freedom fighter. So at thirty-two I ran away from home and married the man I was living with because I got pregnant. I have been happily married ever since. I have grown up by leaps and bounds. I am no longer afraid of sex (I never really was. I just didn't know too much about it). I shouldn't have listed that first, it just popped up.

151

Well for quite a while, actually the longest part of my existence I've been living a double life. I have been a good girl on her way to becoming a good woman. I looked forward to being a good housewife and mother. I often wished that I was smart but I wasn't, my best grades were for discipline. So I didn't make any waves. I just moved on without thinking of seeing what was in back or ahead because I was someplace else. Dreaming of someone else that wasn't me, a someone that traveled and lived somewhere else. It was the only means of escape.

Later on I looked and wondered how I didn't get hit by a truck walking around like a sleepwalker. What the hell I was a non-person to so many, what difference does it make if I create a better world for me, I don't bother anybody. I just do it to myself. It's my world over here nobody else's I can have all the fantasies I want whenever I want them. I am not hurting anybody with it. I am hurting myself by not trying to stay awake, by wishing things away.

Here I am picking up for the 15th time, my back is hurting but it will stop some time. So I dreamed a dream of running away with my friend. She is fed up but she is chicken she rather have a dishwasher and a spic and span house. Her husband is a jerk, a real jerk I know because she told me so. But he is a good provider and she is afraid to go out and do something with herself. So she pretends she is happy. She flirts with other men and feels pretty and desirable for a week then she is out of her mind once again. I can't trust her, she is unreliable. But, she is funny she makes me laugh. Last week she told me I should get a wok, that was really something.

El Paisano
Is a Bird of Good Omen

from Andrea *a novel in Progress*

GLORIA ANZALDÚA

Andrea straddles the mesquite post of the corral. Balanced on the top of it, she watches the white sky dwarf the chaparral, the cattle and horses, the house, and the portal with the guests moving under it. The sun

dominates the land. Always. La tierra. Everywhere, punctuated here and there with mesquite thickets and clumps of prickly pear. Under the quickening hum of the guests' conversation and the clinking of knives on plates, she hears the cackle of the hens clucking over their finds, a fat earthworm or dry grass seeds. On the highest branch of The Mesquite a mockingbird imitates another bird's trill. Under her, the hard roundness of the mesquite post seems an appendage of herself, a fifth limb, one that's also part of the corral, the corral that's part

of the land. The corral is a series of thick posts sunk side by side into the ground with just enough space between them to accommodate, horizontally, half a dozen logs alternating one on top of the other. The logs lock into each other between the paired posts, like people who try pairing, then stacking to accommodate each other. If the tops of the posts aren't flush with the average height their heads are either lopped off to make a tidy corral or they are cast out as

153

deficient, unsuitable. She feels her body flowing from

one post to another until it, too, encircles what the corral encircles. But the gates are wide open, the circle will be incomplete until dusk when the newly calved cows are rounded in for the night. No, not complete until her new house is finished. Anda en la garra—on the rag. During her menses she feels fragile, expansive, the limits of her body stretched beyond her skin, she flows out like a sheet, encompassing, covering trees, people, everything around her. There is still time.

There is still time to change her mind. She shifts her bottom, the post is now on the left side of her cunt. Gently, she sways back and forth. If she does it just right she can bring herself to orgasm. Not as good as during a fast run, the wind whipping the mare's mane, her own hair across her mouth, no one hears her. She wonders: what encircles, what excludes, what sets apart.

"Andrea." Her mother is walking towards her. She's dressed in a pinstriped two-piece suit, white blouse, black hat veiled at the back, white open-toed pumps. Her mother made it a point to dress better than the other women.

"Sí, 'Amá, ¿Qué quieres?" she asks, jumping down.

"What's the matter with you?"

"Everything. Why? What do you care?"

"You look hollow-eyed, hot. I don't want you embarrassing me today."

"The feeling, 'Amá. It's come back."

"No seas tonta, hijita. You must mingle with the guests. And get out of those man's pants. I find it totally incomprehensible why you moon out here like a lost calf and why Zenobio keeps himself hidden all afternoon in the house with

154

your sisters draping themselves around him like a harem."

"And what's the harm in that? Why can't he just do what he wants?"

All day he keeps away from her, waiting for her to act, watching her from the corner of his eye (*Therefore shall a man leave his father and his mother.*) expecting a word from her: But if he's not around to remind her she may never say it.

"Go and change, greñuda, muchacha chiflada. And comb the mesquite leaves out of your hair—go! Chase your sisters out of the house. Tell them to bring out more tortillas de masa y la carne."

"No."

Her mother opens her mouth then closes it. Then more gently, Andrea says, "Why don't *you* go and do that and talk to Doña Inés. Todos la hacen menos." Both turn and look at Doña Inés, Zenobio's mother. She stands alone in the middle of the portal wringing a pair of black gloves. Under a crownless parachute hat her face is emaciated and passive. Her beige jacket hangs loose from her thin shoulders, her black wide hemmed skirt drags on the dirt.

"All she talks about is how well her 'baby' can cook. I suppose if he wanted to she would let him take up sewing," says Andrea's mother.

"If he enjoys cooking, why shouldn't he cook," says Andrea turning away, at once regretting her habit of contradicting her mother, her habit of heaping all her griefs, from infancy to womanhood, on her mother's back. She knows that on top of the stored-up grievances, she will lay future ones. But the thought is an old one, too familiar to explore, and almost at once she forgets her mother.

The land. She never tires of looking at the land. She could never leave the land. The house faces east. It is an oasis in the middle of the brushland. To its right, on the gnarled limbs of The Mesquite, her brothers have roofed a shelter for guests and tables of food. The portal, erected with corrugated aluminum of different lengths and cedar branches that still distill their piny fragrance, looks unnatural. The Mesquite reigns over the portal, the house, the yard. Only The Windmill rivals its height. Perhaps its fifty or sixty-foot-deep roots tap the same underground water source as The Windmill. She wants to tap that deep place, too. Maybe if she stayed still long enough her feet would worm roots into the moist core. Her two things: The Papalote, The Windmill, that she built with her brothers' help and The Mesquite she claimed as soon as she could climb it. Both connected...somehow. The trunk—a black wrung-out piece of cloth whose whorls and twists point toward some

revelation. She studies the gnarls and tries to unravel them. The Mesquite looks like an ancient ballet dancer doing a one-legged twirl, arms and head appealing to the sky. The trunk oozes a black gummy secretion from a lipless vagina mouth. If only she knew how to listen to the tree she would know what the mouth is screaming. She could once. She remembers gazing up at the tree and talking to it in its own language when she was about three. What is it that Tío Efraín is always platitudinizing? "Beautiful women and trees are more apt to be embrujadas." Bewitched. She climbs the corral again to see The Mesquite better. As the wind stirs the tree's limbs, Andrea sways

like The Papalote. Andrea sways, her hair becomes ruffled leaves. The tree is a tree. But is it just a tree. *("Ego jungo ves in matrimonium.")* To the right of the portal, the partially finished house, looking like the gutted side of a cow, two walls up, a skeleton roof, the floor strewn with pieces of lumber and buckets of nails resembling the rotting entrails of the animal. Laughter erupts from a group of men sitting on two thick cedar logs and half a dozen bales of sorghum that lie sprawled in a semi-circle under the portal. She is not part of this half

circle. She is outside of it. *(The priest sprinkles water over*

156

their bowed heads.) Directly west of the house are the corrals. Next to them, towering over the ranch house and corrals, is The Windmill, a permanent silver sunflower. She twists around. The Windmill, the beacon that guides the hands home from a sea of brush and cactus, is moving. The wind has turned the vane. The vane, an arrow shaft, points toward the south. On the vane, the words DE LA CRUZ shine bright in the afternoon sun. Hay algo en al aire. Something is in

the wind. The Windmill's sails rotate faster and faster as the south wind surges louder and louder. Though she sits motionless, Andrea too rotates with the sails. She doesn't have to sit up there, she *is* up there. She feels the guests' sly glances brush over her wild henna hair. She can hear their heads repeating over and over, "strange, too willful and impulsive." They would like to throw a saddle on her, dig their spurs deep into her sides, pull hard on the bridle until her mouth runs red, loses its adamancy. Or, tie her to a post like a wild heifer, tail between her legs, head caught in the trough and

milk her. Sand down her *dentata* to a

toothless grin. Well, she's not going to laugh at their jokes and snide remarks nor smile. Already her mouth hurts from not smiling. She touches her throat, touches

pearls. The string of pearls she didn't wear. She will not wear. Her hands smooth the silk of her dress, the dress she does not wear. She will not wear dresses here. Not here— maybe in another place. No, no, no. Sweat drenches the hair in her armpits. She takes a deep breath. Another. After a while the no's become quiet like baby chicks under the mother hen. She weans her attention away from The Windmill and waits for the everydayness to fold its wings around her again. Warm and safe. Home.

A handful of steers drink at the edge of the waterhole beyond The Windmill. Half a mile beyond the waterhole is the dark green of the lagoon. Andrea blinks and half of her moves to the lagoon's edge. The greedy land slowly sucks at the meager rains it trapped in its hold during January and February. Insidious roots slither silently toward its edge and swells like thin sponges. Low dark clouds crowd the horizon. If only the wind would turn. Huisache and prickly pear fringe the lagoon. The yellow-orange flowers of the cactus and the pale gold of the huisache, the sole colors in the brown and barren land. It is April: the semidesert is in bloom. The huisache's tiny pompom blossoms move gently, dispersing their delicate perfume in the hot wind. Andrea feels the leaves' feathery softness on her face, soft like the heads of newly hatched chicks, crests still wet and yielding. A thorn scratches her cheek dispatching her other half

back. Instantly, the lagoon and huisache are far away. The men's voices grow louder…"Las mujeres, they're more susceptible to it. Their fury is more unbridled than ours. They can't temper their…well, their tempers. And they're fickle by nature."

"What do you know about females? The closest you've been to one is that cow you keep in your kitchen."

"You mean his wife?" There is a roar of laughter.

"No, no," interrupts another, "it gets in their blood, there they boil vile vapors. When they belch they infect everyone near them."

"Yes," says another, "if a pregnant woman comes near them she'll miscarry and lose the child." Andrea pushes

their voices away. Her grandmother was one. And now she. And what else can she do that others can't, besides remembering events before they happen? She jumps off the corral. Walks to The Windmill. As she climbs up, the rough wooden tiles under her hands and feet feel immensely thick and deep. They can plumb the center of the world. Now she's on the platform under the blade and must be wary of wind change—it wouldn't do to get rapped on the head by the sails, by anything. She has to—no, not think, just allow the quiet to seep into her body and wait for the flash to strike 'the knowing.' Today. Zenobio. Her land. Her people. The people not as much hers as the land. Beyond

the lagoon is the monte where the cattle shelter, nibbling mesquite pods or what grass they can find. (*"You* will *go through this ceremony, cabezona."*) The dark clouds are looming nearer. North of the house, to the right, are three lone dark green cedars. Quiet sentinels watching over the land. Always watching. Half a dozen vehicles are parked under them. Some of the guests disembark from old Fords and Chryslers. A Willys Jeep, a relic from the war that has just ended, had earlier emptied a large family from tiny tots to aged grandparents. It looked like a tree at first light vacating chickens that have roosted there all night. A few guests had arrived on horseback. (*"You have to go through with it. You don't want to end up a solterona like your aunt Ramona?"*) Don Efraín had driven his '41 Lincoln Continental Coupé. He gives more care to it than he does his family. He is seen spitting on it then shining out the spots of dirt with the shirt tail under his forearm. He is heard whispering love words to it. The platform

trembles. Andrea blinks. Expands. The other Andrea flows down, down. The men are talking of something else now. "No one can imagine. It was so long ago. That kind of quake, thrown to the ground. The earth became a crazy dancer. It was as if a dissident orchestra had mutinied and each musician had played a different song. So long ago, when the Indians were free." Back. Looking

down she sees it's only her Uncle Efraín scaling up. His arm muscles taut. Her own muscles taut. The fingers grasping the ladder become her fingers. She is beside her uncle. "You shouldn't pretend to be younger and stronger than you are," she tells him, stretching out her hand to help him.

"You're not supposed to know that," he says ignoring her hand. He gives a little hop and lands his scrawny buttocks on the platform. "Saying truths is not the thing to do, hija. People won't stand for it and men will always try to impress you, you know that."

"Why do they have to always prove themselves?" she asks.

"Sepa Dios. ¿Qué te pasa? Your mamá said you were being difficult."

"Difficult is the only way I *can* be with her. It's all this fuss and bother. I can't decide." Andrea remains silent for a while.

"There's nothing to decide, it's all been decided for you. Like it was for me. I wouldn't go through with it a second time, though. Not for all the land in The Valley. Why in my time...Andrea stops listening. The land, people married for it.

"It's peaceful here, like being in another world," says Andrea. "Or another self."

"You're right, hija. It's a tiny island floating above everything."

"That was a nice gift you brought us, tío. It must have taken you weeks to carve it."

"It took me months. Yes, that paisano was a long time coming. But how I loved working on it! Couldn't get it right until I got the idea of carving a base for it. For balance. Had to send my boys out into the brush. They came back with enough cowhorns to make a dozen roadrunners and enough bones for m'ija to paint on for months." His daughter had presented Andrea with a cow pelvic bone with a small hole and a thin strip of cowhide with which to hang it around her neck. On the bone carved and painted: The Mesquite with The Windmill in the background. Andrea puts her hand between her breasts. The bone is warm.

"You've got that look in your eye, my girl. What you need

is some cerveza." They climb down.

Andrea takes her beer which she isn't supposed to be drinking, the frown on her aunts' faces and the male guests' eyes tell her.

Andrea takes her beer to the corral and places it on a post.

Andrea is not anywhere near the corral or a post.

Andrea places her beer on the post where it rocks a bit but doesn't topple. She looks at the women. Andrea does not look

at the women. The bridesmaids, wide pink skirts (they wear identical dresses) swirling around their calves, cast coquettish looks at one muchacho or another as they traffic among the tables ladling out chunks of carne asada, arroz con pollo, and papas con frijoles, serving beer or lemonade or chocolate. Not much to say for their lot until they learn to say no. *(Andrea's bouquet sails into the sun over the heads of the shrieking bridesmaids. Sweat pours down their faces. The flowers hit one girl in the face. Clutching them, she scrambles away laughing. The men will get hit in the face too. Later. "Así son las cosas, mijita," her mother would say every time Andrea complained of the restrictions marriage imposes on people.)* She hasn't eaten since yesterday noon, but that's not why it

happens. That López girl has nice tits and her...Andrea blinks. Andrea leaves

herself—the self that sits atop the corral. The men sit on the bales of hay in their stiff dark cotton suits eating, their felt stetsons on the ground beside them or hanging from the mesquite branches. Some are rolling or smoking their Buglar and drinking, discussing the drought. Now one talks of the quarantine of his cattle by the government, another cuts in with the movidas del compadre Juan. One signals to her but she pretends not to see—feeling angry at the pretense, wanting

161

to hit him in the face. It's only when they're bunched up in herds, alone not one of them would dare look her in the eye. Zenobio brings her a plate of food and leaves before she can say anything. She doesn't touch it—she's no longer there. The músicos are feeding their music with whiskey, fueling the songs' fire before the dance begins, their instruments beside them on the ground like crippled birds. As she picks up her beer her hands start to tingle. The flow of liquid down her throat feels like a wind

milling down her middle. Her hands are fluid. Where does the edge of the glass end and her mouth begin? Then she tries to define the "feeling" but can't and becomes afraid. She smiles. Yes, when she wants to be *gone*, to be *that*, all she has to do is look carefully, focus steadily on something and she takes leave of

herself. The women sit taking turns talking about what their hijos do, what their maridos say. They seem to rush through their words in a desperate attempt to make up for the usual isolation of their lives. Funerals and weddings, the only events that bring them together. Their men and children. Andrea wants to run away. She wants to run to her grandmother and kneeling before her, bury her face in her ample thighs, smell the smell. (*Because the fourth finger of the left hand is the least active finger of the hand least used.*) Her grandmother is sitting on the Windsor chair that Andrea has taken out of the house for her. She sits near but not with the women. Andrea feels removed from the women, from everyone. It seems that she inhabits a space that is not there, impervious to the bodies milling around her, to the food and laughter. There. But not there. Here. But not here. Hearing, yet deaf to the chortles that follow the jokes, the tittering of the young in the backyard. Motionless, feeling nothing, thinking nothing, rooted to the post, not even seeming to breathe. (*But señorita, you must find your certificate of baptism. I never was baptised because I never was born. Mamagrande gave birth to me in her kettle. Mamá's baby was born dead. I was put in its place so she wouldn't grieve its death. Stop it, Andrea. Don't listen to her, Father, she likes to make jokes.*) A world lay in that smell. She would not cook for the man, nor bear his dark moods and snotty children. She would not bolster his spirits when the cattle died off like flies, nor his balls when he dried up. Zenobio is not like the others, he would accept this. Another world lies out there. Perhaps she could be her

self out there. "Fue un escándalo," she had overheard. "Sleeping naked with la serpiente. A huge rattler. A diamond back, the most vicious killer of them all. Her henna hair wild over her body, her body glistening, the serpent entwined around her middle, its head peering from her pubic patch, its dry scaly tail rubbing the silk of her. She lavishes on her pet the warmth she cannot lavish on a man " Rubbing the depression on each side of its

snout, between eye and nostril. Víbora loved that. She would take its tail between her hands and study its hollow, ring-like bulbs at the tail entering the biggest ring and the other rings gradually diminishing in size, each opening to its neighbor. Several times a year, it would shed its skin. A new one would form beneath the old one. Then the old one would be sloughed off. But not completely. It would retain something of the old skin. The old tail sheath would remain loosely fitting over the new one. With each molting another joint would be added. Some would wear away with time. If only she could shed her old skin and grow a new one as easily. She loved to feel the rapid vibrations of the tail. She'd had it since it was a baby, no more than a foot long and thin as a tapeworm. Now it was over eight feet long and as thick as her thigh. Now she had to keep it outside in the nopal thicket— everyone in the house was terrified of it. That she had such a pet in her family and the neighbors could accept more readily than the fact that the snake always returned after its nightly excursions. Even after weeks of absence. The people could stomach

her taming wild bulls and mad dogs

but not a snake. On one of the tables a head of a steer, pit barbecued, is spiraling steam out of its dull gaping

163

eyes toward the branches of The Mesquite. She smells the rich odor, too rich. It's as if her nose were buried in the head. Revulsion pinches her gut. Surely it's not one of her favorites. The wild ones sometimes get caught, too. Her mother had gotten up at three in the morning, spicing the head, wrapping it in burlap, burying it in the ground, and covering it with live coals. It has slowly simmered for ten hours. Don Sebastián, it was told, had taken the entrails of one of his dead cows into his kitchen and laying the bowels over a gridiron had lighted the stove murmuring, "That will make the bruja real hot." Hombre. Why does he fear us. The more female we are the more he fears us. Is it out strength or our

tenderness he fears? The only way not to alarm him is to acquiesce and allow him to lock us up in a room. A will indifferent to his own he cannot abide. How dare we have wills. He wants us to mother him, give him pleasure, grant all his wishes and ask for nothing. Someone puts

a hand on her shoulder. (*God made them male and female.*) Without looking she knows it's Zenobio. What Zenobio fears is her power to evoke in him the naked helplessness of his being. The power to make him aware that he has no control over that feeling. *That* to him is betrayal. But she never takes advantage of him when he is the most exposed. He knows I never will, Andrea thinks, yet...Zenobio grins, puts a pomegranate in her hand then

disappears. She blinks. The pink, blue and white frosted cake lies on the middle of the center table. Looking at the stiff figures of the novia y novio smiling inanely on top. She already feels herself becoming stiff. She touches her arm to reassure herself. Pan de polvo, empanadas de calabaza and pitchers of hot chocolate lie by the cake awaiting la merienda. (*She stands at Zenobio's right hand. The madrinas and padrinos stand behind.*) Tall glass vases with huge red and white roses from her grandmother's jardín flank each end of the table. The stain,

the chocolate stain disfigures the white

lace tablecloth.

Hearing a burst of laughter, Andrea looks down the length of the corral.

Hearing laughter, Andrea refuses to look up.

Andrea looks up. The younger men congregate at one end of the corral. Astride posts, legs dangling, bottoms squirming, they pummel each others' arms as they trade witty nonsenses. She might as well be sitting right

next to them. Secretive whispers, boasts of prowess at roping, at riding, at fucking the cantineras. They ogle the girls, most often the López girl. A few eye the horses in their beautiful sleek flesh snorting water from the trough or standing stiff-legged, tails swishing off flies. (*As is required, I will instruct you in the doctrine. Now, the nature of marriage is obedience...*) This marriage will save us from having to marry, she thinks. She hears the thud of knives that a couple of adolescent boys are throwing at a tree stump out of sight in the backyard. José Manuel had better not come around smirking. The "bullseye" from one of the boys drowns out the laughter of the guests. A young boy tears across the backyard chased by an enraged tom turkey. The boy runs into the rope that some girls are jumping and sprawls amid skirts and squeals and slaps. Soft bodies and soft hands slap

Andrea. She ducks, then turns around furtively to see if anyone is looking. She'll have to burn prickly pear and mesquite pods to feed the cattle this summer if the rains don't come. Everyone will be upset, not so much at her doing a man's work but for doing it better. A group of screeching children surround a boy in a yellow shirt dangling a horned toad over a heap of swarming red ants. The horned toad squirms, body convulsing. The piercing pain in

her arms and hands almost shock her into crying out. She rolls up her sleeves. The red spots on her arms were made from climbing the windmill, from the splinters. And those on the back of her hands? Finally a boy in a purple shirt

165

scatters the children and releases the horned toad. The toad scuttles out of sight under some nopales. (*The two altar boys carry the vessel of holy water to the altar, the sprinkler, and the little basin that will hold the ring. The priest walks behind them.*)

"¡Hijita! Get off of there. A fine hostess you are." Andrea looks down. Her mother again, arms crossed, a scowl on her face.

"I want to be alone, 'Amá."

"Andrea de la Cruz, get down and go greet la familia Flores." The pearls around her neck bubble up and down. "They've just arrived—late as usual."

"They shouldn't have bothered."

"Pórtate bien, Andrea. You must stop this bickering with your cousin."

"All right, but I didn't start it, he did, and if he makes a wrong move I'm going to flatten him." Andrea leaps off raising a little cloud of dust from which her mother backs off, the scowl, a permanent feature now.

"It's not good for women to quarrel with men, especially about...well, it's just not good."

"You mean it's not good for women to have opinions on anything. In fact it's not good for women to do anything."
The Flores' approach and she greets them, but turns away from José Manuel's smirk and outstretched arms.

"Here's your wedding gift. I'm sure Zenobio will like it," he says smiling. She remains silent. He holds the cage out to her, then drops it at her feet, almost on her toes. "The paisano will bring you good fortune," he says, a weasel in his smile.

"I've already received my good fortune," she says. What had ever possessed Zenobio. It's not like José Manuel is the only one around. There's Pete and Mando. (*I hereby proclaim the coming nuptials of Andrea de la Cruz and Zenobio Ríos. Those who wish to bring to light any obstacles that stand in the way of this union, let them come forward. This prenuptial announcement will also be made during the next two misas as befits canon law.*)

"No one can have too much of a good thing," says José Manuel, weasel mustache twitching. "Fried paisano is a remedio for the itch, or so they say." Someone snickers.

"A caged thing never brings anyone luck, least of all the one who captures it," says Andrea.

"How do you like that for thanks," says José Manuel, ears flattening against his skull as he surveys the guests that have bunched up around them. All avoid his beady eyes. It is to Andrea that they always come when they're short of money or water or feed for their cattle. At other times, when their cows go dry, they whisper behind her back, say that fulano saw her cast a stone over her left shoulder toward the west. Or that once she made midnight of high noon. Andrea looks men full in the face. Andrea looks

fully at him, her eyes absorb the hostility emanating from him. Her body full of it. And he knows. He and Zenobio. Innocent, trusting Zenobio. Then "the betrayal" as Zenobio dramatically called it when he told her about it. And she even more stupid—she should have warned Zenobio. Poor Zenobio, duped, seduced, betrayed. She would never forget his pain. Andrea blinks and says, "You are not welcome here," She is herself again.

"I'm always welcome at the house of my aunt."

"Make any trouble and I'll boot you off of my land."

"Your land? You're a woman—or arc you? Women don't

inherit."

"Va 'ber pedo. A fight, a fight," the boy in the yellow shirt chants. José Manuel pushes her once. Twice. As he tries to push her a third time she takes a knife out of her jeans and his hand

runs into it. Shocked, he backs off staring at the blood dripping from his hand. Don Efraín pushes his way through the group. "Now, now, now," he says putting his arm around Andrea and turning her around. Complete silence, all eyes riveted on the blood dripping.

"Consider Zenobio," Don Efraín whispers moving her away while at the same time José Manuel's brother takes José Manuel's arm and pulls him toward the portal. José Manuel muttering, "Should have given her the yerba—would of cured the chingadera out of her."...He swallows the last words, hand on his throat gagging. He turns to find her standing very still, her eyes wide, her gaze aimed directly at his throat. The saliva in his mouth turns to rust, the weasel in his eyes wild with fear. In the future I will not need a knife, she thinks. She stands

holding the cage at eye level with both hands. The paisano cocks its head to one side, then the other, looking at her through first one eye then the other. Killer of rattlers. Killer of alacranes and tarantulas. The bird blinks its fierce eye, film clouding and unclouding it. The bare patch of vivid blue and red skin behind the eye fascinates her. The bird blinks again, the eye clears then films. Clear then clouded, unclouded then filmed, over and over and over. The *feeling*, and a tingling in her hands. The boy in the purple shirt watches her. She opens

the cage door. A beautiful cage made of bleached dry twigs and grass stems. It doesn't move. Just the eye. Clouding and unclouding. The paisano takes off down the back road in a streak so fast it seems to be skimming the ground, long legs churning, tail flat. The road forks out to the right and another branch to the left. Andrea silently urges the paisano

168

to cross the right road from left to right. Squatting, she looks at the track, two toes pointing forward, two toes pointing backward—to mislead the evil spirits, people say. (*Cállate el hocico, Zenobio. You've asked me what time it is a hundred times in the last five minutes. Cállate, she'll be here on time.*) She looks toward the north, clenches her fist and concentrates. Lightning flashes in the north. She counts slowly and when she gets to seven there is a low rumble. She begins to count again and at seven the wind come sweeping over the rancho. Andrea turns to find the boy in the purple shirt looking at her. "Will you teach me how to do that?" he asks. Both smile. Andrea looks for Zenobio. He's not in the house. He's not with José Manuel. He's with his mother on one of the benches that have been set up to accommodate the Flores'. The benches, she notices, close off

the circle. He's standing by the wedding cake laughing at something Don Efraín is saying. They stand close together. Don Efraín never should have married. It's not too late, she thinks. Not too late. Not

too late. "Oh, there you are, corazón," says Don Efraín, putting his arm over Andrea's shoulder. "Oye, paisana, I was just telling your hombre here how lucky you are."

"Ya lo sé." She doesn't want to hear anymore about 'luck.' "I'm bailing him out. And myself. We're rescuing each other, for now anyway."

"What nonsense you talk sometimes, hijita. You sound more and more like your mamagrande everyday. Be careful. People do not tolerate what's different." Zenobio doesn't seem put out by their conversation, she thinks, annoyed with herself and everyone. She's never seen him flustered or even self-conscious. He always looks beautiful. She looks at Don Efraín and studies the sombrero in his hand. The small holes around the crown form a pattern of inverted squares inside of which more holes bisect their angles to form a

cross. Sun wrinkles spread outward around the eyes

gazing at her. Why, he's chuckling at our situation. And pitying it, she realizes. A lizard scurries out from

between her legs. She is partial to lizards. (*Lo cagamos, the ring doesn't fit, says Zenobio. You didn't think it would, did you. It's not supposed to fit. Nothing is supposed to fit so don't start expecting things to, she tells him.*) "Some more mescal, Tío?"

"Yes, but I'll get it. I know you want to be alone to fight with your 'novio'," he says, accentuating the novio. The music starts. The men begin moving all the tables to make room for the dancing. Everyone turns to look at Andrea and Zenobio. Don Efraín is there beside them, urging them to the center of the portal saying, "The bride and groom always start the first dance."

"I don't want to dance with him. Nothing personal, Zeno."

"Cagada, let's get it over with," says Zenobio, putting his arm around her. They stand motionless, freeze a smile for the photographer. They are waltzing smoothly. Her hands on his thin shoulders, his bony hands on her waist. (*For the wife does not rule over her own body, but the husband does; likewise the husband does not rule over his own body...*) She is a substanceless body doing the courting being courted. He is a substanceless body doing the courting being courted.

"Why are you looking at me that way?"

"I feel like not going through with it," she says.

"Tás loca. It's the night before."

"I don't see the point of it. Just why are we doing this. Pa'no casarnos deveras. So we won't have to go through a 'real' marriage? We're being hooked into it. Into doing what's 'done.'" She looks around. Others are dancing. The waltz becomes a polka, a foot-tapping, dust-raising Texas Mexican polka full of ajúas, Andrea walks away, Zenobio follows. They stand on the sidelines watching the dancers. Everyone, old and young, is dancing. The girls left without partners are trying to cajole their young brothers into dancing with them. Two seven-year-old girls dance with each other. Andrea walks up to the López girl who's been turning down man after man, all bunched up around her like cattle around a salt lick, tongues falling out.

"Ven. Baila conmigo." The López girl smiles, her teeth gleam as Andrea takes her into her arms and whirls her around the circle. Andrea's head is full of the music. The strings of the guitar twang inside her skull. The beat becomes her heart-beat, opening her, widening her diaphragm, her hips expanding. Only the tune exists and Belinda López. Throbbing. Her pelvis makes circles around Belinda's navel. She shakes her head and blinks, lips glisten, jaw falls slack. Her spine is undulating. Gradually, she notices that most of the dancing couples have taken root right in the middle of the portal and are staring at the two women, lips thinned and whitening.

"Stop, let go," says Belinda López, teeth whiter than ever.

"Aw come on, you like it."

"Yes. But we're not supposed to."

"I'm tired of the millions of things we're not supposed to do," says Andrea.

"Well, you're the only one that can get away with doing things we're not supposed to do."

"Ay chulita, I'll tell you my secret. I just do them."

"But you're different. They're scared of you. Andrea la Bruja, they call you behind your back, making the sign of the cross when they say your name," she says. She breaks from Andrea's hold, running out of the circle of petrified eyes. Her palpitating breasts affront the men and bring a look of envy to the women's eyes.

Andrea walks back to Zenobio. "¿Qué pendejada fue ésa, Andrea?"

"I did it because I wanted to just like you want to dance with the boy in the purple shirt staring at you," she says.

"What I want and what I do are two different things."

"Oh yeah? What about José Manuel?" says Andrea. "Oh let's stop squabbling. W'ere beginning to sound like we're married already."

"OK, I know what you're thinking. You want to run off and leave me," he says. "But we need each other, Andrea. We understand each other. No one else does. We have to stay together." And when she makes no reply, he says, "Take me with you." They put their arms around each other. The image of a tumbleweed wrapped around a post with the wind whirling past is in her mind. But who is the tumbleweed and who the post? Over Zenobio's shoulder appears the frowning face

of her mother, Andrea feels a vague sense of guilt, a diffused disloyalty. The warmth and affection and love that is her mother's due she lavishes on her grandmother, on Zenobio, on Víbora, on the land.

"I wish we hadn't started building our own home yet," she tells him.

"It'll be finished in a month, then we'll have some privacy."

"You don't know my mother."

"Querida, it won't matter. We can put up with her for a month. And she with us."

"Or, we can skip out. It's not just her, Zeno, it's me.

172

And it's you. We don't fit here. So maybe we won't fit anywhere else, but maybe we will. Maybe there's a place for people like us somewhere."

"You mean in the gavacho world?"

"I don't know. Zenobio, don't look like that."

"I want you to stop talking like this. You're scaring me. Besides, I'm hungry. Let's go eat."

"You gó, I'm not hungry. I'm going to talk to Mamagrande."

Her grandmother is sitting on a bench under The Windmill, arms on her lap, quietly rocking.

"I was waiting for you, mijita." They remain silent. Silence—their way of talking. Finally her grandmother says, "It's a closeness, a connection."

"Yes," says Andrea, "with people and things. But only with certain people and certain things at certain times. It's frightening."

"Only because it's new and unfamiliar. Soon it will become comfortable and in time indispensable."

"I don't mean *that*. I mean other's fear of it and my fear of their fear. Why do I seem evil to them?"

"Because you are wholly yourself. *That* terrifies people who are prisoners of others' upbringing, who are molded by others," says her grandmother.

"I don't know what to believe. It's terrible! I don't want it. It means being alone."

"Which? ¿Tu poder o tu querer?"

173

"Both," she says, surprised that her grandmother knows about su "querer." Yet nothing her grandmother knows really surprises her. "Don't the two go together, Mamagrande?" asks Andrea.

Andrea walks back toward the portal, then turns to go back to the corral. A small group has gathered around José Manuel. He playfully puts a pair of pants over a heifer's head, one of the ladinas. He opens the gate and hits her sharply on the shanks. Blinded she whirls around and around trying to shake off the cloth over her eyes. Frightened and enraged she runs straight toward Andrea. From the guests— an audible sucking in of air. The heifer is almost on top of Andrea. Andrea jerks the pants off her horns. The animal stops dead in her tracks, wild-eyed, spewing rivulets of saliva. Andrea whispers to her and walks into the corral. The wild heifer follows her meekly. Andrea turns and locks the gate. The circle is complete. She ignores the remarks addressed to her, repeating to herself *It is not a sickness, nor is it evil.*

Another melody attaches to the first—I must do it I must do it. An incantation to ward off...A white glare

lays over everything like a fine dust. Another world, a different one, superimposed over the normal one. The land, the people, everything takes on a fused quality. Like figures carved out of the same white rock. What was it like before? Where's the Andrea that left her bed that morning? What was the dream about that woke her up?

She is standing on the banks of a river holding a bucket. She fishes by dropping it into the water and scooping it up. At first she catches a big beautiful paisano. She knows it's a rare one. She throws it back into the river. It metamorphoses into Víbora, her pet snake. Víbora stands on the water flicking her tongue, then with a rattle of her tail, turns and swims for the shore. Once on land, she crawls toward the west. Andrea wakes up saying to herself, a dream about my future.

She hurries back to the portal and sits down beside

Zenobio (*And the two shall become one. And they shall be one flesh.*) who has multiplied and his several selves fan out around him like cards held in a hand. The physical Zenobio draws the others. (*I pronounce you man and...*) These others are Zenobios that she's never met. She feels a tightness in her head and a great wind in her bones.

"¿Pa' dónde vas?" Zenobio asks when she starts to leave.

"Away from here."

She finds herself once more on top of The Windmill. She doesn't remember climbing up.

The world gradually settles down around her, forming a different rockbed. There is nothing that she can compare the feeling with—except maybe dreams. She puts her hands on her temples and presses hard. It must all be part of what could have been or what is, she thinks. The vane now points toward the west. I am that I am. The paisano is a bird of good omen. She descends

from The Windmill and walks slowly to the portal. She dips a broom sprig in water. A fine rain begins to fall. The feathers of an eagle consume all other feathers if they're mixed together. Leaning against the gnarled Mesquite, hair touching some of its leaves, she begins to bid the guests goodbye.

Character Sketch
of a Woman Looking

Elva Pérez-Treviño

A ll those that wish to die today are anxious for tomorrow.
Tomorrow is anyday, each a more violent day of hungry
souls grasping faint images of themselves. Today Milagra
decided that she could not believe in any one thought long
enough to see it give form...take shape.

When thought connects with attention new images form.
They are blessed with a flair for movement, and their trails
mark space with bands of fermented matter: large landscapes
open where none existed before. One thought lets go into a
thousand and more pictures. A new persona births and dies
within split seconds, or it grows horns, tacks on colors and
meaning to everyday existence by waiting...observing...
studying the hues of sunsets leaves an impression of heat.

At thirty Milagra has lost all use of her mind...she is
busy being self-conscious. Too preoccupied with impressions,
she laughs and cries with herself. Either she functions or she
creates...the fine edge of her creativity carves space with a
thin blade...here life slices into profane and sacred...all is
minor divisions.

Today she became sweaty when she caught sight of herself
looking at herself in the mirror: as a reflection she did not
recognize herself. She has been thinking about passion and
tries to envision herself as lover...she seduces herself into a
tangent of thought. She avoids looking at her reflection, but
she needs to see.

Her mind, in order to restore its equilibrium, creates fantasy in another dimension. She paints new visions because she knows that no matter where, she is just a manifestation of static...she represents the ultimate in a process designed to complete divine desire into action. As her connections to pain and knowledge slowly dissolve into a still-picture, a new vision spins off.

"A woman who disowns herself can sit on any beach," mumbles Milagra's mind to itself. Milagra's usual state of waiting leads her into a diffused awareness where her senses do not shatter against rigid barriers. She withdraws to her thinking. She stands before the mirror, immersed in contemplation, desperate to feel anything, even pain...to hurt with the negative can be positive. In the mirror, her face shies. Anxiety, like sweat, springs from old sores.

"How strange! I don't recognize myself...I never look at my face, unless it's to pick at some flaw."

Milagra's contemplation leads to alienated feeling. The absence of firm ground nurtures seeds of knowledge not yet understood: ignorance confronts its lack of self-respect. She embraces the source that makes her look—all the vivid memories of childhood, the want and the desperateness.

"These beasts of malcontent are supposed to die some time...people accept that time will erase the most bitter of life...I don't trust this easy thinking. I see the need of full circles, something continuous in my life that makes sense. I'm uncomfortable not knowing what to choose for myself. After all, what do I do because I want to...how much of my life? And why do I sound so melodramatic about it? What is necessary...which division...which circle?

A woman stands on the beach. The day barely lightens over the water. No gulls screech and the wind whips palm leaves violently. The woman is alone. She scans the blended horizon of sky and ocean. Her footprints wash free with each wave that surrenders onto the harder sand made of cracked shells. On the wet sand tiny crabs scatter, preparing for the new day, scurrying for their food and shelter. The woman stands silent, eyeing the vastness of unfirm terrain, the lack of solid ground halting her deliberate, wandering step.

Anxious to feel relief in this microcosm, in a frenzy she reclaims random moments from her life, no matter how painful or unnecessary. The work involved in testing her instincts for safety, recalling dead and live fears, are the measure of her personhood. The venture of shedding old patterns, of stroking new strengths, creases her forehead. Accepting what she sees in the mirror is a deliberate and necessary process.

The woman sitting isolated underneath the sun shifts her eyes and her head travels full circle. Her gaze focuses on two native women squatting in a palm tree's shade. Her face intrigues them. She moves them out of waiting into purpose. They accept that this woman appears temporarily.

She lights on petal of thought. Her eyes look inward. The women know they must remain a silent refuge for this wandering soul. Her face wears the pout and downcast mask of the Uninvited; her presence remains constant. Both microscope and specimen, she is numbed against the world: another full circle which can respond in full form to its self-containment. She has come to this point and this beach before, but always ignorant of her whereabouts. In her reflection she visits with her only possessions...her sense of self-value, though at times it is a bitter pit.

In the mirror Milagra can see herself, naked body gold-gilded by candle light. Her own hands run from her smooth throat to her shoulders around to her breasts. She cups her left breast and recalls her girlhood, the discovery of being able to lick her own nipple while she masturbates. She grows hot with shame with the recognition of her intense sexual demands, and she fights the feeling of shame. Old pain rears its angry tail. She is sometimes still ashamed of her early introduction to sex. These memories still scare her, make her a cautious woman. Then, from deep within her conflict, she loses sight of herself as her head lowers towards her breast, and forgives that girl. She regresses in honor of that moment and in the mirror Milagra releases her mind. She can be spied sucking her breast. Sounds shift the small candle flames with puffs of movement.

The two native women talk among themselves. Their faces express precise exchange of secrets. Their similar dress blends them into a double vision of brown skin, dark features, and strong bodies. They rest on their haunches, toes flicking sand at insects that pester.

"That one will learn not to wait," Acatl, the older of the two says, motioning with a jut of her chin towards the isolated Milagra.

"We have watched and remained silent for too long. The mornings that she has greeted the same dawn now accumulate the space and time of many years." Santos is still young, and does not express herself well, but plainly enough.

Acatl, greeting new information with a philosopher's fever, replies. "She will learn because in waiting she learns how time and its phases are never linear. When she learns that she can forgive and still not accept what she forgives she will move on to another moment that will no longer concern our silence, nor this dawn." The two native women are two women who exist in the hiatus between what Milagra knows and what she would like to know.

Milagra's head slowly returns to an even level where her eyes meet their reflection in the mirror. She licks her lips and spreads herself open at the crotch. Her finger trace every fold of skin, as her own smell assails her nostrils, she is gone again. She twists thought behind leveled eyes: the look of self-containment can not be negated.

Milagra relaxes her hold on herself and focuses once again on her body. Her hands extract themselves from within her female hole. She turns towards the wash-basin, runs cold water, and splashes her face, neck, and chest. She blows out the candles and moves into the sunny living room. She engages in sorting through what she knows about who she is.

"Are my sisters as scared of daily routine as I am?" Milagra pushes the question as dialogue with herself.

On the beach Acatl and Santos has stripped their wrapped skirts creating a canopy of multi-colored shade. Like mental apparitions they flank Milagra. They become the boundaries of an increased awareness whose presence creates a womb

179

out of all the loose space. Reasons throw off definitions, new meanings attach to life. Milagra breaks one connection and makes others. In another setting through an open window, the sun is seen aging.

"How does that feel Milagra?" She addresses herself. "When I look at myself it feels like I must diminish myself... as I resolve who I am I find I can't forget my audience. All those who have seen who I am...in my ignorance, my response has always been sincere." She finds little comfort in this last thought.

The setting sun throws shadows of swaying mesquites at her feet.

She is drawn by the shadows of tree limbs grappling with the room, a picture of what happens inside her head. She sits on the floor, she sits within the casting rays of the dying sun.

"How much longer do I have to keep thinking about changing...transforming my visions into realities, before I change? I've closed...I'm stuck...on myself...my mind can't breathe...split second leaping from faith to trust is still hard for me. Thinking it over, I don't know how to be vulnerable. How to change neurotic thinking to action...maybe I need to learn to let go."

Recognizing the problem narrows down the choices of deciding: acceptance, change, or death. This is unfamiliar clarity. Words like hallucination and dreams are simple, and easily understood. The firm belief in dreams sets a straight line she can follow.

Acatl and Santos hold firm to the fabric, now a billowing wrap in a new, more gentle wind. A cool shadow forms a larger canopy above the trio. The two native women continue to be a staunch guard. The woman for whom barriers are difficult to erect keeps the guard, the key to her journey, in check with her peripheral vision. She welcomes their beauty as she notices how blowing sand turns their hair white, and she unfolds into their distinct warm odor. Milagra notices their warm smell and accepts her curiosity. Without thinking, she stands up, turns her back against the water and the waiting. Two women of firm step follow her into the thicker terrain, away from the water. Their procession is commanded by a single instinct: to follow the path that travelling day leaves.

"A woman who disowns herself can sit on any beach," Milagra's mind mumbles to itself as it turns outward. Three women walking flow in a single line against the horizon, blot out the setting sun.

Pesadilla

Cherríe Moraga

There came the day when Cecilia began to think about color.

Not the color of trees or painted billboards or the magnificent spreads of color laid down upon the hundreds of Victorians that lined the streets of her hometown city. She began to think about skin color. And the thought took hold of her and would not give; would not let loose. So that every person—man, woman, and child—had its particular grade of shade. And that fact meant all the difference in the world.

Soon her body began to change with this way of seeing. She felt her skin, like a casing, a beige bag into which the guts of her life were poured. And inside it, she swam through her day. Upstream. Downtown. Underground. Always, the shell of this skin, leading her around.

So that nothing seemed fair to her anymore: the war, the rent, the prices, the weather. And it spoiled her time.

And then one day, color moved in with her. Or, at least, that was how she thought of it when the going was the roughest between her and her love. That was how she thought of it after the animal had come and left. Splattered himself all around their new apartment or really the old apartment they had broken their backs to make liveable.

After brushing their way out the front door, leaving the last coat of varnish on the hard-wood floor to dry, Cecilia and Deborah had for the first time in weeks given themselves the afternoon off. They returned in the early evening, exhausted from the heat, and the crowds, and the noise of the subways and slowly began the long trek up to their sixth-floor apartment. *Why couldn't we have found an apartment with an elevator in the building,* Cecilia thought each time she found herself at the bottom of the stairs, arms full of packages, staring up at the long journey ahead of her. But no, *this* was the apartment they had wanted — the one they believed their love could rescue from its previous incarnation.

The woman who lived there before them was said to have had five dogs and five children, crowded into the one bedroom apartment. Each time Juanito came by from across the hall to spy on their working, he had a different version to tell of "La Loca" who had lived there before them. "She was evicted," he would announce, almost proudly, with all the authority an eight-year-old can muster, puffing out his bare brown chest. "She was so dirty, you could smell it down to the basement!"

The signs of filth, yes, still remained. But *that* Cecilia and Deborah believed they could remove — under coats of paint and plaster. The parts of broken toys found in the corners of cupboards, children's crayola markings on the walls, torn pieces of teenage magazines stuck up with dust-covered strips of scotch tape — all indicated too many people in too small a space. ¿Quién sabe la pena que sufría esa mujer? Cecilia thought.

It was the woman's anger, however, that could not be washed out of the apartment walls. There was no obliterating from Cecilia's mind the smell and sight of the dogfood she had found stuffed into the mouth of the bathroom sink — red and raw in its resentment. As Cecilia scraped it out — "la mierda del mundo que coma mierda!" — she tried not to believe that all this was the bad omen she suddenly felt rising hot and thick in her throat.

Finally, making it up to the sixth floor landing, the two women dropped their bags, exhausted and Cecilia drew her keys out from her purse. But before she could turn the key in the lock the door easily gave way. She quickly tried to convince herself that yes, she had been negligent. The last to leave. The first to forget in her fatigue to secure the lock.

But she knew different. Entering the apartment, her heart pounding, Cecilia lead the way down the long hallway—a dark labyrinth to the pesadilla that awaited them. At the end of it, she could see their bedroom, the light burning. A tornado had hit it!

No, this was not the result of some faceless natural disaster. This was a live and breathing thing. An animal. An animal had broken in.

And the women broke down. *What kind of beast* they cried *would do this?* His parts drawn all over their freshly painted walls for them to see and suck and that's what he told them there on the walls.

SUCK MY DICK YOU HOLE

He had wanted money and finding no such thing, but a picture of a woman who could have been a sister or a lover or a momma and no sign of man around, he wrote:

I'M BLACK YOU MOTHERFUCKER BITCH

YOU BUTCH

And Cecilia knew if he had had the time and sense enough he would have even written her lover's name out there upon the bedroom wall.

He wanted Dee, too. Even in his hatred, he wanted Cecilia's lover. Everybody, it seemed, had *something* to say about Deborah's place on the planet.

Seeing his scratches on the wall, both women knew they were

very close to giving it up altogether. Cecilia closing up the thought just as it broke open inside her. Closing in on Deborah, she brought the woman into her arms and they fell against the wall, crying. The animal's scrawl disappearing behind them.

It was the first time in their life together that Cecilia wondered if she were up to the task of such loving.

It had scarcely been a week since they had carried down their five flights of stairs the last torn-up suitcase of the animal's debris. They needed the rest, the relief from the city and found it in the home of friends by the Hudson, drinking iced seltzer with lime in the bake of the sun. The violation, a million miles away from the one hour's drive out of town.

Dee grew blacker as she slept on the deck. And when Cecilia rose to refill her glass it took the greatest rigidity of spine, *not* to bend down and kiss the wet and shining neck of the woman stretched out before her, sound asleep.

Cecilia wanted her. She was afraid to want her.

Closing the sliding glass door behind her, the house hit Cecilia with a cool that she had nearly forgotten amid the heavy humidity of the city. Even the city park could not provide this quality of coolness—cement blocks hovering around it on all fours. This was the kind of coolness that only grew from a ground not hollowed out by tunnels and steaming underground trains.

Berkeley. It reminded her of the hills in Berkeley. The blend of drying jasmine and eucalyptus hot-whipped into a cloudless sky, the scent carrying itself into the bay.

In Brooklyn, she still found it hard to believe she lived by the water. The tops of neighboring ships were to her merely another line of differently-shaped structures rising up from the stiff water-floor. The real mother ocean was three thousand miles behind her.

The kitchen was flooded with sunlight and houseplants—those that hanged and those that seemed to grow right out from under the linoleum floor. Cecilia found herself breathing more deeply than she had in months. She felt calmer somehow. A feeling she had left somewhere, she thought, *back in California.*

But what?...What exactly *was it?*

The smell?

The light? She held the bottle to pour. *Yes, both these things, but...*

"Salud." She mimed a toast in the air, pushing back the thought coming at her, her heart speeding up.

It was...white.
It was whiteness and...safety.

Old lovers that carried their whiteness like freedom/ and breath/ and light. Their shoulders, always straight-backed and sweetly oiled for color. In their faces, the luxury of trust.

It was whiteness and money.

In this way, she had learned to be a lesbian. Not that any of her friends actually had cash on hand. In fact, she was the one among them who came from the least, but who always seemed to have the most—the one that always managed to find something "steady." But there was the ambiance of money: the trips cross-country, the constant career changes, the pure cotton clothing; and yes, the sunshine. In her memory, it was never dark, except at night when it was always quiet and nearly, suburban.

But the feeling she remembered most, the feeling that she could not shake, was of some other presence living amongst them. Some white man somewhere—his name always mono-syllabled:

Tom, Dick, Jack. Like boys, flat-topped and tough—cropping up in a photograph, a telephone call, a letter, who in the crunch, would be their ticket.

Nobody would have said that then (or even thought of it that way). Cecilia certainly wouldn't have. But she could see it now, now that they were gone—the man's threatening and benevolent presence living with them all. They were his daughters after all, as long as they remained without a man.

Blood is blood.

It was that night that Deborah had her attack (or "fit" as Deborah used to describe them, mimicking some 1930 sci-fi version of epileptics or schizophrenics). It was the first time Cecilia had ever witnessed one in Dee, although for years Dee had spoken of them, sometimes beneath a rush of tears.

Standing on her knees in bed, she would go through the motions once again of the man coming down on her with the back of his hand. The hand enlarging as it advanced—broad and blacker than she'd ever seen it. "That's when my fits began," she'd say, then suddenly, "Blahblahblah-blahblah-blahblah! Po' lil cullud girl, me!"

He was the second and last man her mother kicked out.

("My babies come first." Both their mommas could have been found saying the same thing, wrists bent back into hipbones. That's what had brought them together—the dark, definite women of their childhood.)

But that night, there was no joking. Waking to Deborah's absence in the bed, Cecilia quickly got up and entering the bathroom, found her lover thrown back against the tank of the toilet, mouth open, unconscious.

It was not how Cecilia had imagined it. No tongue-gagging. No guttural sounds, no jerking movments. No joke.

187

Gathering the dead weight into her arms, Cecilia brought the heavy head to her chest, holding it there. The weight like a hot rock against her breastbone—the same shape of the fear now forming inside her heart.

And then, as if she had rehearsed the role, she began to rock the body. And the more she rocked, the more the motion slowly began to dissolve the stone inside her chest and allowed, finally for her tears to come. She rocked. She cried. "Oh Deborah, baby, wake up." She cried. "¡Por favor, despierta! ¡Querida, por favor!" She rocked. Until at last, she felt the head stiffen and pull away.

"Get my pills," Deborah moaned.

Cecilia rushed back into the bedroom and began rumaging around in Deborah's bag, trying desperately to find the pills, finally dumping the entire contents onto the floor. There on her knees she felt something turn in her. She suddenly felt her heart like a steel clamp inside her chest, twisting what was only moments ago a living beating fear into a slow cool numbing between her breasts.

Her loving couldn't change a thing.

Cecilia remembered the first time she had ever felt this same sensation of "coldness." Her memory rushing back in flashes to the picture of a woman, her mother, elbows dug into the kitchen table, yellow, the photograph curled into her hand, yellow too, tears streaming down her cheeks.

Again. A river return.

A river whose pull always before that moment had swept Cecilia off her chair and into her mother's arms.

But on that particular day, Cecilia stepped outside the circle of pain her mother poured like hot liquid into the little girl's body, enflaming it. The mother's tears comingling with her own, like communion.

Cecilia didn't understand why her feelings were changing only that they had to change. *Change or die*, she thought. And suddenly she grew stiff and fixed in her chair, hands pressed between her knees, riveted against the tide of rage and regret she knew her mother's memories would call forth. Old wounds still oozing with the blood of sinners in war time.

"I forgive," her mother would announce. "But I never forget."

And mustering up what courage she could, the girl first whispered to herself, then shouted outloud, "You gotta change, Mamá! You gotta let it go!"

When she didn't change. When Cecilia had prayed and pleaded, practiced and preached every form of childish support she could think of, she left the woman. It was years later, but she took a walk right out of that kitchen and family-way of passing on daughter-to-daughter misery. Her momma cursing after her, "You're just like the rest of 'em. You don't know how to love."

"Honey? Are you coming?"

"Yeah, right away, baby." Cecilia grabbed the pills and came back into the bathroom to find Deborah now with eyes open and blinking alive. But Cecilia couldn't rid herself of the feeling in her chest. It was as if a different woman had stepped back into the room and Cecilia now stood somewhere else, outside the room, watching this other one nurse her lover back to health. In silence, giving Deborah the pills. In silence, moving her back to bed. In silence, watching her fall into a deep and exhausted sleep.

Lying awake in bed, the sunlight cracking through the window, Cecilia thought of the times as a child when always she lived her nights like days while the rest of the house slept. Never soundly sleeping like the woman now curled under her arm.

Getting up six and seven times a night, locking and relocking the doors. Praying in whispers the same prayers over and over

189

and over again, nodding into sleep, resisting. Resisting the pictures the dreams would bring. The women, wanting. The men, like flaming devils, swollen with desire.

Locking and re-locking the doors. Keeping the fearful out, while it wrestled inside her without restraint. During those hours before dawn, *anything* was possible—the darkness giving permission for the spirit to shake itself loose in Deborah.

Cecilia wanted Dee. She was afraid to want her. Afraid to feel another woman's body. Like family.

When she discovered the first woman wouldn't change, it had sort of wrapped things up for the rest of them. Still she'd go through the changes of asking for changes como su abuelita during the english mass mouthing spanish a million miles an hour, kissing the crucifix of the rosary wrapped 'round her neck at each and every "amen."

Nothing to disturb her order of things. No matter what was said or done in english, she knew the spanish by heart. In her heart, which long ago forgot the clear young reason for the blessings, the vicious beatings of the breast, the bending to someone else's will.

What frightened Cecilia so was to feel this gradual reawakening in her bones. For weeks her hands had merely skimmed her lover's flesh, never reaching in.

Cecilia pressed her nose into Dee's hair. The sun almost full now in the window, had warmed the fibers into a cushion of heat which promised rest, continuance. In the intake of breath, there was more familiarity, more loss of resistance, more sense of landing *somewhere* than any naming she had tried to do with words inside her head.

Words were *nothing* to the smell.

Pesadilla.

There is a man on the fire escape. He is crouched just below the window sill. I could barely catch the curve of his back descending, but I have seen the movement. I know it is the animal, returned.

The figure suddenly rises to attack:

DEBORAH!!

The dark woman looking in through the glass is as frightened as I am. She is weeping. I will not let her in.

FEBRUARY NOTEBOOK:
A Month in a Nutshell

ALEIDA RODRÍGUEZ

Figures begin to be unrecognizable. Instead of painting objects as they are seen, one paints the experience of seeing... It would seem that in fixing upon the object nearest the cornea, the point of view is as close as possible to the subject and as far as possible from things. But no—the inexorable retreat continues. Not halting even at the cornea, the point of view crosses the last frontier and penetrates into vision itself, into the subject [herself]....Ideas, then, are subjective realities that contain virtual objects, a whole specific world of a new sort, distinct from the world revealed by the eye, and which emerges miraculously from the psychic depths.
　　　—José Ortega y Gasset, "On Point of View in the Arts,"
　　　　from *The Dehumanization of Art.*

For months I've been anticipating an earthquake. I'm in the middle of any activity when I feel its approach, can hear its growl begin in its intestines and swell to its throat. I actually hear the china clinking; the window panes rattle. But nothing doing. Nothing, that is, but expectation. Expectation is doing. It's doing fine. My furniture cracks its own knuckles, stretches from that awful position of just sitting around.

****

The bluejay—scrub jay, actually—today got hungry enough to take peanuts from my open hand, then gradually began to pluck them from my fingers. There are two of them that hang around for handouts, but the other one has either been warned by this bolder one that the back porch is its territory, or it may be inexperienced. It sits in the low branches of the eucalyptus

192

making a whirring sound of either anger or envy.

****

I talk to my therapist about this rumbling in the deep caverns
of me, but she can't know anything yet because I don't. First
things first. What's first? The door. No, not the door, but the
long field that stretches for miles in front of the door. And
before the field, what then? A forest. And before the forest, a
river. And then mountains and another field, and eventually
the coast. Then the sea. But then it gets vertical and we have
to look at what is before the sea, beneath it. Is that getting
closer? Would we be getting closer if we went there? Is it there?
Yes, like the submerged islands.

****

I'm pissed. I want to blow everybody's fucking head off. I want
to scream at them whether or not it's nice. I'm repeatedly told
to be quiet, to be agreeable, and I'm tired of it. I want S and T
and J to go to hell! I'm not going to swallow anymore and it's
me who's deficient just because I'm the only one with complaints. They can't stand anyone around them not having the
same opinions. That's their problem if they can't hold onto
their views just because I disagree. What makes me most sick
is that while they're judging and criticizing me, I'm the one
who gets to be seen as overly critical! And if they indulge
themselves in throwing stones at me, or better yet, ignoring
me, making me invisible, and I happen to protest, they're
surprised: but you look so thick-skinned!

But nothing's wrong with the way they see things—after all,
everyone else who's white agrees with them, and that's how
they know they're right. In other words, it lets them sleep
nights. What about my being the only colored person within
miles of them, and that they don't know what to do with my
expressiveness because they're racist? In their eyes I'm harsh,
I'm critical, I'm opinionated—in other words, I'm foreign, and
not well-mannered enough to keep my thoughts to myself.
And J trying to stop me from getting angry at them only
makes me angrier.

I'm sure they all had a lovely time last night without me going
and having opinions. They had cared enough to ask why SE

193

didn't return to the group, but couldn't bother to tax their brains about why I didn't. But it doesn't matter to J. It's good for her, so she doesn't care how bad it is for me. It's your business, she says. Is it so unreasonable to want support and loyalty from one's lover? She makes a scene over the tiniest move I make that may not include her, but when her turn comes, she wants no intervention. Double standard.

***

This is the third day of my experiment with the jay. Now I have it coming on my hand parrot-style to take the peanuts from my other hand. It's also flying into the kitchen and helping itself to the nuts left lying on the counter. I'm starting to wonder what it is I want from it. How much further can I take it? It is, afterall, a wild bird, and this is certainly an accomplishment. But what? Now that I have made it trust me, trick it? Eat it? Teach it to speak so that it can comfort me? Why do I want it to come inside the house? Am I trying to coax the wild part of me back in? It has no use for a house. It has no complaints. but it wants my peanuts, my offering.

****

After much chasing around the house, when it ventured too far away from the kitchen door, I finally got it in a cage after cornering it in the bathroom with my gardening gloves on. Its mistake was that it stayed at the bathroom window, seduced by the apparent nearness of escape: the park just on the other side of the glass, the acacia in full bloom pressing its yellow cheek against a corner of the house. Now it sits next to me while I draw its portrait, sad and resigned. But it's not such a bad life, just different, I try to convince it. It won't even look at the full cup of peanuts I've put in the cage. It's looking down and making a promise to the scrub jay god that if it ever gets out of this one, it swears, it'll never, never accept food from a human again. Its friends are calling it from the outside in a language I can't understand, so they know it's safe to communicate. Pretty soon the scrub jay army will be knocking on my door with a picture of this one to see if I recognize it. I will deny ever setting eyes on it, but it's all a setup and the jay will hear them at the door and cry: I'm here! The thugs will push past me and liberate the little ingrate. Let them, there are more wild things out there.

But really, I'll let it go when I've shown everyone that I was able to catch it. Its blue is so blue it's difficult to believe it doesn't dye it. That's one thing you can always depend on about wild things: they are what you see. Unlike me. If I had been sincere, I would have continued to offer it peanuts without having to own it. It's finally noticing the cup of nuts. It picks up each one, rattles it in its shell, then throws it to the bottom of its cage with the abandon of an abstract artist to scorn me and my false generosity. It'll go on a hunger strike, if necessary.

Will its beak hurt me, so hard and black like a gun? Can I make it sit on my hand long enough to satisfy me? Difficult questions. It's probably full of mites and now I'm covered with them and the house, everywhere it flew.

Now it has escaped, the pesky bastard! I reached my hand in to see if it'd stand on it, but it tricked me and slid around the opening leaving me looking after it like a fool. But the back door is closed, so it's only a matter of time before I can secure it again.

··*

Got it. Fed it some water through a dropper because it was out of breath after the chase. It needed it, but it didn't appreciate it. Now I have it in Alix's room. Alix's response was one of bravado. Alix is the only one I've been able to show my prize to. She ruffles up her feathers and is not threatened but struts instead. Now they're both in there cracking their peanuts and eyeing each other.

J still hasn't called. The coffee's hot, I can hear it begin to sizzle in the pot. I pour myself a cup. This is a power game J is playing with me and I'm playing with the jay. If I can't get J to listen to me and support me, why, I'm going to catch a little wild creature and make it feel what I feel.

J talks constantly about putting and keeping me in a pumpkin shell like Peter Pumpkineater's wife. This week she chose to be apart on exactly those days when I wouldn't have my car so that I would be confined to the house while she's out in the world. And Peter Pumpkineater put his wife in a pumpkin shell because he couldn't keep her. It seems J doesn't truly want to keep me, but she doesn't want me to go anywhere else either. And why do I let her? Maybe because, like the jay, I'm hungry, I've risked too much, and now I'm caught. This is exactly why she continues to abandon me. I'm already in the cage. She can take her mind off me and go about her business.

****

P and C came over for dinner and were able to see my little catch. C says it will keep coming around for food after I release it. I don't think so, neither does P. I think it will resent me for having tricked it. Although it really can't complain about its treatment—it gets everything Alix gets, even apples and pine nuts. But I really know that's not the point, that's not the thing it values most.

****

Nearly a week has gone by and still no sign of J. She's still the only one who hasn't seen it. Even M and MT saw it when they dropped by to give me some company. They, too, were divided over the issue of whether the jay will come back or not. We mused about it in the doorway to the back porch, watching the jay in its cage. I put the cage outside because I thought that might help, considering J is taking her time about calling and I really can't let it go without her seeing it. I tell this to the jay so that it won't blame me too much—after all, I'd let it go right now if she walked in!

Last day of the month and thanks to our therapy appointment we couldn't continue to indulge ourselves. The skinny Italian blinds in the office shook. I know tomorrow my legs will ache from the steep climb, from trying to see what's beyond this hill.

****

We didn't speak before we got there, but we each got ourselves there, remembering the time and place as though it had been a silent agreement. That seemed important somehow. It left me thinking about all the other places we both know exist and could get there by ourselves, if we just agreed to show up. I've got my car back, and I'd drive anywhere for a compromise.

****

After going by to look at her baby canary which had been born just a week ago, J and I went back to my house so that she could see the scrub jay. I told her I had been saving it for her. She wanted me to let it out right then. But it was night, and I was afraid it would get confused and bump against a tree and be eaten by a cat while unconscious—or something. Anyway, it didn't feel right releasing it just like that. So we did it the next morning (although I had second thoughts because it was raining).

But it was a gorgeous rainy day—the kind that really wants to deliver rain generously and not leave you feeling like someone is crying alone in a windowless room in the center of your chest in the sky—so, I figured, the jay would get a little wet, but I'm sure it would prefer that to staying indoors.

We went together into the kitchen where the jay was in its cage by the stove. I reached in—it was important that it know I was letting it go on purpose, that it was no mistake—and while it jumped and flapped I tried to curve my fingers around its feathered heart. Because that's all it seemed to be now, just a few feathers around this warm beating thing.

I cupped both hands around it and hurled it to the clouds that were as grey as its belly. It flew to the top of the pine and made the rusty-scissors sound it hasn't done in a week—no reason to. It sat on a high branch with its back to me: this is how quickly I can forget you, honey! Then turned its head and peered at my body propped inside a skinny rectangle of darkness over its blue shoulder.

El Viaje

A Fefita.....

Sara Rosel

Muy amontonados cerca de la puerta tratábamos de contar por las luces qué cantidad quedaba. Con la obscuridad se hacía un tanto dificil, pero sin embargo las casi trescientas personas en el lugar teníamos una idea fija: que si nos sequían dejando para el final, nos jodíamos.

Ya cerca de medianoche nos mandaron a hacer fila. Por suerte fui una de las primeras y no sin trabajo consequí un buen lugar que perdí solamente diez minutos después cuando una señora gorda se sentó en el lado derecho, dejándome como única comodidad el tener que apoyarme en una sola nalga.

Como respuesta a un "coño" que pronuncié entre dientes, la gorda se me quedó mirando y comprobé con la poca luz que había que ella trataba de adivinar si yo era hombre o mujer. Evidentemente la voz le había parecido de mujer, pero ahora sus ojos me recorrían de arriba a abajo y cuando nuestras miradas chocaron dejó escapar una disculpa que apenas logré entender. No obstante no cambió su posición y yo tuve que conformarme con seguir en la misma postura, pues ya no había otro sitio libre.

—La noche va estar fría.

Ahora su voz era clara y en un tono tan alto que dudé si

se dirigía a mí o a todos en general.

Pero pronto volteó la cabeza y después de mirarme la ladeó varias veces.

—Me olvidé de traer abrigo. Pero imagínese en el mes en que estamos quién iba a pensar. ¿No cree?

—Sí claro (apenas escuché mi voz).

—¿Cómo?

—Digo que efectivamente no estamos en un mes en que deba hacer tanto frío.

Hizo un signo afirmativo y en ese momento tuve la certeza de que no iba a callarse en todo el viaje. Entonces traté de ganar espacio, pues mi trasero que hasta ese momento se mantenía en equilibrio ya empezaba a tambalearse. Ella se hizo la desentendida y ya estaba pensando que si no se corría un poco la conversación la haría con su abuela. Ella pareció adivinar mis pensamientos y en un gesto exagerado se corrió lo más que pudo y con trabajo. Pues ya yo estaba acalambrada pude apoyar mi nalga izquierda.

—Sí, nunca se sabe con el tiempo, hace sólo unas horas hacía calor.
¿Cuánto cree que durará el viaje?

—Realmente no sé, nunca lo hice antes.

—Sí claro, ninguno de los que aquí estamos.

Sentí un poco de vergüenza por el tono de reproche con que habló y traté de arreglar las cosas.

—Dicen que de diez a doce horas.

Ella pareció satisfecha con mi respuesta, luego pensé que si no la hubiera dado, hubiera sido igual. Evidentemente ella

199

necesitaba con quién hablar y ya todos los demás habían escogido y formado pequeños grupos conversando de diferentes temas.

Como si temiera que por encontrarme más cómoda y por la hora que era, fuera a quedarme dormida, volvió al ataque en un tono tan bajo y misterioso que tuve que sonreír recordando a mi abuela conversando con la vecina, cada una tratando de no hincarse con el alambre de púa que dividía los dos patios. Siempre me mandaban que entrara a la casa. Pero ya sabía de qué hablaban—pues todos los días hacían los mismos comentarios. Ella pareció un poco sorprendida de mi risa y pensando que no la había entendido repitió la pregunta, esta vez un poco más alto.

—¿Usted es casada?

—No.

—Sí, ahora las muchachas se casan muy tarde, le tienen miedo a las obligaciones, sólo piensan en fiestas y diversiones y les aterra parir. Tienen miedo de perder su figura, claro yo no lo digo por usted, que sí me parece una persona asentada.

Era claro que no quería perderme. Pues yo no había dado hasta entonces ninguna muestra de asentimiento, como no fuera tratar de "asentarme" con mis dos nalgas y no le veía la relación.

—En mis tiempos cuando una muchacha tenía quince años, estaba preparada para el matrimonio, ya conocía todas las obligaciones de una casa, y sólo pensaba en encontrar un buen hombre y tener hijos. Así es cómo debe de pensar una mujer a ese edad. No como ahora que con el pretexto del estudio pasan los años y los años y siempre oyes lo mismo, cuando termine la Universidad, cuando termine la Universidad y con ese cuento se pasan la vida. Lo que menos hacen es aprender, porque van a la escuela a pasar el tiempo, para no tener obligaciones, para andar con uno hoy y otro mañana.

—Esa es una minoría.

No pareció darle importancia a lo que dije y yo me juré no volver a abrir la boca y dejarla hablar hasta rendirse.

—No hija, el mundo está al revés, antes los hijos respetaban la opinión de los padres. Ahora se les enfrentan para hacer lo que les da la gana. Las mujeres trabajan y estudian en veinte mierdas que son propias para hombres y el gobierno las apoya porque tienen delirio de ponerle nombre a todo y dicen que eso es la emancipación de la mujer. Yo digo que eso es la degeneración de la mujer. M'hijita te doy un consejo, tú eres joven, busca un buen muchacho, cásate y dedícate a él y a tus hijos y vas a ser muy feliz. Mira a los diez y seis años me casé, tuve una hembra y un varón y hasta que murió mi esposo, que en gloria esté, fuí feliz ocupándome de cosas a las que ahora las mujeres le tienen miedo. Mi hija salió casadita de su casa, pero todo eso va en la crianza, en la crianza. Bueno, yo digo que todas las épocas tienen sus cosas malas pero hay que saber llevar a los hijos por el buen camino.

Realmente ella tenía razón al temer que me durmiera, pues ya sentía ardor en los ojos y aprovechando un momento en que fue al baño recliné la cabeza en mis rodillas. No sé qué tiempo dormí pero fue mucho porque todo mi malestar había pasado. Recordé que estaba en una Iglesia vestida de blanco del brazo de un hombre muy serio. Era toda una ceremonia, hubiera llorado de no sé porqué y de un costado de los bancos salieron varias amigas y entre risas en vez de arroz me tiraron frijoles negros. Mi tía Concha protestaba por la mala educación de mis amistades mientras la madre del novio me miraba con rencor porque a mí me parecía todo muy divertido.

—Durmió bastante, ya casi va a amanecer.

Sin duda ya ella estaba preparada para continuar la charla. Como yo no tenía sueño y quería que pasaran rápidas las horas enderecé mi cuerpo lo más que pude para darle a entender que estaba dispuesta a seguirla escuchando. No puedo precisar si ella captó el gesto por ser muy inteligente o por ser muy conversadora pero el caso es que me dirigió la más agradecida de sus sonrisas y pude ver entonces con la claridad del día que no era tan gorda como había pensado si no era muy estrecho el lugar donde estábamos sentadas. Ella ahora pasaba su dedo índice repetidamente por los ojos tratando de quitar hasta el último vestigio de una mala noche y lo iba limpiando en su vestido al tiempo que me observaba.

—Sí, como le decía anoche, todo anda mal, es imposible vivir en un país donde no hay respeto para nada. Todo se ha perdido. Claro que hay mujeres que se mantienen en su lugar pero la mayoría andan como locas por la calle y son putas, homosexuales, toda clase de gente.

—No le hace usted mucho favor a nuestra especie.

—Que va m'hijita a mí que me digan anticuada. ¿Tú viste la cantidad de tortilleras que andan por ahí? En eso sí estoy de acuerdo con el gobierno que cada vez que cojan a una la lleven presa. Si no el día menos pensado se paran en una esquina y lo dicen a gritos, reclamando derechos. Eso sí tiene bueno el país. Y ¿Qué será de nosotros las personas decentes?

Fue interrumpida por un grito unánime. Todos trataban de incorporarse y al hacerlo me di cuenta de que andábamos en flotilla. Aparte del barco que nos conducía había otros quince o veinte y todos se saludaban con risa nerviosa porque ya se veía a lo lejos la costa de los Estados Unidos. El capitán dio la orden de sentarse y se trató de calmar la impaciencia de unos niños con chocolates y otras chucherías.

—Mi hija y su esposo deben de estan en Cayo Hueso esperándome. Porque yo vine más bien por eso. Tengo dos nietos que no conozco. ¿Por qué se fue Usted de Cuba?

—Porque no estoy de acuerdo con lo único que usted le encuentra bueno al gobierno, porque soy lesbiana y porque quiero, como usted dijo, pararme en una esquina a gritar y exigir mis derechos.

Un poco de chocolate a manera de baba, corrió por su mandíbula. Pero ya yo estaba caminando en dirección a la proa,

202

sin duda estaba más sorprendida que ella. Era la primera vez en mi vida que podía decir lo que sentía entre personas "decentes."

Ya cerca se veía el puente con muchas personas agitando las manos. Mi mirada pasó de éste al agua azul. Curioso, no sentí miedo y yo sabía que nadie me estaba esperando.

El bacalao viene de más lejos y se come aquí

AURORA LEVINS MORALES

Passports

1

I've been packing for a month. Useless packing because I always end up taking the clothes out again to wear. Last week I bought a new suitcase. A small one. I decided to travel as light as I can. The weight of my own fears is more than enough for me. I've been coughing uncontrollably for three weeks, my chest too tight for breath. I keep on believing that one clear inhalation of that wet warm air will cure me, like stepping into a humidifier. I don't believe any of this is real. I panic regularly. I can't go! I don't want to go. I don't want to know the answers to my questions: will it be different? Do I belong? Is it home?

2

Now it's time for the ritual: the immigrant going home. Suddenly I become aware of us all, a little group of foreigners, all homesick, all exiles in San Francisco, a city of out-of-towners. Sitting in living rooms in last minute visits, everyone presses addresses into my hand, asks me to bring them...tokens, reminders, something to hold in the hand, keep on a shelf, taste. "Bring me a güiro, some panapén to cook, don't come back without something, anything, from Loíza Aldea." Proof that they can go back anytime, are going soon, probably next year, that they really want to, that they don't need to: a passport (I remember doing it myself), proof of a fading citizenship, an open door.

3

On the plane, the first plane, to New York, I write about sex, trying to measure off, summarize these last almost seven years, a period of my life that's ending with this journey home. I find myself making lists of lovers (as we fly over snowy mountains, the dusty plains, green cornfields) trying to remember which year, and was it April or May, and instead of getting analytical, trying to find out something revealing, see some pattern in my long list of dissatisfactions, I just list them and close the book, and close my eyes. Soon enough, after all, I'm in New York.

4

Early morning, winging southeast. I decided to watch the movie, to fill the time until Puerto Rico appears in the windows. I have to keep reminding myself to feel, to breathe, to stay alive. "I wish I had taken a picture of the people standing in line, that immigrant crowd with their bags and cardboard boxes and the children in pretty-for-abuelita dresses and tucked-in shirts. I was such a child in my organdies and checked shifts, and Ricardo all tucked and belted with this hair cut short, but that was the other journey: grandparents and tíos and tías in North and us going to visit..."

5

These must be the southern latitudes. I imagine the water is lighter, richer, carbonated with sunlight. I scan the dark lines in the distance: islands or cloud shadows? They hand out the hot towels and my ears begin to pop. I still can't see a thing. It must be under those rainfilled clouds. We stoop lower, circling. The humidity is condensing on the outside of the windows. Then at the last minute, the grey folds back: a patch of turquoise sea, a line of white surf, green palms, and far away, where the rain is falling, the mountains.

Esa Noche La Luna Caía En Gotas De Luz

Deperté, pensando que ya amanecía, que debía irme para que no me cogiera el día, ni los vecinos. Tito dormía. Poco a poco me desenredé de su cuerpo y me vestí a la luz de las voces roncas de los gallos. "¿Ya te vas?" Me recuerda de lo de la puerta, que hay que levantarla pá que no chille, y se duerme de nuevo.

Afuera la luna se derrama en una llovizna finita. El cafetal, los guineos recién sembrados, la tierra roja del camino, mi piel recién acariciada: todo se empapa de luna. ¡Qué truca de la noche! Faltan horas todavía. Paso por paso, calladita, tomo el camino hasta mi casa por el aire florecido en la hora más secreta del barrio, cuando hasta los perros se esconden debajo de las casas. Quise cantar. Quise hablar en poesía, pero cuando llegué por fin a mi puerta, tenía la garganta amarrada de silencio y luz, y florecitas minúsculas de luna llena por toda mi piel.

Sí Los Escritores Son Así

I tell Lencho and Sefa I'm working on a book of stories. Sefa's sharp black eyes flash all over her wrinkled face. Snoot in the air and everything akimbo she says, "Hm! A mí no me vayas a poner ahí con mi nombre, nah! Don't you go putting me in there with my name." Lencho is reasonableness personified, explaining to the unenlightened... "But, Sefa, eso no es ná, ¿verdad que eso no es ná, Dori? There's nothing wrong with that." I say OK, I'll change your name. What name shall I give you? Lencho confirms that this is something writers do. César did the same thing when he wrote the novel about the crime in El 22. He says "Ponle Tomasa." Sefa bridles in mock indignation, smirks, looks at me challengingly. "Ay, Lori, you really are too much, tú sí que eres tremenda! Y que Tomasa!" Then, beginning to reminisce, "I knew an old lady named, Tomasa once. She used to wear one of those dresses de antes, from the old days, with a deso here, you know, of lace... *her* name was Tomasa..."

Lencho is delighted with the project. If he sees me writing he stands stock still, grinning, until I look up and catch the expression of delighted respect and pride on his face. Then he tiptoes out of the room. One night when he's drunk he asks me to dedicate a book to him. I promise. For the way his face lit up when I told him I was a writer. For his pride: "I passed the drivers' test first time round, even though I can't read. Some of those school kids have to take it three or four times before they pass." And of course for love.

206

Just like César is the refrain. Lencho is deeply proud of having known him. Once when he was waiting for his government pension settlement, after the accident to his leg, he complained to César about the delay. The next week César wrote it up in his column in the *Imparcial*, and the very next day Lencho got his check by special messenger. He's never forgotten this basic lesson on the power of journalism, and now… "Just like César… *he* used to take down everything you said, too. He asked me all sorts of things when he wrote *Cosas De Aquí*… César liked to get up early, too… but he liked sweets, y ésta no." He recognizes all the symptoms.

Meanwhile Sefa punctuates the conversation, exclaiming, "¡Mira si la nena no sabe ná! She doesn't know *much*, does she? ¡Mira si no sabe la nena!"

Algunas Cosas No Cambian

The first night I spend with Tito I am amazed at how easy it is. As if we were old lovers returning to a familiar bed. Later I prop myself on one elbow and ask: So what have you been doing for the last fifteen years? He tells me: school, a carpentry job, got married, time served in the north, washing dishes in New Jersey and two months in jail because he was stopped driving without a license and didn't speak English. Three children, a girl and two boys. More time in the north, this time in Brooklyn with his cousin Cuni. The marriage falling apart. Haydée living with her mother who looks after the kids. I tell my own story as succinctly: school, work, lovers, changes of address.

The miraculous thing is that it works. We're caught up. I've known Tito since I was six. He hasn't seen me in ten years, and it doesn't seem to matter at all. He tells me Don Paco's store is gone, did I notice, and his sister is living in New York. Remember Caín, you know, El Múcaro, he married a woman with five kids. He reminds me of how he used to steal kisses from me in the lunch line and I remind him of how my father threatened to cut his balls off if he didn't quit it.

This affair requires no courtship. It's all been done in advance. My first day back in the barrio I run into Tito at the store. He asks me if I'm married. I say nope. He says,
"You know how I've always felt about you."

"MmmHmm"

"We need to talk," he demands.

"OK, where?"

"The rock."

I grin. "Neutral territory, huh?"

"Exacto."

The big boulder between our houses where we used to eat stolen tangerines and plan trouble. OK, I say, just like I did when I was ten...I'll wait for you at the rock.

Vivir Es Un Peligro... Y Muerto No Se Puede Vivir

She was a beautiful girl. I remember her at twelve or thirteen, a quick, intelligent face. Bright. She was always in and out of César and Jane's house. They half adopted her, taught her to read, lent her books. Then Jane died and César moved back to the city with his son and Jane's mother Maga.

I asked Tito about her. "She's not pretty any more," was all he would say. She was one week under fourteen when she ran away with her first man. He turned out to be a thief, got caught and went to jail. While he was inside she fell in love with his brother. The first one got out, got his own sister in trouble and took rat poison. He died in the road between her parents house and ours. Years ago I heard she was living in Cabo Rojo. Twenty-three years old, five kids.

Last week Carmen showed me a picture of her, surrounded by children in a living room somewhere in Massachussetts where she lives with her third husband. I didn't recognize her. This afternoon I was out driving with Lencho. We stopped at the place where the road widens before it becomes a razorback between two 500 foot ravines and winds down in to Bartolo. I asked him, "Do you remember Charo?" "¡Cómo no!" he said, "Muchacha inteligente." "She was beautiful, too, wasn't she?" Lencho gazed off toward the silhouette of the farm, a far away crest of pines in a distance his eyes can no longer reach. He sighed. "A flower...era una flor."

El Bacalao Viene de Más Lejos Y Se Come

1

I dream it's my childhood again. The house is as it used to be: none of the damage has been done. Glass sparkles in the windowpanes. The tiles are all in place in the floor, the wood solid and well painted. The trees stand back from the house and the garden is cleared. The drying platform is unbroken. Little yellow planes fly over, cute stubby ones, and Mami runs out to wave at them and they waggle their wings, just like they used to. Then I see that the house is ruined. The cement of the platform is crumbled and the wilderness has reclaimed everything. The whole barrio is overgrown. There are no houses, no paths, nothing but trees and vines. It's been abandoned for years and everything is gone. I know that now the little planes will be lost out at sea. They can't find their way back to land, and I can never return.

I wake sobbing in Tito's arms, pouring out my dream and all the grief of my loss. He strokes my hair and says yes, I know. I know how you feel. I know what you mean. Until I fall asleep again, no more an exile than Tito, living with his loneliness or Cheíto across the way or Haydée up the hill or Caín down the road, all of us grown here and watching it die. No more a stranger than anyone who grows up.

2

There are things I will always know and people who will always expect me to. The difference between a *niño* and a *chamaluco*. What an orange tastes like hot off the tree and eaten on the run. What Don Paco's store smelled like on a rainy day: rum, dust, damp wood, butchers paper, stale candy and the steaming road. I will always remember Angela Báez and Carmen Ana Ríos and Ofelia Ramos who lived in an old wooden house on the way to school. I will always recognize the taste of bacalao cooked up with onions and the look of geraniums planted in battered Sultan cans.

When I came back, I expected to be foreign. To have to introduce myself, explain. I found I was familiar, expected to show up sometime, as all the immigrant children of the barrio are expected. The barrio nodded its head to me, asked after my family, called by my name.

3

I didn't marry Tito. he wanted me to. He asked me about once a day. Now that I'm gone he writes:

> I can't change how I feel. I understand. You have your whole life there and I know how important your writing is and your politics. I know you won't leave that. Let's not argue. Que el tiempo lo decida. Meanwhile, its raining here. A lizard has moved into our room. She looks at me as if she wanted to talk and I feed her sugar from my finger...

Sitting at a desk surrounded by the New England fall, I ask myself again...Do I belong? The understanding comes slowly. No. I don't belong to Indiera. I never will. But Indiera belongs to me.

I come from a long line of eloquent illiterates whose history reveals what words don't say.

Vengo de una larga línea de analfabetas elocuentes cuya historia revela lo que callan las palabras.

Lorna Dee Cervantes

211

Zulema

> yo ya enterré a tus muertos
> bajo un trigal al viento
>
> Lucha Corpi

I

The story that Zulema heard that November morning in 1914 changed her forever, and for the rest of her life she had to deal with the consequences of what she was told on that long-ago Tuesday morning. All during the previous night she had listened to sporadic gunshots across the river where the Federales were shooting at the Villistas. The noise and the unfamiliar bed had made her wake up long before the bells of San Agustín Church pealed their daily calling to the faithful, and at six o'clock when the first sounds from the belfry echoed in the distance, Zulema got up, blessed herself, then knelt down to say her morning prayers. She heard Mariana moving around in the next room and wondered if the disturbances in the night had also made her get up earlier than usual.

Mariana looked different this morning, puffy around the eyes and rather tense as she prepared the coffee and tortillas de harina. Zulema sensed that she had interrupted her aunt as she came into the kitchen but Mariana instinctively left her comal to kiss the child. "Te tengo muchas noticias," Mariana whispered as she put her arms around Zulema's slender body. Then, as she moved back to the stove and stirred

212

the chocolate she was preparing for the child, Mariana told her the story.

Her voice sounded a little forced and her face was solemn and weary. Zulema would later try to recall the scene but all she could remember was Mariana's parlor and the voice that had been pitched higher than usual. In this tone Mariana told her that her new brother had arrived during the night, tired from his journey, but happy and fat and kicking with gusto.

The night had been full of activity, she continued. In addition to the new baby's arrival and the shooting on the other side, a messenger had come from San Antonio asking Zulema's mother to come immediately to take care of her other sister Carmen who had suddenly come down with a serious case of pneumonia. Isabel had left right away with the messenger, leaving her new-born baby behind with the rest of the family. As soon as Carmen got better she'd be back. Give my Zulemita and Miguelito a kiss and tell them that I'll be home soon. Those had been her last words as she left, Mariana said.

"Tú te quedarás conmigo por un rato," she continued. Miguel would stay with his father and his grandmother, and the baby would be with Doña Julia who lived across the street and also had a small infant whom she was nursing. It had all been arranged.

II

Thirty-five years later, sitting on Zulema's bedroom floor, propped on some thick pillows she had made especially for me, I heard many different versions of what I later realized was the same story. During my afternoon visits I listened to Zulema's calm, deep voice as she invented one tale after another with superbly eccentric characters who continued to dance and whirl about in my own accelerated imagination. Some of the stories were simple duplications of tales which Mariana had told her but most of the narratives were Zulema's own inventions. Often Mariana would join us, sitting on the rocking chair with her eyes closed as though she were reliving the episodes which Zulema was describing.

Now and then Mariana would open her eyes and then lean forward to listen more closely. She would shake her head and correct Zulema. "No, no fue así." And she would turn to me with her own version of the story that I had just heard. It was difficult for me to decide whose narrative I liked most, for they each had their way with description and knew just when to pause for the maximum of effect. But I suppose that at that time I tended to think that Mariana's "bola de años," as she referred to her advancing age, gave her an edge over Zulema's rendition.

I soon learned that Zulema had a favorite story. It was the one about the soldadera Victoriana, who, at the height of the revolution, had crossed to this side to wait for her lover Joaquín. For a while people coming from her pueblo in Zacatecas would confirm her belief that Joaquín was still alive but as the years passed, everyone simply forgot about Victoriana. She continued her vigil until that unexpected afternoon when the people had found her thirty years later, sitting in the same chair where she had first sat down to wait, covered with cobwebs and red dust but with a glowing expression, with her rusted rifle at her feet.

I never got tired of Zulema's cuento, for each time she'd recite it, she would pretend it was the first time she had told me about Victoriana and she would embellish the story with a few more details. The climax was always the same, though. She'd describe how Victoriana had been unable to recognize the man whose memory she had loved all those years for when the newspapers printed Victoriana's story, Joaquín came, out of curiosity, to see her and she had not singled him out from all the other visitors she had greeted that afternoon. He, not being the campesino she had fallen in love with but a very important businessman, was alternately amused and mortified by the moths and butterflies entangled in the cobwebs of her silver hair.

Zulema would conclude the story with Victoriana boarding the Ferrocarriles Nacionales Mexicanos, while the townspeople waved a sad farewell to the splendid and flamboyant figure who had enlivened their routine lives for a brief while. She too waved to the people as the train pulled away, taking her back to her pueblo, where she hoped to locate some of the relatives she had last seen in Bachimba claiming their rifles, and riding off into the distance to be swept into the force of the revolution.

Unknown endings, unfinished lives. That was the subject of most of Zulema's narratives but I cannot remember when I first began to notice this. On the day after my sixth birthday I sensed something different. Zulema changed the story from fantasy to biography and for the first time mentioned Isabel to me. She took a photograph from her missal and passed the edge-worn picture to me. "¿Sabes quién es?"

I immediately recognized the photo as a copy of one that my mother had. "Es tu mamá," I responded right away. "Mi abuelita Isabel."

I often opened the top drawer of my mother's dresser just to steal a peep at the clear-eyed young woman in the tucked lace blouse who looked back at me with soft gentle eyes. No one had ever told me very much about her except that she was my father's mother who had died when my uncle Luis was born. Each of the boys had been reared by a different surrogate mother who didn't find it appropriate to talk to them about Isabel possibly to spare them from the memories which they would otherwise not have. Up to then I knew very little about her.

"Murió cuando tenía veinte y cuatro anõs. Yo tenía seis entonces," Zulema looked pained as she spoke. "Mariana deveras me tomó el pelo diciéndome que mamá se había ido con la Tía Carmen."

Zulema's shoulders began to heave and suddenly she was sobbing uncontrollably, holding the photo to her breast. Through her tears she managed to tell me how she had waited for days on end for her mother to return on that first winter when Isabel had gone away without a word to her. Whenever she'd hear people pass by on the street she'd run to the door to see who it might be. The clanging of the streetcar that passed right in front of the house seemed to sound especially for her, and every time she'd see Julia nursing the baby she'd wonder if Luisito was hungry for his own mother. She began to feel abandoned and to talk about her feelings; yet, everyone maintained the story which Mariana had uttered. When, when, when she asked her aunt, and Mariana had finally said, "Cuando termine la guerra, volverá."

And so the eight year-old Zulema had become interested

215

in the war. At night whenever she heard gunfire or ambulances she'd cry herself to sleep. As soon as the bugles of the infantry began each morning, she would catch her breath. In the afternoons after her classes she'd go down by the river to look across its banks at the war-torn nation on the other side. Her eyes closed, praying as intensely as she could, she would wish the war away, while imagining her mother coming to her in her lovely white cotton dress with the ruffles at the neck. But Zulema could sense that she would not be back for a long time, for everyday she was aware of the dozens of people who continued to cross the bridge with their belongings in wheelbarrows or in suitcases of every sort or even in knapsacks slung across their back. Sometimes her father would give work around the store or in the ranch to some of the people who had just arrived, and Zulema would take advantage of their personal accounts to ask them many questions about the war before they moved on further north. No one had any idea when the revolution would end and many of them no longer cared about it except for the manner in which it had altered the course of their lives. Their main preoccupation was with the death and destruction over which they had absolutely no control.

Zulema soon became apprehensive with all the talk of death. When she heard the refugees talk about the death of their loved ones, she began to associate their experiences with the loss of her own mother and slowly she began to doubt the story about her mother's return. One day she tried to tell Carmela—who had just joined her father's household—about her mother and she realized that she could no longer form a clear image of her. The memory was itself becoming a memory that was slowly fading.

On the day of her birthday in 1917 she had let everyone know that she realized the war was supposed to be over and still her mother had not come back. "Sé que se perdió," she told everyone. Then she looked directly at Mariana and stated in a tone of finality, "Yo ya no tengo mamá."

And that same day she had started to tell her own stories. She took Miguelito and Luisito to her room and sat them down on the floor, while she lay down on her bed looking up at the ceiling. "Les voy a contar un cuento de nunca acabar," she

216

began, as she started to narrate her own version of the Sleeping Beauty who had been put under a spell by her wicked stepmother. She was supposed to be awakened by the kiss of a gorgeous prince but that never really happened. She turned to her brothers and asked them if they knew why the prince had not found Sleeping Beauty. Then without giving them a chance to answer, for this was supposed to be her very own story, she continued with melodramatic gestures.

The prince could not find Sleeping Beauty, she whispered, because a revolution broke out just as he was setting out on his journey and word arrived that his white horse was being confiscated by Emiliano Zapata. So now the prince had to find his way around on foot, and not accustomed to looking out for himself, he had no idea what direction he should take. He decided to return to his castle but when he got there he found that it had been blown to bits, and the revolutionaries had declared that he was no longer a prince. Consequently, he could not complete his mission and poor Sleeping Beauty was left forgotten in the woods and since she could not live without the prince because they needed each other to exist, she simply had no future, and remained out there in the dark woods forever and ever. Pretty soon no one could even remember, much less care, about the troubles of that poor Little Sleeping Beauty who had been foolish enough to think that she needed to live in a castle with a prince. And so without realizing what they had done, the revolutionaries had managed to get rid of all those princes as well as all the silly, pampered Sleeping Beauties.

That afternoon I listened to Zulema for many hours as she recited one such story after another through her tears and frequent lapses into silence. From the beginning, she said, her brothers did not like her plots because they considered her endings to be strange and, at times, morbid. She had tried occasionally to tell her stories to her father but he was not the least bit interested in them. Mariana, who perhaps best understood what she was trying to say, assumed that she could change her endings. Therefore, Zulema felt that for lack of an audience she had been fated to keep them to herself all of those years. I was the only one who had let her tell the stories the way she wanted them to be, she lamented.

217

"Zulema, a mí me gustan tus cuentos," I reassured her as I undid her braids, then ran my small fingers through her hair.

I looked at her through my own tears. Unlike Mariana and the picture we had of Isabel, Zulema seemed quite ordinary-looking with her long hair parted in the middle and plaited into thick braids which she wore criss-crossed on top of her head. She did not look like my mother either, whose hair was swept away from her face and wrapped around a hair piece pinned to the front of her head in keeping with the fashion of the day. I much preferred Zulema's hair, though, which I loved to unbraid and then brush out, its soft waves reaching down to her waist as it straightened out.

That afternoon I gave her particular attention and made her prettier than usual by weaving a red satin ribbon into her braids as she continued with the narrative which had gone unshared all those years. She skipped the elaboration she gave to her other tales and was direct and terse as she described the main event that had shaped her life. She was not really blaming Mariana nor her father, for they had obviously been trying to save her from the very pain which they had inadvertently caused. By the time she was twelve she had definitely given up on her mother coming back, although occasionally she still thought she saw her sitting there in her rocking chair when she opened a door in her father's house. Whenever that happened, she'd see a luminous creature for a brief instant, holding a baby but the light radiating from them did not permit her to see their faces. That was about the time she took to opening all the doors in the house. Gradually she became fascinated wtih opening trunks and boxes as well.

On one of the days when she had been visiting her father and Amanda, she found herself alone in the room where he kept his papers. She started poking into his desk and in a drawer, underneath some photos and albums, she uncovered the announcement which she, unknowingly, had been looking for all those months. It was in the shape of a large card with black borders: *ISABEL MENDOZA CARDENAS, esposa de José María del Valle—1890-1914.* She read those words over and over, then finished the rest of the announcement which indicated that she was survived by three children, Zulema,

218

Miguel and Luis.

Zulema put the card back where she had found it. After that she no longer opened doors nor boxes in Mariana's house either. She began getting up at six o'clock so that she could attend daily mass at San Agustín where she remained until it was time to go to school. Gradually she began to lose interest in what was happening in her classes, and one day she decided to stay in church all day. For several weeks she sat in the huge church where the incense soothed her memories and the candles she lit brightened the semi-darkness. Soon el Padre Salinas began to notice that the candles were disappearing, and hardly any money was being left in the offering box to cover their cost. The next day he caught her sitting in the front pew facing the virgin and child, lighting two or three candles at a time and when those burned down in their green votive glass, relighting fresh ones.

Just about the time that el Padre Salinas approached Mariana about the church expense, the teacher paid José María a visit. He did not bother to discuss the matter with his daughter but instead talked to his sister-in-law. Mariana then told Zulema that her father wished to keep her at home, for she could not be trusted to go out on her own anymore. From then on she would not be allowed to go anywhere without being accompanied by either one of the cousins or the aunts.

Zulema had not minded the restrictions at all. In fact, she had never felt herself the object of so much attention as she now did. Mariana began to teach her how to make traditional dishes like mole de gallina for which they would spend a good part of a day grinding the sesame seeds on the metate as well as the peanuts and pastillas de chocolate. When they had prepared all the ingredients for the sauce and before they started to simmer it for hours, they would go out to the gallinero to pick out two or three full-grown chickens. After one or two lessons Zulema learned how to wring the chicken by the neck before cutting off its head with a machete. She loved preparing capirotada and leche quemada for desserts, and the first time she prepared the entire meal for a table of twelve she relished all the compliments she got, especially for her calabaza con puerco.

Doña Julia taught her to crochet blouses and gloves as

well as tablecloths and bedspreads which she made for herself and her cousins to be used at weddings, first communion parties or fiestas de quinceañeras. When she herself turned fifteen she was honored with a dance attended by all of her relatives, their friends and friends of her father who all danced to the music of a local combo with the happy honoree until the early hours of the morning. Between dances everyone kept going back to the bottomless urn of tamales de venado and the steaming pots of cinnamon coffee and all the side dishes of barbacoa, guacamole, arroz, frijoles borrachos and warm freshly grilled gorditas.

That was the first time she had met Carlos with whom she had danced many times during the evening. A few days later he had called on her father asking permission to visit her at home, and she began to be kidded about having a novio by the girls and by the older women in Mariana's colcha-making group. Zulema had just smiled shyly at the questions that were asked of her, and she pretended to concentrate on her stitches. Her first quilt was made of white flannel on one side, satin on the other, with a two-inch flounce which she gave to her cousin Elena when her third baby was born. Soon she began to fill up her own trunk with the essentials for her future life, and when she married Carlos she brought to her home all the basic requirements which a seventeen-year-old bride needed to begin her new life.

After Zulema's and Carlos's first child had been born, Mariana came to live with them, and for more than twenty years the three of them had seen the family expand, then contract as the older sons went off to study in Austin and the youngest daughter married, like her mother, at seventeen.

Zulema had tried to get each one of her children interested in listening to her stories but all four felt that they were silly and repetitive. So, it wasn't until I started making daily requests for recitations about all those extravagant creatures that she began to reconsider the reasons for the various vacuums in her life.

"Es lo que más me ha gustado, contar cuentos," Zulema sighed. She had calmed down as the afternoon had faded into a soft crepuscular mood.

"A mí también," I smiled as I tucked at her red ribbons.

Just then the door opened, and my cousin Marica turned on the light. "What are the two of you doing sitting there in the dark? Ay, mamá, you look so silly with those ribbons." "She does not," I contradicted. "She looks just great." Marica waved her hand as if to brush aside the comment. "You two, with your silly little games. Come on. I've brought a trayful of fried chicken and potato salad. Mariana's fixing some flan for dessert. I'm going to start to set the table." "We'll come in a minute," Zulema answered. "Déjanos terminar aquí." As soon as we were alone again, Zulema looked at me very intently. "Vamos a guardar todo esto en secreto. Pobre Mariana. Hace tanto tiempo que murió mamá. Ya ni para qué andar haciendo borloteos."

III

I reread the entry I had made for April 15, changed a few words with my new ballpoint, then closed the journal and laid it on my lap. I felt the smooth surface of the deep burgundy leather cover and recalled how pleased I was last Christmas when Mariana and Zulema had given me the book. This afternoon the sun was particularly brilliant, and since I had forgotten my sunglasses in the rush to get to the bus station, I closed my eyes against the glare and tried to sleep. After a few minutes I opened my eyes to check on the time. Another two and a half hours before I would arrive. From the empty seat next to me I picked up the magazine which I had bought at the Greyhound shop in San Antonio and leafed through it. News of Cuba, Vietnam, Laos. A terrible picture of Barbra Streisand and a cute one of the Beatles. I leaned against the window and stretched my legs out across the two seats. From that position I could see the other passengers around me. The woman two rows up on my left reminded me of Florinda's mother with her heavily teased hair. I closed my eyes again.

I had never met Florinda's mother but from the story my sister had told me I had a pretty good idea of how she looked on the day she had left Cuba five years ago. For almost a year she had let her hair grow very long in preparation for the day they would all leave. When the day arrived, she teased it

221

into a very high beehive. The inner layers of her hair had been divided into three sections. First she had twisted a finger-wide French roll which she fastened down with pins encrusted with precious jewels; a small fortune I was told. This small twist was covered with a larger one held up by more jeweled hairpins. The outer top layer neatly covered the cache, over which a heavy lacquer was sprayed. Almost as if to mock fate she had decorated her coiffure with pink and white gauze butterflies attached to thin wires which held them to her hair. According to Florinda her mother had looked so outrageous that no one bothered much with her and she had smuggled a sizeable sum with which the family had set up a small fabric shop which now, four years later, was a thriving business.

I opened my eyes and lit a cigarette. From the angle at which the sun was hitting me, the smoke from the cigarette resembled swirls of thick fog which reminded me of the movie version of Juan Preciado's search for his father as he roamed the villages in the land of the dead amid tumultuous vapors.

"Esta es mi novela favorita," I had pointed out to Zulema and Mariana, "aunque hay mucho en ella que estoy segura de que no entiendo," and with that I had introduced them to the espíritus of Comala. During my last Thanksgiving break, we had been reading *Pedro Páramo* aloud from the paperback copies I had given them as gifts. Mariana and I did most of the reading although Zulema sometimes took her turn also. We had a grand time sipping Cuervo añejo as we commented on what we had just read. Mariana, in particular, seemed to enjoy the characters at the Rancho Media Luna, for they were part of an era which she could well remember. Zulema, as I had expected, identified with Dolores, whose fate had also been shaped by the early death of her mother.

"Los espíritus siempre siguen afectando a los que les sobreviven," Mariana sighed. "Aquí mismo tenemos el ejemplo de Zulema, quien sufrió tanto después de la muerte de Isabel."

Zulema and I looked at one another. Fifty years after the death of her sister, Mariana was finally commenting on it.

¿Por qué dices eso, Mariana?" I questioned softly.

"Es que los murmullos se ponen más fuertes cada día,"

she answered, extending her hands on the armrest, then closing her eyes and rocking herself back and forth. The conversation had ended; at least, she did not want any more questions. Mariana looked intently at us and murmured, "Ya es tiempo." Then she continued to astonish us by saying that she wanted to take us to Isabel's burial place.

As I drove the car to the cemetery in absolute silence, my mind was full of questions. Like the rest of the family I had completely succumbed to the story of Isabel's departure and had never even asked where she had been buried. For fifteen years, ever since the day when Zulema had told me her version of her mother's death, I had removed Isabel from the world of the corporal and had placed her in the realm of the spirits. I wondered if Zulema was as shocked as I was since she too had not said a word during the trip.

"Vamos por este camino," Mariana had led us through the old part of the cemetery until we had come to a grave with a bouquet of marigolds in a red tin can half-buried in front of a tombstone marked with the same inscription as on the death announcement which Zulema had read so long ago. ISABEL MENDOZA CARDENAS, 1890-1914. In just two more days she would have been dead for fifty years and all this time she had been within reach. I was stunned and looked at Zulema whose lower lip began to tremble. Little whimpering sounds started to come out of her mouth and Mariana put her arm around her niece's shoulder, then rested her head against it.

"Yo nunca supe cómo remediar lo que pasó," she said simply. It was obvious that she finally wanted to talk, and since her legs were hurting her, we moved to a white wrought-iron bench a few feet away. The three of us sat in silence for a while. Then Mariana began to tell us about how difficult it had been for her to tell the story which the family had chosen for the children on the night that Isabel had died. She had made adjustments in her life from the very beginning when, instead of attending the novena for her dead sister with the rest of the family, she had stayed home with Zulema. When the child had started showing her suspicions, she had begun to doubt the decision to protect her from the truth.

But after a few years they themselves had nearly accepted the story as true and tacitly believed it would be much more

223

difficult to adjust to a new reality than to live with the pattern that had been set. "No sabía qué hacer," Mariana said over and over.

Then she told us about her weekly visits to the cemetery as her way of keeping the memory of Isabel alive for herself. For years she had sneaked away on the bus with her bouquet of three marigolds which she placed in a constantly recycling Folger's tin. As the years progressed her visits became more and more sporadic. Just a few days ago, however, she had brought the small bouquet we had just seen.

Looking at Mariana's rheumatic limbs I wondered how she had managed to maintain the manner she had chosen to honor her long-dead sister. "Uno hace lo que tiene que hacer," she affirmed as we headed back towards the car.

During the rest of the day I kept wondering how to fit together all the pieces of the story. After I got back to my dorm room, I started writing extensive entries in a loose-leaf journal. One day in early December I stuffed my notes into an envelope and mailed it off to them, with instructions to save the pages for me. A few weeks later I received my leather bound book as a present.

I reached over to feel it, again, then opened my eyes. We had arrived. As the bus made its way through city streets, I gathered my belongings and moved to the front. The instant we pulled into the terminal, I saw Patricia waiting for me.

"Is she still alive?" I asked my sister as I got into the car.

"She's been hanging on but she won't last much longer," she answered as she sped to the hospital. "This morning she had another heart attack and the doctor is not sure she'll pull through this time."

As I opened the door of room 306 I heard the murmur of prayers. Young Father Murphy was reciting the prayers of the Extreme Unction, and blessing the thin body on the hospital bed. My mother whispered to me, "She died about fifteen minutes ago."

I felt everyone's eyes on me as I walked up to the bed, then bent down to kiss the smooth shallow cheeks as tears streamed down my face. For a long time I looked at the body without saying anything; then I suddenly knew what I had to do.

I borrowed my sister's car and drove across the river to the church by the first plaza where I had often seen offerings of tin milagros pinned on the saints' clothing. At the small religious shop next to the church I found hundreds of milagros for sale in many different shapes, sizes and materials. I bypassed the large ones and knew I could not afford the gold ones; so, I carefully selected from the half-inch tin offerings those in the shape of human profiles, hearts and tongues of fire. The volunteer at the shop looked surprised when I told her I wanted five dozen of each but she patiently waited while I made my selection, then she put the milagros into three small plastic bags. I got back in the car and drove a few blocks to the flower market where I purchased bunches of marigolds, which I asked to have divided up into small bouquets of three flowers tied with a thin white ribbon. They took up most of the back seat and the customs inspector remarked on my collection of flowers "para los muertos." My next stop was the stationery shop where I bought a small box of red cinnamon-scented candles. Then, as I headed for Brewster Funeral Parlor where I intended to leave my purchases for a while, I passed a record shop. I slammed on the brakes, doubleparked and ran in to inquire if they sold small 45's that were blank. As a matter of fact, replied the clerk, they had three such records left from a very old special stock. I rushed back to the car and continued on to the funeral parlor where I discussed my intentions with the chief administrator who dubiously gave me permission to carry out my ideas only after I had explained my reasons at least five times.

At the agreed-upon hour, I returned to the funeral parlor and for the next three or four hours I carried out my task; after that the corpse would be ready to be viewed by family and friends. My back hurt from being bent for so long but I continued sewing the milagros unto the white satin lining on the inside cover of the casket. By applying three tight stitches through the tiny hole on each tin sculpture I made three arcs—the faces on the outer row, the tongues in the middle and the hearts on the inner row. When I finished with the milagros, I stepped back to get a better view of how pretty they looked, each with its accompanying tiny red ribbon. When the lid was closed they would be a lovely sight to have from inside, I thought. Next I arranged the marigolds on the casket forming a halo effect above the corpse so that its spirit could savor the smell of the flowers. I arranged the candles all in a row in front of the casket hoping that their scent could also reach her. And finally, I placed the three records on the left side of the body. "Fill them with your favorite stories," I whispered.

For a long time I sat in the semi-darkness, allowing myself to be mesmerized by the smell of the flowers and the perfumed glow of the candles. I knew then that I did not want to see anyone tonight and that very shortly someone would be coming to sit out the early morning vigil.

I got up and walked up to the coffin once again. The milagros looked absolutely splendid. I looked at the dearly beloved figure for the last time before I walked out of the funeral parlor knowing that I would not be going to the burial ceremony the next afternoon.

Instead I went home and immediately began to write in my journal. For two days I wrote until I filled all of its pages. Then I gave my thick book to Patricia asking her to see what I had just finished.

She started at the beginning and read for several hours. At times I would see her shake her head and make almost inaudible sounds. Finally, when she finished she closed the book, but kept her hand on top of it.

"No," she said, "no fue así." As she spoke a stern expression crossed her face. "It's not been at all the way you've presented it. You've mixed up some of the stories which Mariana and Zulema have told you which might not even be true in the first place. I've heard other versions from Tía Carmen, and, in fact, from Zulema herself. Mariana would never even recognize herself if you ever showed this to her."

"I'm not sure what you are trying to do," Patricia continued "but what you have here is not at all what really happened."

"Lo que tienes aquí no es lo que pasó."

BIOGRAPHIES

Amina Susan Ali (formerly Amina Muñoz) a woman poet who fixes telephone equipment for a living. Born 31 years ago in New York City. Started writing in 1974 when I discovered the Frederick Douglass Creative Arts Center in Harlem. Currently an active member of the Feminist Writers Guild. Have read at the Nuyorican Poets' Cafe, Galería Morivivi and the Women's Salon, among other places. My work has appeared in *Heresies, Revista Chicano-Riqueña, Third Woman, Womanspirit, Essence* and in the anthology *Nuyorican Poetry*. At present, I am involved with becoming a mother for the first time (April, 1983). My current passions include eating, sleeping, and trying to save money.

Gloria Anzaldúa is a Chicana poeta from South Texas presently completing her book, *La Serpiente Que Se Come Su Cola: The Autobiography of a Chicana Lesbian*. She is also the co-editor of *This Bridge Called My Back: Writings by Radical Women of Color* (Persephone, 1981).

Cenen—African Puerto Rican born in New York City. "My work is me, even when the words I write or the images I paint say what my conscious mind has not yet acknowledged."

Myrtha Chabrán—I was born in Vega Alta, Puerto Rico on April 6, 1934. My family was part of the exodus to the United States in the 40's, but we went to California instead of New York. I went to school because I wanted to be a writer, but instead I became an activist and an academic. Now that my sons are grown, I am trying to grow up to become a writer.

Cícera Fernándes de Oliveira is a woman from the under-developed Northeast of Brazil. She was married at 14, then deserted by her husband and moved to Rio de Janeiro. The work included in this anthology is an excerpt from *Cícera: A Woman's Fate.*

Carolina María de Jesús was born in 1913 in Sacramento state of Minas Gerais in Brazil's interior. A black woman with only 2 years of education she spent the greater part of her adult life in the slum "Favelas" of São Paulo with her 3 children. In 1958 she published a book of tremendous social impact, *Child of the Dark* which tells of the constant struggle she waged amidst poverty, violence, racism, and the stigma she suffered for rejecting life with a man. The cuento appearing in this volume is the beginning of an unfinished novel. Carolina María de Jesús, whose work has been translated into many languages, died in 1982.

Myriam Díaz-Diocaretz is a Chilean poet, translator and critic. She has published one book of poetry, *Que No Se Pueden Decir* (1982), and a translation of Adrienne Rich's poetry with a foreword which is in press in Spain. She has done work on Faulkner, Wallace Stevens, Black American Women Poets, and is doing translations of June Jordan's work. She is on the editorial board of *13th Moon* and *Third Woman.* She is working on another book of poetry and prose, *Conversaciones con mi Nana.* At the time of this writing, Myriam is living in Spain.

Roberta Fernández has been a visiting lecturer in Women's Studies at the University of Massachusetts, during the fall semester, 1982, and a visiting lecturer in Afro-American Studies at Smith College in the Spring, 1983. During a four-year lectureship at Mills College in the San Francisco Bay Area, she established PRISMA, which she now edits independently. Her work has been published in *Tin Tan, Prisma, Revista Chicano-Riqueña,* the *Massachusetts Review,* and the anthology *A Decade of Hispanic Literature.* She is also the author of *Thirteen Hands Make a Rainbow,* short stories on the Mexican folk arts for young adults. She was born in

Laredo, Texas. The stories appearing in *Cuentos* are part of a series of stories dealing with creative expressions of the women of the Southwest.

Rocky Gámez was born and raised in the lower Rio Grande Valley of Texas, the location of most of her stories. She is presently living and working in the San Francisco Bay Area.

Alma M. Gómez—Born January 15, 1953 in the Caribbean section of New York City's Lower East Side. Family history includes Puerto Rican parents who taught her "that once you discover words you discover your history and that to speak a true word is to transform the world." Six brothers/no sisters/ and four cats. Part-time proposal writer, teacher and consultant. Currently working as a social work administrator in a community mental health center in the South-Central Bronx.

Milagros Pérez Huth:
    Date of Birth   —February 3, 1940
    Place of Birth —Humacao, Puerto Rico
    Marital Status—Married
    Height   —5ft. 2in.
    Weight   —115 lbs.
    Mother   —3 sons

Gloria Liberman: El trabajo de Gloria Liberman se ha publicado en Chile en *el Diario Ilustrado*, 1965, en *la Revista Estudios Atacamemos* de la Universidad de Chile, 1973-4, y en la revista *"Kardias"* 2 y 3 de la Universidad de Chile 1978-9 respectivamente. Gloria nació en Santiago, Chile en 1953, y ha viajado extensamente desarollando sus experiencias en el campo de estudios humanísticos, particularmente Ciencias Sociales y Communicación. Como historiadora y publicista en Santiago donde reside y pertenece al Círculo de Estudios de la Mujer, se ha dedicado a coordinar diversas actividades de gran importancia social para la mujer chilena.

Aurora Levins Morales was born February 24, 1954 (one week before Lolita Lebron led the attack on Congress) in the coffee-farming barrio of Indiera in Western Puerto Rico. "I am Jewish and Puerto Rican and drawing strength from both traditions." When I was 5, I learned to write and have been writing, with more and more confidence and joy, ever since. I am fascinated by history, colors and the sea. I live and work in the San Francisco Bay Area. My writing has been published in *This Bridge Called My Back, Gay Community News, Coming Up, Revista Chicano-Riqueña* and other places. My mother, Rosario Morales, and I are working on a book together, to be published by Crossing Press.

Cherríe Moraga was born in Los Angeles in 1952. Since then, she has lived in Berkeley, San Francisco, Botson and now Brooklyn. In 1981, she co-edited with Gloria Anzaldúa, *This Bridge Called My Back: Writings by Radical Women of Color* (Persephone Press). In the Fall of 1983, the first book of her own writings, *Loving in the War Years: Lo Que Nunca Pasó Por Sus Labios* was published by South End Press.

Rosario Morales — I'm a New York Puerto Rican, born in 1930, been a radical since I was 19. I've farmed in Puerto Rico, studied anthropology, borne and raised three delightful people. Now I write, sew fabric, and look forward to old age: "¡Ciudado Vejez, aquí viene doña Rosario!"

Elva Pérez-Treviño — Born and raised Mexican, third generation Tejana in San Antonio, Texas, I write in response to the political implications of being born Mexican in South Texas. It has been the stark beauty of dark skin Mexicanismo in the landscape and environment that has allowed the magical philosophy of my Raza to survive within me in the form of *el espíritu Mexicano,* luminous source of faith and trust. There is a certain dignity and sense of self-value knowing my indigenous roots are founded in La Tierra Del Sol and the seven tribes of Aztlán. The fiction I compose is inspired by the compassion that has been stirred by other Mexicanos and the women of all nationalities.

Aleida Rodríguez was born on a kitchen table in Guines, Havana, Cuba six years before the Revolution. Since 1967, she's lived in Los Angeles where, since 1978, she has been involved in small press publishing, and co-editing. She publishes (along with her lover, Jacqueline DeAngelis) *Rara Avis Magazine* and *Books of a Feather*. Her work has been published in small press magazines across the U.S. including *BACHY, Beyond Baroque, Chrysalis, De Colores, 13th Moon;* and anthologized in *Lesbian Fiction An Anthology* (Persephone Press, 1981) & *Fiesta in Aztlán* (Capra Press, 1982). In 1981 she was awarded second place in the Woman of Promise National Poetry Competition sponsored by the Feminist Writers Guild. She was a recipient of an NEA Creative Writing Fellowship Grant for 1981-1982.

Mariana Romo-Carmona — En la narrativa de Mariana Romo-Carmona, la mujer existe siempre como personaje principal. Aunque no comenzó a escribir seriamente hasta los últimos años, a los doce leía cuentos por la radio en un programa para niños en Calama. Años más tarde, en Connecticut, Mariana fue la locutora de su propio programa de radio feminista. Su trabajo ha aparecido en publicaciones como *"Fight Back! Feminist Resistance to Male Violence,* (Cleis Press, 1981), *Sojourner, Gay Community News,* y diario *El Sur, Concepción* (1979). M. Romo-Carmona nació en Santiago, Chile en 1952 y emigró a los Estados Unidos en 1966. Actualmente vive en New York y es editora con Kitchen Table Press.

Sara Rosel nació el 9 de septiembre en Oriente, Cuba. Hizo estudios de historia. Se ha dedicado a la poesía desde hace algunos años. Esta es su primera publicación y su primer intento de escribir cuento o narrativa. Sara vive y estudia en Iowa City, Iowa.

Lake Sagaris, 26 años, Santiago, Chile. Estudió Creación Literaria en la Universidad de Columbia Británica, donde recibió su título de Bachiller en Bellas Artes. Volvió a Santiago en 1981, donde trabaja como profesora de idiomas y traductora. Ha publicado poesía y cuentos en revistas chilenas, norteamericanas y canadienses (*Minnesota Review; La Gota Pura; La Ciruela; Event Magazine; Prism: International; Room of One's Own; Other Than Review*). En este momento, está traduciendo la primera antología de literatura canadiense para edición en español. Trabaja en inglés y castellano. Miembro de la Sociedad de Escritores de Chile. Ganadora del concurso "Palabra Para el Hombre" Agrupación Cultural Universitaria, Universidad de Chile, 1981.

Lus María Umpierre: I am a native of San Juan, Puerto Rico who came to the United States in 1974. I was born in the worst slum area in San Juan at the time, called "La Veintiuna" (the place where the short story takes place). For years we lived 16 person in a house with enormous burdens. From 1974-1978 I attended Bryn Mawr College in Pennsylvania under a Fellowship. Since 1978, I am an Assistant Professor of Caribbean Literature at Rutgers University. From 1981 to 1982, I was a Visiting Scholar at the University of Kansas under a National Research Council Fellowship. My creative writing has been published in *Mairena, Plaza, Revista Chicano-Riqueña, Taller literario, Bilingual Review* among others. I also have two books of poems: *Una puertorriqueña en Penna* and *En el país de las maravillas* (Third Woman Press).

Luz Selenia Vásquez: I am a New York born and raised Puerto Rican Feminist who comes from a long line of story tellers. I have often been described as a "survivor". Currently, I am in my 4th year of medical school. In order to reach this goal I have had to undergo the politicization process that comes with struggling inside the monster. I take myself seriously in the roles of doctor and writer, and see both as ways to organize within the Third World community. Like many, I did not have a "Dick and Jane" childhood. I find myself now converting much of those painful times into positive energy and learning to be happy.

Helena María Viramontes was born in East Los Angeles in 1954 to an urban family of eleven. She is currently living in Los Angeles. For Helena, the celebration of Chicano Life and Literature are inseparable. She has been writing fiction since 1975, committing herself to the promotion, publication and exposure of Chicano Literature in general, Chicana Literature in particular. She has been co-ordinator of the L.A. Latino

Writers Association, Literary Editor of *Xhisme Arte Magazine,* and organizer of both community and university poetry/fiction readings. Her publications include two First Prize Fiction from *Statement Magazine* for her short stories "Reqiuem for the Poor" and "Broken Webb"; another First Prize Fiction award from the Irvine Chicano Literary Contest for her story "Birthday," among other works of fiction.

Iris M. Zavala is a poet, novelist, writer, professor and Marxist. Her most recent work is a collection of poems. *Que nadie muera sin amar el mar* (1982) and a novel *Kiliagonía* (1980), as well as a three-volume *Social History of Spanish Literature,* of which she is co-author. She has just finished a new novel, *Nocturna mas no funesta, de noche mi pluma escribe* an allegation against repressive cultures and institutions, placed in the XVII century in San Germán. She is a native of Ponce, Puerto Rico. Her work has been published in Latin America, Europe and the United States. At the time of this writing, Iris is living in Holland.

Glossary

NOTE: *English translations appear here in the order the Spanish appears in the text.*

By Word of Mouth

mi abuelita constantemente en la cocina, con la cuchara en la olla...Tú sabes...
My grandma always in the kitchen, with the ladle in the pot...
You know...

cuentos   stories

mujeres en lucha   women in struggle

las raíces de la cultura de silencio
the roots of the culture of silence

el poder de la palabra   the power of the word

quiénes somos   who we are

los cubanos son así   Cubans are like that

los puertorriqueños no saben hablar
Puerto Ricans don't speak right

la mezcla   the mixture

esperanza   hope

nuestros deseos   our desires

nuestras voces   our voices

Amanda

lentejuelas de conchanacar   sequins made of mother-of-pearl

telas de tornasol   iridescent-colored fabrics

¿Te gusta, muchacha?   Do you like it, girl?

chismes   gossip

¡Qué preguntona!   What a busy-body!

chongo   chignon

hechicera   someone who performs black or white magic using
  potions of herbs and weeds

muñequitos   little dolls

ancianas   old women

morral   knapsack

hierbas   herbs

brujas   witches

rebozo   wrap, shawl

"La Señora le manda un recado a su mamá"
"The lady has a message for your mother."

Mire lo que hizo la bruja.   Look at what the witch has done.

Pobre Librada. ¿Por qué le echas la culpa de tal cosa?
Poor Librada. Why are you holding her responsible for such a thing?

*"Oye, Amanda, me podrías hacer el traje más hermoso de todo
el mundo? ¿Uno como el que una bruja le diera a su hija favorita?
¡Que sea tan horrible que a todos les encante!"*
"Listen, Amanda, would you make me an absolutely gorgeous
outfit? One which a witch might give to a favorite daughter? One
that is so horrible that it will just enchant everyone!"

"¿Y para qué diablos quieres tal cosa?"
"Why in the world do you want such a thing?"

*"No mas lo quiero de secreto. No creas que voy a asustar a los
vecinos."*

"I just want to have it for my very own, as a secret. Don't think that I'm going to scare the neighbors with it."

"Pues mire usted, chulita, estoy tan ocupada que no puedo decirle ni que sí ni que no. Uno de estos días, cuando Dios me dé tiempo, quizás lo pueda considerar, pero hasta entonces yo no ando haciendo promesas a nadie."

"Look here, sweetheart, I am so busy that I can't say either yes or no. One of these days, when God gives me some time, I might be able to consider your request. But for now I cannot make any promises to anyone."

lechuza   owl, or as it is used here: a white screeching bird

Es de gata   It's made of cat.

cascabeles   little bells, jingle bells

linternas   fireflies

Júdases   spiraling firecrackers which shoot off in multicolors and which are shaped like Judas the Apostle; used ritualistically throughout Mexico and in the US bordertowns

chicharras   cicadas, a chirping insect found throughout the Southwest

I Never Told My Children Stories

"Gracias a Dios, mi hijita tiene un hombre bueno que la cuide."
"Thank God, my little girl has a good man to take care of her."

Sin Luz

¿Qué quieres?...¡No, Viejo, estoy cansada...por favor!
What do you want? No Viejo, I'm tired...please.

¡Quítate, Viejo!" ¿Estás Loco?"
Get away from me. Are you   crazy?

nalgas   ass, rear-end

El Paisano is a Bird of Good Omen

Sí, 'Ama que quieres?   Yes mama, what do you want?

No seas tonta, hijita.   Don't be silly.

Todas la hacen menos   Everyone ignores her

cabezona   hardheaded

cerveza   beer

carne asada   roast meat

arroz con pollo   chicken with rice

papas con frijoles   beans with potatoes

así son las cosas   that's the way things are

movidas del compadre Juan   compadre Juan's deals

hijos   sons, sons and daughters

maridos   husbands

fue un escándalo   it was shocking

bruja   witch

novia y novio   bride and groom

empanadas de calabaza   pumpkin turnovers

la merienda   the meal

madrinas and padrinos   wedding party

jardín   garden

cantineras   bar maids

pórtate bien   behave yourself

fulano   so and so

chingadera   fuck

alacranes   scorpions

cállate el hocico   shut your snout

ya lo sé   I already know it

lo cagamos   we fucked it up

mescal   liquor made from the maguey plant

'tas loca   you're crazy

ajúas   Mexican power yells

ven, baila conmigo   come, dance with me

Ay chulita   oh honey

qué pendejada es ésa   what kind of crap is that

gavacho   honky

tu poder o tu querer   your power or your love

pá dónde vas   where are you going

Pesadilla

¿Quién sabe la pena que sufría esa mujer?
Who knows the pain this woman has suffered?

La mierda del mundo que coma mierda.
The shit of the world that eats shit.

Pesadilla   nightmare

El bacalao viene de más lejos y se come aquí

algunas cosas no cambian   some things don't change

bacalao   dry salt cod

chamaluco   a variety of banana

¡cómo no!   of course,

el bacalao viene de más lejos y se come aquí
proverb: salt cod comes from farther away and we eat it here.
(When one complains that something or someone is too far away
and therefore the idea is impossible).

múcaro   owl

muchacha inteligente   bright girl

que el tiempo lo decida   let time decide

los escritores son así   that's how writers are

vivir es un peligro, y muerto no se puede vivir
proverb: living is a danger, and dead you can't live at all.

Zulema

tortillas de harina   flour tortillas

comal   flat stone cooking pan

"Te tengo muchas noticias."   I have lots of news for you.

"Tú te quedarás conmigo por un rato."
"You will stay with me for a while."

No, no fue así.   No. It was not like that.

bola de años   accumulating years

soldadera   woman soldier of the Mexican Revolution

campesino   peasant

"¿Sabes quién es?"   "Do you know who it is?"

"Es tu mamá."   "It's your mother."

"Mi abuelita Isabel."   "My grandmother Isabel."

"Murió cuando tenía veinte y cuatro años. Yo tenía seis entonces."
"She died when she was twenty four. I was six years old then."

"Mariana deveras me tomó el pelo diciéndome que mamá se había ido con la Tía Carmen."   Mariana really pulled my leg, telling me that mother had gone away with Aunt Carmen."

"Cuando termine la guerra, volverá."
"When the war is over, she will come back."

"Sé que se perdió."   "I know that she got lost."

"Yo ya no tengo mamá."   "I no longer have a mother."

239

"Les voy a contar un cuento de nunca acabar."
"Once upon a time…"

"Zulema, a mí me gustan tus cuentos."
"Zulema, I like your stories."

mole de gallina   chicken mole (a Pre-columbian dish)

metate   a grinding stone (a Pre-columbian method)

pastillas de chocolate   chocolate squares

gallinero   chicken coop

capirotada and *leche quemada*
desserts: bread pudding & carmelized milk

calabaza de puerco   pork and squash dish

fiestas de quinceañeras   fifteen-year-old birthday parties

tamales de venado   tamales made with venison

barbacoa   meat baked in a pit

arroz   rice

frijoles borrachos   beans cooked in beer

gorditas   extra thick corn tortillas

novio   boyfriend

"Es lo que más me ha gustado, contar cuentos."
"It's what I have most enjoyed, story-telling."

flan   custard

"Déjanos terminar aquí."   "Let us finish here."

"Vamos a guardar todo esto en secreto. Pobre Mariana. Hace tanto tiempo que murió mamá. Ya ni para qué andar haciendo borloteos."
"Let's keep this to ourselves. Poor Mariana. It's been such a long time since mother died. There's no point in creating problems now."

"Esta es mi novela favorita…aunque hay mucho en ella que estoy segura de que no entiendo."
"This is my favorite novel…even though I'm sure there's a lot in it that I don't understand."

añejo   especially aged

"Los espíritus siempre siguen afectando a los que les sobreviven."
"The souls always continue to influence those who live after them."

"Aquí mismo tenemos el ejemplo de Zulema, quien sufrió tanto después de la muerte de Isabel."
"Even here we have the example of Zulema, who suffered so much after the death of Isabel."

"Es que los murmullos se ponen más fuertes cada día."
"It's just that the murmurs get stronger by the day."

"Ya es tiempo."   "It's time now."

"Vamos por este camino."   "Let's go through this path."

"Yo nunca supe cómo remediar lo que pasó."
I never knew how to remedy what had happened."

"No sabía qué hacer."   "I did not know what to do."

"Uno hace lo que tiene que hacer."
"One does what one feels obligated to do."

milagros   little offerings made of tin

para los muertos   for the dead

"No, no fue así."   "No, it was not like that."

"Lo que tienes aquí no es lo que pasó."
"What you have here is not what happened."